D0899269

# Introduction to International Arbitration Practice

# Introduction to International Arbitration Practice

## 1001 Questions and Answers

Pierre A. Karrer

Wolters Kluwer
Law & Business

*Published by:*
Kluwer Law International
PO Box 316
2400 AH Alphen aan den Rijn
The Netherlands
Website: www.kluwerlaw.com


*Sold and distributed in North, Central and South America by:*
Aspen Publishers, Inc.
7201 McKinney Circle
Frederick, MD 21704
United States of America
Email: customer.service@aspenpublishers.com


*Sold and distributed in all other countries by:*
Turpin Distribution Services Ltd
Stratton Business Park
Pegasus Drive, Biggleswade
Bedfordshire SG18 8TQ
United Kingdom
Email: kluwerlaw@turpin-distribution.com

*Printed on acid-free paper.*

ISBN 978-90-411-5289-3

Printed and Bound by CPI Group (UK) Ltd, Croydon, CR0 4YY.

# About the Author

**Pierre A. Karrer** has been in private practice for over 40 years and practices as a full-time arbitrator from his "boutique" premises in Zurich, Switzerland. He has been chairman and arbitrator in well over 300 international commercial arbitrations all over the world.

He is Honorary President of the Swiss Arbitration Association, former Court Member of ICC, former Vice President of the Stockholm Institute, former Vice President of the LCIA, FCIArb, and listed arbitrator in numerous arbitral institutions worldwide.

After studies in Zurich, Göttingen, Padova, and The Hague, he obtained a Dr.iur. (*summa cum laude*) from the University of Zurich, and an LL.M. from Yale. He taught at the Tulane University School of Law in New Orleans, Louisiana, and at other universities.

He chairs arbitrations in English, French, German, and Italian. He also speaks Dutch and some Spanish. Contact: karrer@pierrekarrer.com.

# Table of Contents

Table of Contents

# Preface

The present book is for students and young practitioners of international arbitration. Nowadays, they have much better theoretical knowledge of the arbitration process, and far easier access to the sources of international arbitration law than today's seasoned arbitrators had at their age. But they are obviously still in the process of building up practical experience. This book tries to help them by summing up and updating life-time personal experience in the field, but in a simple, practical and commonsense fashion. Hence, questions and answers.

If one conducts an arbitration, one must institute a dialogue. This is a dialogue about instituting that dialogue.

# Acknowledgments

This is to thank my editor Eleanor Taylor and my assistants Marc Fauvrelle, Christine Zeder and Silvia Gerber.

# International Contracts and Dispute Resolution

**1.  Q: Let us start at the time when the Contract is negotiated and closed. Why are Contracts getting longer and longer?**

A: This is one of the many effects of computer technology on commercial life and the law. Still, Contracts have actually not changed in their legal nature.

**2.  Q: Which is?**

A: Contracts provide a description of what the Parties say should or should not happen. They also say what *should* happen *if* some things happen that *should* happen or should *not* happen. From an economic point of view, Contracts in this way allocate commercial risk between the Parties.

Thanks to computers, it is now possible to describe these things in great detail, and so this is what Contracts do nowadays.

This is often done in a modular fashion. One can refer to a text available from elsewhere, or copy and paste it in. Accordingly, many Contracts are multi-tiered, which is a typical modular technique. For instance, a construction Contract may have about a dozen levels of law, some general and abstract, some special and concrete. A dozen different documents in a hierarchy specified (one hopes) in the top document. Plus the law applicable to each of these levels.

Another effect is that once a template is available it will be copied, even if it is in a language, and refers to a law, that the Parties would otherwise not have used. One of the many reasons why we use written English more and more is that we use computers more and more, and our templates are in English.

1

**3. Q: Are templates sometimes copied mindlessly?**

A: It happens, and this keeps lawyers busy.

**4. Q: And this leads to arbitrations?**

A: Not necessarily, but imperfect Contracts may aggravate rather than avoid disputes.

**5. Q: Does this also lead to more Anglo-American law being adopted?**

A: At least indirectly, yes. Even if the applicable law clause provides for some civil law to apply, the agreement may include clauses that are geared to common law concepts. Two thirds of the world lives with civil law systems, yet because English is the *lingua franca,* and many English-speaking countries are among the economically dominant, common law concepts are often adopted.

**6. Q: An example?**

A: The American client's favorite template has a clause excluding liability for "consequential damages." With some difficulty, one *can* apply this common law concept even in a civil law Contract. However, in civil law, liability for damages for gross negligence cannot be excluded, even if they are only consequential, so the clause may mislead.

**7. Q: Can one avoid the influx of English law through the use of the English language?**

A: A friend of mine suggests this "We-write-English-but-we-think-German" language: "The English expressions used do not imply an English law understanding of the obligations of the Parties. English is used only as a means of communication."

**8. Q: Is this a good idea?**

A: Most of the time, no. This will just raise suspicion, thus be counterproductive.

**9. Q: Do more complex Contracts lead to more disputes, or fewer?**

A: Computerization makes it possible to enter into more complex Contracts than was possible in earlier times. For instance, instead of just designing and building a production line, the supplier of a complex production line may also be required to train personnel locally, and this may involve problems different from designing and producing plant and equipment and delivering it to a site.

Ideally, if one deals with many questions expressly, all in one document that is well thought through, this should lead to fewer disputes. Remember, Contracts are designed to say what should happen if a particular event occurs. The more complete and detailed a Contract is, the more one can hope that it will cover even rare events.

**10.  Q: Surely is it not possible to foresee all possible disputes and avoid them?**

A: Of course not, but one can, and should try.

For instance, the Contract may provide for payment in a particular currency. It is foreseeable that that particular currency may be *devalued* dramatically at some time in the future. The Contract may providently provide for a mechanism to redress the balance between the obligations of a Party that must pay in the now devalued currency, and those of the Party that must provide goods and services for which it pays in a different (by now) stronger currency.

It may however happen – and did happen at some point with the Russian Ruble – that the value of a currency unexpectedly goes *up* dramatically. In this particular case, few Parties had foreseen that *this* might happen, and they had not provided anything expressly for it.

So, while detailed regulations may help to avoid disputes, not everything that may subsequently occur may have been foreseen. The Parties may then differ about what a particular provision provides, and whether it is designed to deal with something that did in fact happen, or something different. In our Ruble devaluation example, the dispute was whether one could use the Ruble devaluation clause by analogy, and if so, how.

Thus, the complexity of Contracts increased, but so did the complexity of the disputes. The sums in dispute increased, but not necessarily the number of disputes.

**11.  Q: Apart from crafty wording of the Contract, are there other ways to minimize disputes?**

A: Yes. A long-term agreement can avoid disputes early on by the use of a milestone system. At each milestone, the correct performance is ascertained by some objective testing, involving somebody else, and part payment is then made. This way, at any given time, neither Party is in the uncomfortable position where *it* has performed almost all its obligations required by the Contract, but is now reluctant to go forward because the other Party has hardly performed at all.

Often, some simple dispute resolution mechanism is already built in at various milestones of a complex Contract, so that the performance of the Contract as a whole will not be held up by a relatively minor dispute. Ideally, disputes are resolved as one goes.

### 12. Q: This is not arbitration, is it?

A: No, here we are talking about regular meetings by site managers or higher levels of management, or amicable dispute resolution by dispute review boards and the like.

### 13. Q: And if this does not work, you go to arbitration?

A: Not so fast. You then try to negotiate a more complex, *overall* solution, an amendment to the agreement perhaps.

### 14. Q: Then arbitration?

A: Preferably not. The best arbitration is the arbitration that you can avoid.

### 15. Q: Through mediation or conciliation?

A: Exactly. Incidentally, the difference between the two is not important here.

### 16. Q: If nothing works, arbitration is the last resort?

A: Yes. But the other ways of resolving disputes (negotiation, mediation, conciliation, etc.) would probably not work if there was not the threat (and dread) of an arbitration down the road.

### 17. Q: Whose questions does this book try to answer? Those of in-house counsel or Party Advisors? Those of outside counsel or Party Representatives? Or those of arbitrators?

A: All three. Roughly, our focus will be first on questions from Party Advisors, who, at the time of making a Contract, try to serve the needs of their clients,[1] then questions from Party Representatives, who, in the initial phase of an arbitration, seek to optimize their client's position,[2] and last, questions from Arbitrators, concerning most of the arbitration itself and how to conduct it in the best interest of all concerned.[3]

However, on occasion our focus will switch to questions from other participants in the process. One should not forget right from the start that in an arbitration many participants interact.

Moreover, one faces a protracted process, and early decisions may have repercussions many months or years later.

---

1. See questions 19 et seq.
2. See questions 239 et seq.
3. See questions 347 et seq.

**18.   Q: Does this mean that the reader should approach the subject of international arbitration as an entire process, rather than taking the limited view of a particular participant at a particular stage of the process?**

A: Yes. In fact, in our last chapters, we will even look briefly at international commercial arbitration from a historical and philosophical point of view.[4] This should be of interest and help to *all* participants as they think more deeply about the process.

---

4. See questions 944 et seq.

# CHAPTER 1

# Arbitration Agreement and Applicable Law Clause

## (a) Arbitration Agreement

**19. Q: What is the best arbitration agreement?**

A: A difficult question to answer. When one negotiates an arbitration agreement, one does not know whether there will be an arbitration (hopefully not), about what, and how important it will be. Still, the Parties must decide as best they can.

**20. Q: So you have to ask what can go wrong in the Contract and how the client may be affected?**

A: Yes. But many things can go wrong, mostly unexpected and hard to assess.

**21. Q: Often one Party has the main obligation to do something, say a contractor, while the other Party only has an obligation to pay money, say an employer. Does this help?**

A: Not really. Generally there is this distinction, but think again. Even the Party whose primary obligation is to pay money may have to do certain other things. Equally, the Party that must do certain things may sometimes not do them because it runs out of money. It is therefore not always easy to predict who is likely to be Claimant and who is likely to be Respondent. Moreover, there is the possibility of a counterclaim, and, in the end, of an Award of costs.

**22.   Q: Make a decision on the basis of incomplete information? Is this not difficult?**

A: Sure, but no more difficult than any other business decision. It is just in the nature of business decisions that they must be taken on incomplete information. And as with any difficulty, you should divide it up and solve every aspect separately. This is the method that Descartes taught us.

**23.   Q: How can you maximize your chances to make the right decision about your arbitration clause?**

A: Do not adopt an old template mindlessly. Do not fiddle too much with an arbitration clause.

**24.   Q: Is this not contradictory advice?**

A: Admittedly. But it is easy to discuss arbitration with an arbitration specialist. A simple phone call will cost little, if anything, and may save millions.

**25.   Q: Before one makes that phone call, should one prepare?**

A: Last minute? Not even. There is normally no time to do that.

If you want to prepare, do this much earlier, by acquiring an understanding of international arbitration in general.

**26.   Q: What should one do?**

A: Keep a mental picture of an *entire* arbitration all the way from the beginning to the end. That is, from the arbitration agreement all the way to enforcing a favorable Award. You can gain this from experience.

**27.   Q: If your experience is limited?**

A: You may read a practical book like this one. It goes through an international arbitration roughly chronologically, but always within the context of the entire arbitral process.

**28.   Q: The first question in practice is probably, should one insert an arbitration clause and provide for arbitration in the first place?**

A: Not all answers are easy, but this one is. In an international setting the practical answer is clearly, *yes*.

**29. Q: But why not use State Courts? They are reasonably good and even cheap in some countries.**

A: Good to hear, but unfortunately this misses the point. The question is not "arbitration or litigation." There is the other Party, which will not be eager to come here and litigate in our courts.

If you do not provide for arbitration, you may be forced to go before some State Court in some faraway jurisdiction, to you an unattractive option, unless the Parties agree on a neutral State Court.

In an international commercial setting, international arbitration is therefore almost the only game in town.

**30. Q: Many say that conciliation or mediation is better than arbitration. Are they wrong?**

A: No, but unfortunately the question is not "mediation *or* arbitration." What do you do if conciliation or mediation does not work? You go to arbitration. It is the last resort.[5] So you need arbitration in the end.

**31. Q: Should one then provide in the arbitration clause for conciliation or mediation first?**

A: Beware of the *courtesy trap* in arbitration agreements. Many arbitration agreements indeed provide that, before arbitration, the Parties must try to negotiate a settlement. This is well-meaning, but it often leads to disastrous results.

When the arbitration is finally commenced, the other Party may not be so well-meaning. It may say that there was not enough friendly negotiation, and that commencing the arbitration is premature. And it may say this again and again. Saying this costs the other Party nothing and gains it time.

**32. Q: How do you avoid this cheap trick?**

A: If you use a multi-tiered arbitration agreement, you should provide clear criteria for determining *when* friendly negotiation has been unsuccessful and arbitration may commence.

In any event, the Party that wishes to commence arbitration must establish its right clearly, by at least a letter setting out the negotiation attempts, and saying that, in its view, the friendly negotiation has now come to an end.

---

5. See question 16.

If the clause provides for specific deadlines, it is particularly important not to miss one of the contractual deadlines, or the right to arbitrate may be lost.

Beware of clauses and Parties that talk not just about negotiation, but embellish it with "in utmost good faith" and other flowery language. Hypocrites are dangerous.

**33.   Q: Can we not just sit still, and we will never have to sue? If the other Party is forced to sue us right here in our State Courts, will we not have a home turf advantage?**

A: This is short-sighted and too risky.[6] Think again. A Party may unexpectedly find itself in the position of Claimant, or of Counterclaimant. If it wins, it may all of a sudden wish to enforce the Award. Suddenly arbitration becomes attractive to it after all.

**34.   Q: What then should the arbitration clause provide?**

A: Avoid fancy language. The simplest clause is the best.

**35.   Q: If the simplest is the best, why not be pragmatic and easy and always take the same simple arbitration agreement – stay with the clause under which one has had success in the past, and, conversely, avoid those clauses under which one has been unsuccessful?**

A: Many indeed proceed in this way.

Even more than 20 years after the downfall of the Soviet Union, Russian Parties still like to go to Stockholm because people who did this earlier were not put in jail, or worse. Same reasoning in China. Nothing against Stockholm, but there are other possible places.

The legal counsel of a major automobile manufacturer once proudly showed a roomful of people the arbitration clause that he used regularly. It was outdated by more than 20 years. It would just barely have worked if put to the test.

## (b)   Institutional or *Ad hoc*

**36.   Q: If simplest is the best, then what is so complex about an arbitration agreement? For instance, should one use institutional arbitration, or should one go for *ad hoc* arbitration?**

A: Another easy one. Normally, institutional arbitration is to be preferred. Arbitral Institutions even regularly provide excellent model clauses that in their experience work, and they often have extensive experience.

---

6. See question 20.

**37.  Q: Some people say that there is plenty of *ad hoc* arbitration out there. Is this not true?**

A: This is probably incorrect, especially for ordinary cases. Do not rush into agreeing on *ad hoc* arbitration without having discussed this thoroughly with an (international) arbitration specialist.

**38.  Q: Why is *ad hoc* arbitration not used so much? Does it not save the cost of an Arbitral Institution?**

A: Imagine an *ad hoc* arbitration against a recalcitrant Party. You would be in State Court right from the beginning, and again, and again – just what arbitration is designed to avoid.

One should not be overeager to save money, or, as they say in England, penny-wise and pound-foolish (an important idea in all aspects of international arbitration).

The service provided by a reputable Arbitral Institution is usually worth its price. Think of the scrutiny of draft Awards by the ICC Court – you profit, practically for free, from the experience of some of the world's most respected specialists. Just look at the list of ICC Court Members on the ICC Website.

**39.  Q: Which is the best Arbitral Institution? We love the local Arbitral Institution right where we are. Friendly and competent people. And not too expensive. Rather cheaper than ICC.**

A: *You* may like your Arbitral Institution, and it may be very good and even cheap, but it may not appeal much to the other Party, and it takes two Parties to agree.

**40.  Q: But we definitely do not want to go to the other Party's country and the Arbitral Institutions that they have there. These are likely to be biased in *their* favor.**

A: You may think so, and perhaps you even have a point. But the other side may well be – rightly or wrongly – wary of *your* local Arbitral Institution, and that is perhaps why they do not want to come here.

**41.  Q: So one will probably be forced to agree on a neutral Arbitral Institution and a neutral place or seat of arbitration?**

A: Yes.

**42.   Q: Suppose we have now decided on institutional arbitration. There are then three questions that all need to be answered at the time of making the agreement: Which Arbitral Institution?[7] Which seat of the arbitration?[8] Which applicable law?[9]**

A: Yes. While the answer to the three questions will, in each case, be short and easy to state, they involve a complex analysis, especially of procedural questions.[10] And there will be a further question as well, to be answered right when the arbitration agreement is made and there is no arbitration in sight.

**43.   Q: Namely?**

A: The language of the arbitration.[11]

**44.   Q: What about the idea that one should not talk or even think about bad things that could happen, because that *causes* them to happen?**

A: This is nonsense, of course.

Choosing a *suitable Arbitral Institution* is not easy, especially since a Party is not alone in this. There is always the other side. The other Party will think about all these matters also. It may agree to arbitration and making it institutional arbitration. So far, so good. But, beyond these points, it may, as the result of its own analysis, have ideas of its own, different from yours.

As in any business negotiation, each side may have its preferred outcome, but may have to settle for something else as part of an overall compromise. So in the end, the agreement on some points may not be for one's first option, but for a second or third option.

There may, however, also be some deal-breakers. But these will break not only the agreement to arbitrate but the entire commercial deal. Sometimes to negotiators, the commercial deal appears more important than a foreseeable dispute resolution system. They should think twice, because without a reasonable dispute resolution system disputes are more likely to arise.

**45.   Q: Because dispute resolution agreements are designed to *prevent* disputes?**

A: Exactly. This is their most valuable function.

---

7. See questions 47 et seq.
8. See questions 56 et seq.
9. See questions 686 et seq.
10. See questions 77 et seq.
11. See questions 140 et seq.

**46.   Q: Being everybody's second or even third choice gives an Arbitral Institution a good share of the market?**

A: This is one of the reasons for the ICC's success.


**47.   Q: Which Arbitral Institution should one pick? The ICC?**

A: This is a good choice, or another Arbitral Institution that has been tried and tested. Not one of the about two hundred pushy Arbitral Institutions eager for cases.


**48.   Q: Are there differences between Arbitration Rules?**

A: Among the leading Arbitral Institutions, hardly. They tend to follow fashions.


**49.   Q: On what then do Arbitral Institutions compete?**

A: On the quality of their arbitrators and staff.


**50.   Q: And on price?**

A: Yes, but this should be secondary. A badly run arbitration will be costly. The costs of the Arbitral Institution, and even the arbitrators, are only a fraction of the whole cost.


**51.   Q: Why are we talking in this book so much about ICC arbitration and less about other well-regarded systems, such as LCIA, Swiss Rules, Stockholm Rules, ICDR, Hong Kong International Arbitration Centre, and Singapore International Arbitration Centre?**

A: Mostly to keep things practical and simple.

ICC has a truly international system that is used all over the world.


**52.   Q: But its system is not particularly simple?**

A: Admittedly the ICC system is in some respects slightly more complicated than other leading systems, but not all that much.


**53.   Q: What is the main difference?**

A: ICC arbitration is highly *administered*. The ICC Court and its Secretariat exercise functions that the Arbitral Tribunal must often perform itself in other institutional arbitration systems, and always in *ad hoc* arbitration.

13

**54.   Q: Why this involvement of the ICC Court and the Secretariat?**

A: Other Arbitral Institutions also offer world-wide arbitration services, but most of their arbitrations have a local seat (London, Stockholm, Switzerland, Hong Kong, or Singapore) with some local arbitrators. Often even local law is applicable. And they are heavily used by local Parties.

By contrast, the ICC is the only truly international Arbitral Institution, and is designed to work really everywhere, with all kinds of arbitrators. Besides, once you understand how the ICC works, you will understand the other systems also. This is why in this book we will depart from the usual pedagogical principle that you should start with what is simple and then add more and more complexity.

**55.   Q: Are there things that one should watch out for in exotic Arbitration Rules and seats?**

A: Yes, read them carefully.

If the *lex arbitri* does not give an Arbitral Tribunal the power to issue Provisional Measures, the Arbitration Rules should expressly provide for this, but this may not be effective.

In some arbitration systems, the language of the arbitration *must* be a language not often spoken outside the seat. So provide for a suitable language in the arbitration clause if this is allowed!

In some systems, the arbitrators must be chosen from a list. Many unknown persons without international experience are listed. In some lists, old or dead persons appear. So, in practice, the choice is extremely limited.

If the *lex arbitri* does not provide that the Arbitral Tribunal can decide on arbitration and Party Representation costs, the Parties should agree on this in the arbitration clause, or the State Courts at the seat will have to set the arbitration costs.[12] In Sweden, if the seat is in Sweden, even in institutional arbitration, the Award must specify which Swedish State Court may review the arbitration costs. Beware of State Court involvement. Many state judges think that arbitrators earn too much too easily.

One should study the costs schedule. There are international arbitration systems where foreign arbitrators are paid very badly, or must be paid directly by a foreign Party. With such a system, it will be difficult or expensive to appoint a suitable arbitrator.

If the Arbitral Institution is exotic, the arbitrators should insist on being paid as they go and reserve the right to step down if they are not.

In one arbitration with an exotic seat, the Presiding Arbitrator was told by the Arbitral Institution that Party R was owned by the Ruler's family. The Presiding Arbitrator said:

---

12. See questions 850 et seq.

"Thank you, interesting, but not relevant." The Arbitral Institution told him again, and a *third* time. The Presiding Arbitrator did not like this.

## (c)  Seat, *Lex Arbitri*

**56.  Q: Is it true that by choosing the seat one chooses the *lex arbitri*?**

A: Yes. Most people think so, except in France.

**57.  Q: What does *lex arbitri* mean?**

A: The arbitration law of the seat. In some jurisdictions (e.g. France, Switzerland), there is a dual system for domestic and international arbitration. So you should make sure that you are in *international* arbitration. In Switzerland, even domestic Parties can opt into international arbitration. This is advisable.

**58.  Q: Will the arbitration be conducted at the seat?**

A: Not necessarily. Most people emphasize that there is no need to meet at the seat. It is a *legal* concept. Choosing the seat means choosing the *lex arbitri*.

But note that for French theory, this is too easy and indeed wrong; the place of arbitration is chosen just for convenience, and should have no legal significance at all.[13]

**59.  Q: Here, we go with the majority view?**

A: Yes, we start with the theoretical concept that by choosing the seat, the Parties indeed choose the *lex arbitri*, as accepted everywhere except France. We will come to French philosophy towards the end of our conversation.[14]

**60.  Q: What is the best seat? That is, the best *lex arbitri*?**

A: The question should not be asked this way. There are many differences between the arbitration *laws* of various jurisdictions, and we mentioned some of them already.[15] But differences in law are not the *only* relevant consideration when choosing a *seat*. Otherwise we would arbitrate in Djibouti all the time, or in India. Both have arbitration statutes that read well, but in reality other seats are more popular.

---

13. See questions 956 et seq.
14. See questions 956, 961 et seq.
15. See question 55.

15

**61. Q: What is relevant beside the law?**

A: The local State Court system is not equally attractive everywhere, to mention just one aspect.

**62. Q: Other aspects?**

A: Many, including: ease of travel; accommodation; hearing rooms; Court Reporters; visas; currency control; climate; corruption; food; cleanliness; political stability; political and cultural neutrality; reliability and neutrality of the legal system; tax considerations; VAT or withholding tax on arbitrators' fees; quality of local arbitrators and local bar; quality of the court system; language considerations; convenient geographical location; telecommunication; airports; hotels; restaurants; and banks that work well.

**63. Q: Now the substance of the arbitration law at the seat.**

A: An easy way to find out where the arbitration laws differ is to use a book which presents the various arbitration laws according to a particular grid or questionnaire. These go from the relatively superficial, often published by international law firms, sometimes pushing those jurisdictions where they have offices, to in-depth comparative law and practice analysis.

**64. Q: Apart from exotic specialties,[16] where are the main differences?**

A: An important difference is in the *tiers of judicial review of Awards*. This goes from three, as in England, to two as in France, Germany, and Belgium, to just one, as in Switzerland and Austria. This has a major impact on speed.

**65. Q: Having fewer tiers of judicial review saves time and money, correct?**

A: Time, yes. Fewer tiers save time, especially if you think of the Swiss Federal Supreme Court, which more often than not decides setting aside proceedings in less than five months, and almost always in less than seven.

**66. Q: And costs?**

A: With respect to costs, it all depends on the rates charged by the reviewing courts. For instance, one should know that the rate before the Austrian Supreme Court is 5% of the value in dispute on review. The Austrians say that 5% was reached by roughly adding

---

16. See question 55.

up the court fees that were payable in the three tiers before that system was replaced by the one-tier system.

### 67.   Q: This means that reviewing an Award in Austria may cost far more than the arbitration with three arbitrators and the Arbitral Institution?

A: Yes. The costs of three tiers were outrageous, and having almost the same cost for just one tier hardly makesit any better. Fine as Austrian arbitration law is otherwise, this one feature means that, in practice, it is foolish to try to set aside an Austrian arbitral Award.

### 68.   Q: In other words, in practical terms, forget setting aside in Austria?

A: Yes, and time will tell whether the "Lex Storme" idea will be more successful in Austria than it was in Belgium, or whether this feature of Austrian arbitration law will be corrected, as we all hope.

### 69.   Q: Other differences in the *lex arbitri*?

A: What also differs is the *extent* of judicial review of facts and laws. If much of the dispute is repeated before State Courts, why go to arbitration in the first place?

If English law was the applicable law, in England, an appeal on a point of law is possible. So if you like English law, go elsewhere. If you like to go to London, have another law than English law apply. Otherwise, you will see your case in the hands of people with wigs, and they will take years to further English law at your (considerable) expense.

Another difference is in the procedure adopted to *ascertain the applicable law*.

### 70.   Q: Must "foreign" law be proved by Expert Reports?

A: Proving "foreign" law is still popular in some jurisdictions, but there is no requirement for this even in the arbitration laws there.[17]

What is more tricky is the question whether *iura novit curia* applies. The question is how far the right to be heard goes. Does it also include the idea that Party should not be *surprised* by the Arbitral Tribunal applying a certain principle of law, or a particular provision, without having had an opportunity to comment?

If so, the question then is, *when* a principle of law or a legal provision is surprising, because the Parties should also know the law, *ignorantia juris nocet*. If a legal principle is mentioned, but not its implementation in all its facets, is it surprising if one of its implementations or facets is applied?

---

17. See English Arbitration Act 1996, Art. 34(2)(g).

### 71.  Q: An example?

A: In many laws, there is the principle of good faith. One implementation of that principle may be the entire law of unfair competition. If provisions on unfair competition law are unexpectedly applied, is this still surprising if the principle of good faith has been mentioned?

### 72.  Q: Let us go deeper. For which questions does the *lex arbitri* matter?

A: Arbitration is comparative law in action.

Let us start with the fundamental distinction or characterization of questions of *substance versus procedure*.

### 73.  Q: What is the purpose of procedure?

A: An Arbitral Tribunal must (1) find the facts and (2) apply the law to the facts as found. Procedure is about identifying the method that the Arbitral Tribunal will apply to do one and then the other. Substance is about applying the identified method to one and then the other.

### 74.  Q: Does the same law apply to substance and procedure?

A: No. Substantive law questions will be governed by the substantive law applicable to the merits (which may be chosen expressly by the Parties in their agreement, or determined indirectly by the Arbitral Institution's Arbitration Rules, or by the *lex arbitri*).

By contrast, procedural questions in an arbitration are often answered in a fundamentally different way.

### 75.  Q: The difficulty is that in some jurisdictions, many questions are characterized as procedural that elsewhere are characterized as substantive. Is there a good way to distinguish between substance and procedure?

A: This distinction is for the *lex arbitri* to make. Unfortunately, you will not find much of an answer there. But here is the way one could do it:

In doubtful cases one should characterize a question as substantive. From a *functional* point of view, one should characterize as substantive all questions that have a substantial impact on the outcome of the case apart from the facts of the case. Therefore, the following questions should be characterized as substantive questions of law:

- who must provide what under the Contract;
- deadlines to observe;
- deadlines of *mise en demeure;*
- statute of limitations;
- interest;
- presumptions and burden of proof;
- whether an interest worthy of protection exists to justify issuing a declaratory judgment;
- *locus standi*; and
- set-off.

By contrast, where the equal treatment of the Parties and their right to be heard must be guaranteed, in short, procedural due process, one should characterize a question as procedural.

One should pay attention to the notion that procedural law is the handmaiden of substantive law. Procedural questions should remain without substantial influence on the outcome of the dispute. Therefore, long-term predictability is less important.

Accordingly, the following should be characterized as procedural:

- all questions aptly listed in Section. 34 Arbitration Act 1996 (even if the *lex arbitri* is not English);
- the duty to particularize allegations within reason;
- singular procedural provisions of the applicable substantive law such as limitations on proof, for instance, exclusion of parol evidence and prohibition to use as evidence information illegally obtained (exclusionary rule);
- taking of evidence;
- questions covered by the IBA Rules of Evidence 2010, including assessment of the evidence and adverse inferences if evidence is withheld;
- advances and recourse of the Party that made the advance against the defaulting Party;
- security for Party Representation costs; and
- assessing and allocating costs.

**76.   Q: Is this just an autonomous distinction that you are suggesting? Would it not be better to look to the way the procedural law of the *lex arbitri* distinguishes substance from procedure?**

A: No. When a system draws the substance versus procedure distinction for local purposes, this is influenced by local factors, particularly, the court system, the legal profession, legal tradition, and the division of powers in a federal system. None of this is important in international arbitration.

## (d)   Procedure before the Arbitral Tribunal

**77.   Q: Is it correct that on procedural questions the *lex arbitri* applies?**

A: No. We only discussed[18] the way to *distinguish* between substance and procedure. The procedure before the Arbitral Tribunal is, however, another matter.

The *lex arbitri* often lets the Parties agree directly on the overall procedure to be applied in the arbitration itself, but the Parties rarely agree.

**78.   Q: In writing?**

A: No need. An unambiguous agreement should suffice.

**79.   Q: Could the Parties or the Arbitral Tribunal refer to a code of civil procedure?**

A: Yes, but this rarely happens, fortunately.

**80.   Q: Why fortunately?**

A: Because codes of civil procedure are designed for domestic State Court litigation, mostly between local Parties, not international arbitration.

**81.   Q: So Parties should design their own civil procedure? Surely a difficult task?**

A: This should be left to the Arbitral Tribunal.

Arbitral Tribunals have considerable discretion. Due process must be observed, that is all.

**82.   Q: Does this mean that, in reality, an Arbitral Tribunal will shape its own procedure?**

A: Yes, more often than not.[19]

---

18. See questions 72 et seq.
19. See questions 96 et seq. An earlier version of the following discussion was published by the author as "Don't be afraid – a pep talk" in Arbitration, 1999, pp. 24–25. The author thanks the Chartered Institute of Arbitrators and Sweet & Maxwell for their permission to use the earlier publication.

**83.  Q: Should this be done by an Order or an Award?**

A: All measures taken by an Arbitral Tribunal regarding procedure are qualified as Procedural Orders, not as arbitral Awards.[20]

**84.  Q: But an Arbitral Tribunal's decision accepting or declining jurisdiction is procedural, yet an Award?**

A: Yes, a procedural Award. Some purists insist that an Award is necessarily a decision that *awards* something. However, the law [21] then corrects this linguistic problem which arises only in English, not in other languages. It does not arise with the French "sentence."

**85.  Q: How does one distinguish between Procedural Orders and Awards on the merits?**

A: Arbitral decisions are considered *orders* if they may be changed by the Arbitral Tribunal itself at any time. Within reason, because the procedure should be foreseeable for the Parties.

By contrast, an Award, once made, cannot be changed even by those who made it. It is *res iudicata*. However, it may still be set aside by a State Court on limited grounds.

**86.  Q: Some people say that the mandatory parts of the *lex arbitri* apply. Is this not true?**

A: It is of course true that mandatory law in the *lex arbitri* must apply at the seat. But the question is, what is mandatory in the *lex arbitri*. Hardly anything.

**87.  Q: The "contradictoire," as the French say?**

A: Yes, or the right to be heard.

**88.  Q: Equal treatment?**

A: Yes, if this is different.

---

20. See Karrer in Tijdschrift voor Arbitrage, 2004/2 Art. No. 20, pp. 57–62, "Awards and Orders – Labels Matter After All". The author thanks Kluwer Law International for the permission to use the earlier publication.
21. Singapore Arbitration Act, section 10.

**89.  Q: Anything else?**

A: Nothing. One could simply summarize that "due process" must be applied. These two words say it all.

**90.  Q: So the Arbitral Tribunal need not be too much afraid?**

A: No. Too many arbitrators conduct their arbitrations as if the courts were still breathing down their necks. They constantly worry whether someone, somewhere, somehow, might say that they misconducted themselves. Or, to use the newer English phrase, that some serious irregularity crept into their Award. So they walk slowly with circumspection.

However, if you want to walk straight, do not look at your feet too much. Of course, avoid obstacles, but the best way is to have a goal and to go straight towards it undaunted.

**91.  Q: Which goal?**

A: Your goal should be to treat the Parties equally and give them a fair opportunity to present their case, in other words, due process, and then to issue your Award quickly. If you do that, there is no need to worry. You cannot go wrong. Everything else follows from these principles.

**92.  Q: Should you proceed in this way right from the start?**

A: Yes. In the first phase of an arbitration, it is particularly important to apply your mind to devising a *procedure* that fulfills these goals. In order to treat the Parties equally, you will try to proceed in a manner that is equally comfortable for both, or, if worse comes to worst, equally uncomfortable for both. This will automatically rule out the method of following what the Party Representatives, or just one of them, may be used to, or what is normal before the State Courts at the seat of the arbitration, but is foreign to the Parties themselves. Or still worse, what the members of the Arbitral Tribunal may normally do in a State Court at home.

**93.  Q: Do you ask the Parties for their input each time?**

A: Many Arbitral Tribunals do this, but it is good enough to tell the Parties once and for all, right from the start, that they have "general liberty to apply," so you need not ask again and again.[22]

---

22. See Annex (F), First Letter of the Arbitral Tribunal to the Parties, at the end.

**94.  Q: Will the procedure be oral or in writing?**

A: A mix.

If the Parties are to be given a reasonable opportunity to present their case, you will seek the right balance between a procedure in writing and an oral procedure. A procedure in writing gives everybody the opportunity to prepare for a hearing without unfair surprise. An oral procedure gives an even better opportunity for a dialog between the Parties themselves, and with the Arbitral Tribunal, but requires people who can think on their feet.

**95.  Q: And so with the procedure on presenting the evidence?**

A: There also, if you are to treat the Parties equally and give them a fair opportunity to present their case, you will strike a balance between giving the Parties an opportunity to prepare witnesses and draw up Witness Statements, and spontaneous oral testimony in response to probing questions from the other Party and the Arbitral Tribunal.

Where the evidence is technical, it becomes even clearer that you should not proceed along a pre-set path, but rather seek to achieve the goals just mentioned.

**96.  Q: Similarly concerning the assessment of the evidence?**

A: Yes. You will devise the right mix between oral presentations, which can be spontaneous while everybody's memory is still fresh, and Post-Hearing Briefs, which can be more complex and based on a full Transcript of the hearing.

**97.  Q: Oral summations may be difficult for non-native speakers of English?**

A: Yes, and this may lead to forgoing oral summation altogether and having Post-Hearing Briefs only.[23]

**98.  Q: In a complex case, is there not a risk that the Arbitral Tribunal may not get the procedure absolutely right from the start?**

A: True, but do not worry. The beauty about procedure is that little harm is done until an Award is rendered that is *affected* by a procedural mistake. If you err, this is not yet the end. You are not on a tightrope. Even if you trip, you will not fall to your death. If a Party thinks that you went wrong, it will often tell you spontaneously. You should even encourage the Parties to tell you if they believe that you committed a procedural mistake. Ask them, say, at the end of each hearing day. Procedural mistakes can almost

---

23. See Annex (L), Procedural Order No. 1, para. 54.

always be fully rectified on the spot. You can re-establish the balance between the Parties. You can reopen a reasonable opportunity for a Party to present its case.

**99.    Q: Some Party Representatives are given to comment nastily each time the Arbitral Tribunal does something that displeases their client. How should an Arbitral Tribunal react to this?**

A: It should first humbly ask itself whether the Party Representative has a point.

**100.    Q: If not?**

A: Preferably, not react at all. Understand that this is a cultural thing. Some lawyers believe that they must impress their clients. Some believe that in arbitration they can use their aggressivity that is repressed in litigation. Some (rightly) believe that little harm results from complaining while not complaining may be dangerous.

**101.    Q: What happens if a Party holds back and says nothing?**

A: It may then indeed have lost or waived its right to complain, see Article 39 ICC Rules.

**102.    Q: Has this ever been applied?**

A: Yes. There was a multi-billion case in Switzerland that was decided by the Swiss Federal Supreme Court on this very basis, and many other cases.

This waiver principle is also important when an arbitrator is challenged. No prompt complaint, no right to challenge.[24]

**103.    Q: If a Party complains, does this not antagonize the Arbitral Tribunal?**

A: A bit, but a Party Representative should not be too afraid of antagonizing the Arbitral Tribunal.

One can complain with elegance. This is a test of a lawyer's ability to be mellifluous. Say: "As my duty to my clients requires, I must immediately draw the honorable Arbitral Tribunal's attention to this: If the Arbitral Tribunal continues to refuse to hear witness X, it will violate my clients' right to be heard." "Are you threatening us?" "The risk is to my client. I am trying to help the honorable Arbitral Tribunal issue an Award that will stand. We all need such an Award."

---

24. See questions 310 et seq.

In such a case, it is not good enough to raise the *question* whether the Arbitral Tribunal has committed a procedural error. The error must be identified as such in no uncertain terms.

It is recommended to promptly send a letter stating the protest once again. It is also recommended to tell the Arbitral Tribunal how the error could be rectified and present a motion to that effect.

### 104. Q: Is it really necessary for the Party to tell the Arbitral Tribunal *how* its mistake could be remedied?

A: The Swiss Federal Supreme Court thinks so, but this in my view cannot be right. It is the Arbitral Tribunal's duty not to commit procedural errors in the first place, and if it does, then it is *its* duty to figure out how its error can be remedied. It is a not a Party's duty to identify *the right method* to achieve a correct procedure in the first place, let alone to identify the right method to correct a mistake. If the method that it proposes is ineffective, this should not be held against the protesting Party. Accordingly, it should be sufficient for the Party to point out the mistake in no uncertain terms.

### 105. Q: What can an Arbitral Tribunal do to stay out of procedural trouble?

A: At the end of each series of hearings, the Parties' attention should be drawn to Article 39 ICC Rules or the equivalent applicable provision. This should be stated in the Transcript and then in the Award. The Parties' answers, if they point out what they believe to have been a procedural error, should be set out *verbatim* in the Transcript, and discussed in the Award.

If a Party sees that it may lose, it sometimes tries to improve its position by last-minute offers of proof, particularly additional Party-appointed Experts' Reports or motions that the Arbitral Tribunal itself appoint an Expert. If the Arbitral Tribunal refuses, the Party will say that its right to be heard has been violated. This should be prevented in Procedural Order No. 1.[25]

### 106. Q: How can an Arbitral Tribunal deal with the paper tsunami?

A: The secret to good case management by an Arbitral Tribunal is knowing what to read and worry about, and what should be left alone, at least for the time being.

If you receive a written submission, for instance, do not study it too deeply straight away. Let the Counterparty have a look at it first. Perhaps it will argue that some points are irrelevant. Perhaps it will even move that some portion should be completely

---

25. See Annex (L), Procedural Order No. 1, paras 44, 46.

disregarded and struck from the record. It is then downright harmful if you have read those portions too well. It is best not to read them at all until they belong in the record.[26]

### 107. Q: Can assistants help with this?

A: Yes. Arbitrators need to be shielded from certain information, yet need to make decisions. A screen can be the solution.

### 108. Q: This is mechanical work?

A: It is, so there is no problem at all with somebody else other than the Arbitral Tribunal performing it.

### 109. Q: But what will you do if you have to *decide* on whether a particular document is privileged or covered by a confidentiality requirement?

A: This is more difficult. There, a *decision* must be made.

### 110. Q: But then the Arbitral Tribunal will have to see the document, and if it decides that it should not have seen the document, it will have to erase this from its memory?

A: Yes, and therefore a better way is to appoint a *confidentiality adviser*. This person will look at the documents and decide which ones should go into the record and which ones should remain outside.

### 111. Q: Would this be a lawyer? Which law would this lawyer apply?

A: This would normally be a lawyer, and the law to be applied should be determined by the Arbitral Tribunal when the task of the confidentiality adviser is set.

For instance, in one case, the client-attorney privilege invoked by both Parties was the same because they used lawyers from the same jurisdiction. It made sense to have a confidentiality adviser from that same jurisdiction, in the person of a senior lawyer experienced in applying the bar rules of that particular jurisdiction.

### 112. Q: Is a confidentiality advisor just a helper for the Arbitral Tribunal or is he or she an arbitrator *pro tanto*?

A: The latter. Whoever makes a decision that cannot be changed is an arbitrator. This is a special decision method. This must be organized in detail, with the Parties heard

---

26. See questions 469 et seq.

*and involved.* A confidentiality advisor is subject to the same conflict rules as any arbitrator.

### 113.   Q: Are there other types of special decision makers playing the role of an arbitrator *pro tanto*?

A: One can use a *document production master* who will handle the entire document production process. This is a cumbersome process which, if the Parties agree, may be farmed out to a specialist.

### 114.   Q: A specialist who makes decisions?

A: Yes. The decision may also be about how burdensome production of certain types of documents would be.

### 115.   Q: This specialist is then again a special arbitrator?

A: Yes.

### 116.   Q: Are there not cumbersome special problems with respect to Party-appointed Experts?

A: Yes, and there an *expert coordinator* or *expert facilitator* could have a role in communicating with the Party-appointed Experts, bringing them together, making sure they answer the questions that they are being asked, that they send each other the documents that they should send, and the like. This far, all this is still mechanical.

### 117.   Q: But there may be a decision to make. Should the expert facilitator then be a special decision maker, and thus an arbitrator?

A: Not necessarily. Rather, the decision should then be made by the Arbitral Tribunal itself. The difficulty is that Experts play an important role in the Arbitral Tribunal's decision, yet normally have no legal training, and sometimes little understanding of the due process requirements that should be met in arbitration. The Arbitral Tribunal should be concerned about this. It should make preventing trouble its own task.

### 118.   Q: Is all this not giving procedure too much weight?

A: No. Concentrating your mind on the procedural aspects in the first phase of an arbitration is a good thing. It keeps the Arbitral Tribunal from starting to worry too early about the facts of the case or even about the law. If the Arbitral Tribunal has already made up its mind about the facts and the law halfway through, the Parties will not have a reasonable opportunity to present their case. An Arbitral Tribunal will not treat the Parties equally if it tells them, even before it is done, which Party is going to lose. If, however, the Arbitral Tribunal genuinely has not thought much about the facts of the case and about the law, there is little risk that it will jump to conclusions. The Arbitral Tribunal can even tell the Parties that they should not leave the hearing thinking that they are about to win or lose because of what the Arbitral Tribunal said or did not say. It can tell them that the Arbitral Tribunal has no idea at all about the outcome. It will be easy to tell them that, because it will be true.

**119.    Q: Does this mean that the Arbitral Tribunal should not discuss the facts and the law internally from the start, on a provisional basis?**

A: No, but the discussion must really be on a provisional basis, and not prejudge any point.[27]

## (e)    Interpretation of Arbitration Agreements, Pathological Arbitration Agreements[28]

**120.    Q: Sometimes it is clear what the particular arbitration agreement says, but it is not clear what it means. How do you then proceed with the interpretation of a possibly pathological arbitration clause?**

A: First, ask whether the clause provides for arbitration in the first place.

This does not necessarily follow from the use of the word "arbitration," if the context shows that what the Parties called "arbitration" is actually some sort of conciliation or mediation. However, without more, the word "arbitration" should be understood to indeed mean arbitration.

If the Parties use a different word, perhaps even "mediation," one must again look at the context to understand what the Parties meant.

**121.    Q: Which law applies to the construction or interpretation of an arbitration agreement?**

A: This is easy to determine if there is an applicable law clause specifically for this purpose. But this is right only if the clause refers specifically to the arbitration agreement.

Otherwise, if the arbitration agreement is clear enough to determine the *seat* of the arbitration, hence the *lex arbitri*, the better view is that the private law of the *lex arbitri*

---

27. See question 737.
28. An earlier version of this subchapter was published by the author under the title "Pathological Arbitration Clauses – Malpractice, Diagnosis, and Therapy, Festschrift für Thomas Bär und Robert Karrer, Ed. Nedim Peter Vogt et al., 1997, pp 109-126. The author thanks the copyright owners for the permission to use the earlier publication.

should be used to interpret the separable arbitration clause (if it is valid, which is a different question). Thus, if the arbitration clause provides for arbitration in Germany, German substantive law[29] will apply to the interpretation of the arbitration clause, even if the Parties have chosen a different law to apply to their Contract as a whole.

All this follows from the idea that the arbitration agreement is a separable agreement, and it is separately governed generally by the *lex arbitri*, not by the law applicable to the substance of the agreement.

**122. Q: Even if the law applicable to the substance of the agreement was chosen by the Parties?**

A: Yes. Normally the seat was also chosen by the Parties, and that was a more specific choice.

**123. Q: If the text is so unclear that it is not possible to determine where the seat of the arbitration should be, what then?**

A: This presupposes that the Parties did not agree, in their otherwise pathological arbitration clause, for a particular Arbitral Institution to run the arbitration. If they did, the Arbitration Rules of that Arbitral Institution may determine the seat of the arbitration (perhaps by default), or empower a particular body within the Arbitral Institution to determine the seat of the arbitration. Once that has happened, you will take it from there.

**124. Q: If there is no Arbitral Institution to determine the seat, what do you do?**

A: In one such *ad hoc* case, the Presiding Arbitrator wrote the Parties an innocent-sounding letter about where the first meeting might be conducted, and incidentally, that town would be the seat. The Parties said, fine. That town became the seat.

**125. Q: So you trick the Parties into agreeing on a seat? But if they do not agree on the seat?**

A: A difficult question. One may try to have the Parties agree that the Arbitral Tribunal, if and when it is in place, will have to determine the seat.

---

29. BGB (Bürgerliches Gesetzbuch).

**126.  Q: However, you may need a seat to put an Arbitral Tribunal in place. What if *that* part is pathological?**

A: First, something reasonably easy. Contract interpretation should correct errors in geography or information. The more specific element should dominate over the more general, according to the principle *"lex specialis derogat legi generali."*

**127.  Q: Examples?**

A: "Uncitral in Geneva" means Uncitral (the Arbitral Institution which is in Vienna) Arbitration Rules, seat of the arbitration Geneva. "Stockholm, Swiss" means Stockholm, Sweden. "Zurich, Sweden" means Zurich, Switzerland.

**128.  Q: Have there really been cases like this?**

A: Yes. All these examples *did* happen.

There is no justification in my opinion for the ICC practice of putting the place of arbitration in Paris simply because the word "Paris" appears somewhere in the clause, and no other place of arbitration was selected. For instance, if the clause provides for "arbitrato della camera di commercio internazionale di Parigi," the word "di" makes it perfectly plain that all the Parties wished was to identify the Arbitral Institution (as Parties do in one quarter of all ICC clauses), not agree on a seat. One quarter of all ICC arbitrations in Paris wind up there because of this, in my view indefensible, practice of the ICC claiming that the Parties *chose* Paris when they did no such thing.

**129.  Q: What do you do if only a country of arbitration is named, not the place?**

A: The *lex arbitri* of that particular country will either provide that this means a particular city, usually the capital of the country, or it may entitle a court or the Arbitral Tribunal itself to determine the seat of the arbitration *within* the country. The latter solution, however, presupposes that one succeeded in putting the Arbitral Tribunal in place.

**130.  Q: Again the hen-and-the-egg problem?**

A: Yes.

**131.   Q: What do you do if it is not clear which Arbitral Institution is meant, perhaps because an Arbitral Institution was named that does not exist under that precise name?**

A: Sometimes one can identify the Arbitral Institution all the same. In English, capitalization of a word points to institutional arbitration, since Arbitral Institutions have names that one normally capitalizes. One may then try to identify the Arbitral Institution that was meant. Some parts of the names of Arbitral Institutions are not specific and are often wrongly translated, such as "institution," "Institute," "chamber," "commerce," and "trade." The word "international" does not necessarily point to the ICC since it is used by many other Arbitral Institutions as well. The words "court," "panel" and "college" are not helpful because they also apply in *ad hoc* arbitration.

Sometimes there is a prominent Arbitral Institution in a particular city, and one can assume, if the name roughly fits, that this is the one that was meant. However, the mere *statistical* likelihood that a particular Arbitral Institution was meant should not be sufficient for it to be understood to have been chosen in this particular case.

**132.   Q: What do you do if the chosen Arbitral Institution has disappeared?**

A: Did it have an official successor? Then this is what was meant.

If it has no successor (or some people simply *claim* to be successors, but are not), then there is no Arbitral Institution left. This happened with the Arbitral Institution of the now-defunct GDR in East Berlin. It had no successor, not even the private "Schiedsgericht Berlin" which tried to inherit its cases.

**133.   Q: If the chosen Arbitral Institution never existed or no longer exists, will the clause still be valid as an arbitration clause?**

A: Even then, the Parties must be understood to have primarily chosen arbitration at the seat (Berlin), and only secondarily the Arbitral Institution, and, in any event, not court litigation elsewhere. So this will be *ad hoc* arbitration at the chosen seat.

**134.   Q: Even if the chosen Arbitral Institution was supposed to do more than just launch the arbitration, and, as with the ICC, provide support for the Arbitral Tribunal and scrutiny of Awards?**

A: Yes.

**135.  Q: What if some additional pathological elements concern the proper constitution of the Arbitral Tribunal?**

A: Yes, and this does not invalidate the arbitration clause as such. The Parties may have provided for a judge of the particular country to be an arbitrator, when in that particular country judges are specifically not allowed to act as arbitrators. Such provisions should be considered not to have been written at all and be severed from the arbitration clause, leaving the valid parts of the clause intact.

The same thing should apply to *pathological choice of law clauses*. Such clauses have nothing to do with the arbitration as such, and do not invalidate the arbitration clause.

Particularly difficult questions arise if the Parties provide for *conditions* for arbitration that can hardly be met, in particular, unreasonably short deadlines. If the Parties cannot agree to remove such an obstacle, this may well defeat an otherwise perfectly valid clause.

**136.  Q: In sum, one should avoid the dangers of the "midnight clause," correct?**

A: Yes. Actual "midnight clauses" are rare, but many clauses are not well thought through. A phone call to an arbitration lawyer at the seat can help and will cost little. Fortunately, many disputes arise that will be solved amicably. Still, there are cases when the magic goes out of the relationship, and a clause that was lightly negotiated suddenly becomes important. Some mistakes that could easily have been avoided at the negotiation stage may then cost many millions. To be sure, by that time the person that negotiated the clause has long been fired or has retired, but the cost to the company may be huge.

**137.  Q: So you have to think of many things when you negotiate an arbitration agreement?**

A: True, but keep smiling. The result should still be a simple arbitration agreement. Complicated arbitration agreements may well turn out to be inadequate when a dispute arises. What you need is a mechanism that, once the dispute has arisen, will put the right *people* in charge, give them the necessary leeway to design an adequate procedure, and get going.

**138.  Q: Suppose, we have spent time and money on drafting a wonderful arbitration clause, but now there are no problems in the performance of the Contract. Is this not a waste of time?**

A: No. Our good arbitration and applicable law clauses may well have helped *avoid* problems, and this was money well spent.

## (f)   Language of the Arbitration[30]

**139.   Q: Should the arbitration agreement specify the language of the arbitration in advance?**

A: Preferably. Disputes about the language of the arbitration are tedious and costly, and ultimately have little impact on the outcome.


**140.   Q: Does the seat determine the language of the arbitration?**

A: No. This is a procedural question; it is to be decided by the Parties or the Arbitral Tribunal. At the beginning of an arbitration the language question may be troublesome. It also has an impact on the selection of arbitrators.


**141.   Q: Parties in an arbitration often insist that their own language should be the language of arbitration, and they try to have this included in the arbitration agreement. Why?**

A: This normally comes from the clients. They believe that, if their own language is used, they will be able to follow the proceedings and have an advantage over their opponents.


**142.   Q: This is unrealistic?**

A: Yes. Following an arbitration for days is not easy for non-lawyers, even if they understand the language well. But how can one tell this to one's client in a tactful way?

That their lawyers did not talk the clients out of this idea is a telling sign of the client-lawyer relationship on that side at the time.


**143.   Q: The opponents may, in a tit for tat reaction, insist on their own language also?**

A: Yes.


**144.   Q: Is it then not a good compromise to simply use *both* languages?**

A: No, unfortunately. Conducting an arbitration with two languages on an equal footing is possible, but cumbersome. It may be possible to use lawyers on both sides and three arbitrators who can all handle the same two languages at the same time. But the supposed (overestimated) advantages for the clients will then often vanish.

---

30. See Annex (L), Procedural Order No. 1, paras 25 et seq.

Language is not always an obstacle. There was a very pleasant arbitration where the language played no role at all. Four languages (English, French, Italian, and German) were used indifferently by all the participants, without *any* interpretation. The file contained documents in these four languages, and even two more. In that particular arbitration the language question was never even mentioned!

Normally, however, even using two languages without interpretation is cumbersome, let alone more. Somebody, somewhere, will need interpretation, and once an interpreter is present, one might as well take advantage of having the same interpreter all around.

In any event, if the Award will be scrutinized by the Arbitral Institution, then at an early stage one should determine the language that will be used in the Award. There are rare cases where the ICC accepts Terms of Reference in two languages, but the Award should preferably be in English, French, Spanish, or German. For ICC Scrutiny, draft Awards in these languages need not be translated, because the ICC Court uses committees that can handle these particular languages. However, if the case is likely to go before a plenary session of the ICC Court, because a State Party is involved or a dissenting opinion is to be expected, English is recommended because it is far more widely understood at the ICC than French.[31]

### 145. Q: One may prefer another world language, say Arabic or Chinese?

A: Yes, but the Arbitral Tribunal then seldom has control over the quality of the translation of its Award as submitted to the Arbitral Institution.

### 146. Q: Are translations sometimes disastrous?

A: Indeed. Here are two stories that happened at the ICC. There was an Award in Arabic. As is well known, there is an Islamic calendar with lunar months. A lunar month is shorter than one twelfth of the solar year. Some lunar calendars correct this by inserting extra days or extra months, but the Islamic calendar is truly lunar. The beginning of the year accordingly moves around. It can be in the summer. Now, the ICC's translator of the Award simply called the first lunar month January, the second lunar month February, etc. As a result, the whole chronology was warped.

In another case, the original language of the draft Award was Dutch. The ICC worked on the basis of an English translation. The translation was poor. It introduced mistakes into the draft Award that were not there in the Dutch original. Fortunately, the ICC Court was able to detect this and spare itself the embarrassment of drawing the Arbitral Tribunal's attention to mistakes that the Arbitral Tribunal had not made, just the ICC translators.

---

31. See questions 908 et seq.

**147.   Q: Is the language question also a question of prestige?**

A: Unfortunately it sometimes is. Language should be a way to understand each other. However, when politics come in, language may unfortunately become a symbol of national or ethnic identity. As is well known, when these matters come in, plus – even worse – religion, disputes and even wars can result.

**148.   Q: Most Arbitral Tribunals give priority to the language of the arbitration agreement and make that the language of the arbitration. Anything wrong with this?**

A: No. The Parties used a particular language when they were hoping for a fruitful business relationship, and were able to speak that language at that time. One can say that it is not unfair to ask them to use that language when a dispute needs to be resolved between them, arising from the Contract that they made in that language.

**149.   Q: Is there not a difference between small talk and friendly talk, and a fight about sometimes important sums of money?**

A: Yes, and that should be taken into account. Still, the disadvantages of using several languages are so great that they far outweigh the difficulties of having many participants use a language that is not their first.

**150.   Q: Does having one language as a language of the arbitration mean that all witnesses must speak that language? Surely, some just cannot do it.**

A: No. Witnesses should be allowed to speak the language in which they can best tell the truth. There is even a human rights aspect here.

**151.   Q: Some witnesses are quite good in the language of the arbitration (English normally), but they nevertheless prefer to use their own language. They believe that this gives them more time to think about their answers. Should this be encouraged?**

A: No. A witness who is slow and struggles a bit with language will have the Arbitral Tribunal's sympathy and attention, and be more effective than a witness that speaks through a slick interpreter.

**152.   Q: Should opposing counsel attempt to embarrass a witness about the language in which the witness chose to testify?**

A: This is a waste of time and often backfires. Arbitral Tribunals have sympathy for witnesses.

**153.   Q: Should lawyers appearing on behalf of a Party use the language of the arbitration?**

A: Yes. One should expect counsel to be able to speak the language of the arbitration fluently, or they have not been properly selected.

One should be kind, but there are limits. There was a case when, at the ICC initial Case Management Conference, a Party appeared with just one local lawyer who struggled with English. By speaking (too) fast, the Arbitral Tribunal did its best to impress on the client that the lawyer should be replaced. This worked to everybody's relief, possibly even that of the lawyer in question.

Sometimes somebody important in a law firm suddenly appears at the Evidentiary Hearing and wishes to address the Arbitral Tribunal in person and impress the client, but is incapable of speaking the language of the arbitration (as is the client). This person should be important enough to ask somebody else in the firm to interpret. The Arbitral Tribunal should try and suggest that the interpretation be entrusted to a more junior lawyer in the firm who is competent at speaking the language of the arbitration (and is likely to have drafted the speech).

**154.   Q: What about Tribunal-appointed Experts? Should they be able to render their report and answer questions in the language of the arbitration?**

A: This is much to be preferred. If Experts submit their reports by way of translation, and answer live questions in a language that needs to be interpreted, they will hardly understand the questions and simply not make themselves understood to lay people such as the arbitrators. The language problems will overwhelm the technical difficulties.

Experts should also be understood by the Experts on behalf of the other side. In practical terms, this means that they should all render their reports in the *same* language, normally the language of the arbitration.

**155.   Q: Should interpretation be simultaneous or consecutive? Surely, simultaneous interpretation saves time.**

A: A frequent misconception. Simultaneous interpretation saves time only if the interpretation is perfect. Consecutive interpretation costs less than half and is not much slower than simultaneous interpretation. It has the advantage that somebody in both Parties' teams will be able to check whether the interpretation is correct.

One often sees two interpreters, one on each side, who take turns at interpreting (which is tiring), and the other interpreter immediately checks on the interpretation. This is the method that should be used if the language of the testimony is not known to any of the members of the Arbitral Tribunal.

**156.  Q: How do you make sure that the interpreters are good without knowing both languages yourself?**

A: It has happened that an Arbitral Tribunal interviewed several candidates and gave them an examination.

**157.  Q: What was the examination?**

A: The Arbitral Tribunal just gave the interpreters a newspaper text in the language that it did not know. It asked for a translation. Embarrassing! Some of the translations made no sense. Fortunately, one of the translations was perfectly understandable and made sense. Obviously the interpreter who had provided that translation was picked.

**158.  Q: Should an interpreter be a sworn interpreter admitted as a court interpreter in the country of his or her activity?**

A: No. Even good professional interpreters may lack experience with international live testimony. Experience shows that sworn interpreters are often not as good as people from a Party who are familiar with the subject matter of the dispute.

**159.  Q: But will that interpreter from the Party not warp the testimony?**

A: No, if the interpretation is subsequent and is immediately checked by somebody from the other side.

The Arbitral Tribunal should always insist that small portions be interpreted *at once*, say, sentence-by-sentence.

**160.  Q: What should be done about cultural aspects of language?**

A: The Arbitral Tribunal should insist on a truly *verbatim* interpretation.

There is the probably apocryphal story about a Japanese witness who took five minutes to answer a question, and the interpreter then interpreted the answer as "No."

The Arbitral Tribunal should patiently listen to the sentence-by-sentence *verbatim* interpretation of the five minutes "no." The interpreter should be told from the start not to provide a "cultural" interpretation, and that the Arbitral Tribunal will have to deal with the cultural aspects by itself.

**161. Q: Who should tell this to the interpreter?**

A: The full Arbitral Tribunal should informally discuss the interpreters' task with the interpreters directly, and well in advance. The Party Representatives should be allowed to listen in to this.

**162. Q: Is there not a problem with interpreting yes and no? If an Indian person shakes his or her head, this means "yes." In some languages, "yes" means, "This is true," in others, "I agree with you," and in still others, "I understand what you are saying," or even, "I do not understand what you are saying, but please keep going."**

A: True. One should be aware of the "yes and no" problem and take the necessary measures.

**163. Q: Namely? What can a questioner do about this?**

A: Questions should be put as short statements, then asking, "correct?" Avoid negative questions. Avoid questions that require a "no" answer. If the answer is not clear, ask again.

**164. Q: Is there not just one translation, the correct one?**

A: No, this is a frequent misconception.

An interpreter or translator needs to know the *purpose* of the translation and should translate accordingly.

Just think of security warnings for drugs. To serve the particular warning purpose, the translation must sound as if originally written in the target language. The patient must find the warnings easy to understand. That they were translated from another language is irrelevant for the purpose. Security warnings may even differ from market to market because of all kinds of cultural contexts.

Or think of poetry. Ideally, the translation of a poem should read as well as the original.

At the other extreme, take a statutory text. If one translates this too smoothly, the translation is likely to be misleading, because in the target language the context of the legal system may be different. One may start translating a legal text just word by word. But a good legal translator may even include some reference to the original text in the original language, or provide an explanation, and will not be afraid of making the translation into the target language sound like the translation that it is.

**165. Q: Example?**

A: An example from German and Swiss constitutional law: The Federal Constitution of the United States of America has a bicameral federal constitutional system, and both Germany and Switzerland were influenced by the Federal Constitution of the United States and likewise have federal constitutions with bicameral systems.

The Upper House in Parliament in the United States is called the "Senate."

In Germany, the upper house is called "Bundesrat." "Federal Council" will be a correct literal translation of this, but nobody outside Germany will understand what is meant.

In Switzerland, the same name, "Bundesrat" or "Federal Council," is the name of the *Federal Government!* So for a Swiss, the literal translation, "Federal Council" for the German Upper House or "Bundesrat" would be downright misleading.

If you translate Germany's "Bundesrat" as "Chamber of the member State Governments," this is perhaps cumbersome, but a correct description that most people will understand.

In Switzerland, the Upper House is called "Ständerat." This could be translated literally as "Council of the States," but most people would then believe that this is closely similar to the German "Bundesrat," which it is not. The Member State governments have nothing to do with the Swiss Upper House. People will have a better understanding if you translate the Swiss "Ständerat" by "Senate." Admittedly, this word is not used in Swiss constitutional law, but the Swiss Ständerat is closely modeled on the United States Senate – two members per Member State (called "canton" or "Stand" in Switzerland), but elected, and independent from the State/Cantonal Governments, just as the Senators in the United States.

**166. Q: What is the legal position of an interpreter?**

A: The legal position is the same as that of an Expert, but with a limited scope of expertise, namely the skill to interpret a particular text or a particular statement, often testimony by a witness.

As we saw, a controversy about the correctness of an interpretation is best resolved right then and there on the spot, by having the interpretation checked by an interpretation-checker from the other Party.[32]

**167. Q: Is the interpretation-checker then an Expert also?**

A: Yes. Incidentally, the interpreters from both sides may, on occasion, work together to prepare a common translation of a document while everybody else has lunch. Hunger helps.

---

32. See question 159.

**168.  Q: Well, if an interpreter is an Expert, should he or she be admonished to do his or her best to provide a correct interpretation?**

A: Yes, this should be done, but admittedly is often omitted.

**169.  Q: If it is omitted, should the interpretation be disregarded?**

A: No. This is then simply a situation where there is a procedural irregularity which a Party must flag so that it can be corrected on the spot.[33] If none of the Parties objects, any procedural defect that they perceived is remedied,[34] Article 39 ICC Rules.

**170.  Q: So an interpreter has a different legal nature than a confidentiality advisor?**

A: Yes. An interpreter renders no decisions. By contrast, a confidentiality advisor actually renders *decisions* that the Parties and the Arbitral Tribunal will be required to follow. The confidentiality advisor should be seen as an *arbitrator* with a limited range of decision-making power, rendering decisions which will be *res iudicata*. For the Arbitral Tribunal, the confidentiality advisor is a parallel arbitrator, and is instituted not by the Arbitral Tribunal, but actually by the Parties themselves.

The confidentiality advisor is used to screen the Arbitral Tribunal from having to make decisions about documents which, if excluded, should be disregarded, which is difficult for an Arbitral Tribunal to do if it has seen those documents and must erase them from its mind.[35]

## (g)  Applicable Law Clause

**171.  Q: Should the agreement specify the law applicable to the merits?**

A: Yes, but separately, not in the arbitration clause itself. We will discuss the applicable law much later.[36]

However, if there is another separate agreement between the same Parties, and perhaps others, and those other agreements refer to the arbitration clause, make sure that they also refer to the applicable law clause.

---

33. Art. 23 subsec. 4 ICC Rules.
34. Art. 39 ICC Rules.
35. See question 169.
36. See questions 665 et seq.

**172.  Q: Are there further questions that, at the time of making the agreement, an arbitration clause should preferably answer?**

A: No.

Occasionally, writers advocate arbitration clauses that are loaded up with numerous details. Usually, these writers once lost an arbitration on a certain point and now wish to make sure that this will not happen to them again! However, the other side will rarely agree to such a loaded clause, and it will lead to unnecessary and expensive controversy.

CHAPTER 2

# Performing International Contracts, Pre-arbitration Problems

## (a)  Performing International Contracts[37]

### 173.  Q: How should a Party go about performing an international Contract?

A: This is a management task that deserves attention from the outset, at the time the Contract is negotiated. Problems may arise in connection with operating in a different working or regulatory environment. Many international disputes have their root in technical or personnel problems, or both.

### 174.  Q: What kind of technical problems?

A: A company may have developed and successfully commercialized a technology. Now, in a new Contract, it undertakes to apply the technology in a different environment.

The problems connected with operating in a *different environment* may easily be underestimated. Some of these problems are genuinely technical, such as those arising from different temperatures, different humidity, salty air, or the use of different raw materials.

The regulatory environment may also be different, starting with bringing in people and importing equipment and raw materials.

---

37. An earlier version of this subchapter was published by the author under the title "Starting International Arbitration – Pitfalls in the Runway", Swiss Essays on International Arbitration, Ed. Claude Reymond/Eugène Bucher, Schulthess Verlag, Zurich, 1984, pp. 139-145. The author thanks Schulthess Verlag for the permission to use the earlier publication.

Often technical problems also arise in connection with the size of the project. A company now seeks to apply its successful technology on a larger scale, and at an even faster rate. *Increasing the size* of equipment may lead to problems because, for example, length increases linearly, but surface and, even more so, volume and weight, increase exponentially.

### 175. Q: Is a human factor also involved?

A: Often more than the technical factor. At the home office, experienced people draft well-thought-out Contracts. Later, when technical problems arise, perhaps on a faraway site where people are all by themselves, the demands on them increase dramatically. Good people solve problems as they arise. Others let them go out of hand.

Many problems that later surface in performing international Contracts can be traced back to simple difficulties in communication between people on both sides. Their language and communication skills may initially look good, but turn out to be insufficient for unexpected problems. Small difficulties can then snowball.

### 176. Q: Does this mean that management should pay attention to putting together the right team to perform an international Contract?

A: Yes, and not just at the outset, but all the way into a possible arbitration.

*Keeping* the right team throughout personnel changes is important.[38] In one project, a Party's chief engineer went on maternity leave. Nobody replaced her and the lower-level personnel just muddled through. Suddenly the team had lost its capability to deal with major unforeseen problems. Ultimately this led to an arbitration that might well otherwise have been avoided.

### 177. Q: Other management mistakes?

A: It is surprising how often nobody on the team required to perform an international Contract (negotiated by others), is aware of what the Contract actually provides. Particularly with respect to deadlines. The relationship on site may be friendly and informal, but if nobody knows what the deadlines are, there will be a great temptation to let the timetable slip, and to reduce the personnel on site and use them on other projects. Unresolved problems may then grow, and the relationship sours.

---

38. See Annex (A), Our Arbitration Team, and Theirs, Internal Party Worksheet.

**178.   Q: Are there tell-tale signs of trouble in the performance of an international Contract?**

A: There are. Some Parties employ special *letter-writers*. These letter-writers, unlike most of the others, *have* studied the Contract in depth. Their task is to write and complain about every problem. They are native speakers, and they write well. It is not as good as solving the problems, but it is better (for that Party) than doing nothing. If the other Party then shrugs off this avalanche of letters, "just written for the record," the problems may escalate.

A diligent Party should insist that the regular meetings provided for in the Contract are actually conducted. It may be unwise to cancel such meetings, even if they are formal and boring. Important matters may be first brought up at a coffee break.

Do not let the other Party draw up the minutes. Drawing up minutes of meetings is of course tedious, but the minutes-taker determines what was said, and, in a subsequent arbitration, an Arbitral Tribunal may rely on the minutes.

**179.   Q: The minutes may not have been agreed, do they then mean nothing?**

A: This is non-lawyers' law.

**180.   Q: What is non-lawyers' law?**

A: A formalistic and mechanical view of the law often held by engineers, sometimes assorted by wishful thinking that what somebody *thought* might be relevant.

**181.   Q: There is usually a clause providing that incorrect or insufficient minutes must be challenged immediately.**

A: Yes. To challenge minutes is not pleasant, but is still necessary. Even better, avoid the nitpicking role by preparing the minutes yourself. If nobody protested promptly against minutes, it is no good to say that the minutes were not countersigned or agreed at the time. They are still the best available evidence of what was said or not said. Arguing otherwise will be difficult.

**182.   Q: Is this to say that the law is written for those who are awake, not for those who are asleep?**

A: Yes, this has been true since Roman times.

**183.   Q: As long as lawyers are not involved, things are not yet so bad? Or are they?**

A: To be sure, once the lawyers get involved this spells trouble. Once a Party involves its lawyers in the dispute, at the very least it hopes the other side will submit the matter to its legal department, or to its outside lawyers. This is normally a sign that earlier attempts at negotiating a settlement have failed, or that the other Party's management was hard to reach. The other Party should seize this last opportunity.

However, a Party may already have consulted its lawyers at an earlier stage, and simply not revealed this to the other side to avoid escalating the dispute.

Another reason may be that, in expectation of a looming arbitration, the more diligent Party was carefully maneuvering for procedural advantages, and preparing a surprise move without disturbing the other side's sleep.

**184.   Q: Are there specific things that a Party can do to prepare for a possible arbitration?**

A: Absolutely. Without alerting the other side, a Party should *gather proof* of the facts on the ground. Even if everything looks bright, a Party should be aware that one day it may have to prove the facts. For this, it may need to take pictures on site regularly, which is easy and cheap enough to do. But then make sure that you can prove who took the picture, when, from which point, looking in which direction, and what may be seen on the picture (the "w" questions). Writing a few words about this (preferably not on the picture itself) costs little, and may have a significant impact on the outcome of an arbitration.

Leave documents as they are; do not let people comment *on* them in handwriting. Always immediately identify the author of handwritten notes (perhaps by a name stamp – easy and legible). Always date documents (yes, again by a stamp). Take a leaf from what auditors do.

This may also be the moment to involve your outside Experts. They should be selected with care. Their reports should be written in a way that will be usable in a future arbitration. For instance, in English.[39]

## (b)   Pre-arbitration Problems: Strategic Choices

**185.   Q: There comes a moment when a Party believes that it must go to arbitration. What should it then do?**

A: First, it should ask itself whether all other avenues have been sufficiently explored, including high-level negotiations and mediation.

---

39. See questions 573 et seq.

It should ask itself whether commercial arbitration is the only feasible route, or whether investment protection arbitration is a reasonable possibility. It also needs to consider who the Claimant should be. Several companies in the same group? The shareholders as well?

**186.   Q: This may involve the home state and its foreign trade services?**

A: Yes. This is a matter for top management.

**187.   Q: If commercial arbitration is selected, is it then just a matter of calling the lawyers?**

A: It is dangerous for a Party to get involved in a commercial arbitration unprepared. It is even worse for management to then believe, good riddance, that it is simply a matter for the lawyers and possibly outside Experts. Outside lawyers and Experts cannot correct management's earlier mistakes.

**188.   Q: Are arbitrations won and lost by outside lawyers?**

A: Rarely. Occasionally one sees fundamental strategic mistakes, especially from lawyers who are too close to their client and just follow the client's ideas. Beware of clients who are perhaps engineers and have non-lawyers' ideas about the law.

**189.   Q: Can one expect that Party Representatives will try to speed up an arbitration?**

A: No, although they *will* call for speed – the speed of others. In their own case, Party Representatives will normally see it as their task to maximize their clients' chances of success, and most clients will see it the same way. Their philosophy will be that everything that can be done to win should be done. No stone should be left unturned, no avenue left unexplored. If that takes more time, so be it.

**190.   Q: Why is this?**

A: Compared to the amounts at stake, the costs of an arbitration are modest, even the most expensive part of the arbitration, namely counsels' fees.

**191.   Q: Are Arbitrators interested in moving expeditiously?**

A: Those who are paid *ad valorem* are interested.

**192.  Q: If the arbitrators are not paid *ad valorem*, are they less interested in the speed and efficiency of the proceedings?**

A: Less so, certainly. Still, an arbitrator has an interest in conducting many arbitrations at any given time, and many arbitrations over time. In other words, they try to minimize production time, also in the interest of efficiency. A fast moving Arbitral Tribunal is likely to concentrate on the essential points and will provide the Parties better value for money.

**193.  Q: Are Arbitral Institutions interested in a reputation for working fast?**

A: Yes. It is therefore surprising that some Arbitral Institutions are slow and bureaucratic.

For instance, some Arbitral Institutions do not document their arbitrators as soon as they have been confirmed. Instead, they wait until the entire Arbitral Tribunal is in place, so they can organise delivery to everyone at the same time.

Some Arbitral Institutions can act only with the signature of some important and busy person. This does not help the efficiency of the process.

Institutions should compete on speed, quality, and price. In reality one sees little of this.

**194.  Q: Does one encounter teams that are poorly organized?**

A: Yes, unfortunately very often.

**195.  Q: Should there be non-lawyers on the team?**

A: Yes, though it all depends on the nature of the case. Is it mostly factual, mostly technical, or essentially legal?

**196.  Q: If it is essentially legal, you will need mostly lawyers?**

A: Yes, but which lawyers?

It is amazing to see how often Parties are represented by legal teams comprising a group of the Party's friends, and their friends' friends, many of them local to the city or country of the Party's headquarters.

Some lawyers are eager to participate in an arbitration because they think that it is interesting and glamorous. As a result, Party Representation teams are often far too large.[40]

A multi-billion arbitration between some German companies and a Dutch company had its seat in Switzerland. The applicable law clause provided for an unusual mix of Swiss, Dutch and German law. The German companies had a team of some 40 German lawyers, one Dutch, and two Swiss. There was no recognizable leader.

The Dutch Party had a smaller team with a Dutch leader. There were some Dutch lawyers and a Swiss, but no German lawyers. It is difficult to say which team was more sensibly composed. Probably the Dutch team.

### 197. Q: So many people from different jurisdictions! Can a good lawyer not learn about foreign law?

A: Yes, however one often sees teams composed without anyone having taken the trouble to read the applicable Arbitration Rules, the *lex arbitri*, the applicable law (a statute book or case law), and some elementary books about these foreign laws. In a Vienna arbitration, the only Englishman in the room repeatedly said: "In English law …" He apparently thought that all decent laws were the same as English law, or should be. The Arbitral Tribunal told him several times that English law was irrelevant, but to no avail. A lawyer such as this does a disservice to the client. That is why it is better to have a team of lawyers, with a leader who will coordinate the work of the specialists.

### 198. Q: What is the right legal team for an arbitration?

A: The legal team should cover various areas. One needs two lawyers covering the *arbitration law* at the seat (the *lex arbitri*) and possibly aspects of dealing with the *Arbitral Institution*; two lawyers dealing with the *applicable law* (or more laws, if non-Contractual questions arise); and perhaps one or two people, including probably an in-house lawyer, responsible for *liaising with management*. There should also be some people, possibly in-house, understanding the *technical aspects* of the dispute.

It should be clear who is going to be the *leader* of the team. Some decisions will have to be made and they should not be made by a committee.[41]

### 199. Q: Why two of each type?

A: This is going to be a long battle, and one should not depend on just one person for anything.

---

40. See Annex (A), Our Arbitration Team, and Theirs, Internal Party Worksheet.
41. See Annex (A), Our Arbitration Team, and Theirs, Internal Party Worksheet.

**200.   Q: Must there also be a back-up team at home?**

A: Yes, people who will not appear in the arbitration. Tell them right from the start what their important behind-the-scene role will be, and that they will remain at their desks, close to all necessary resources, ready to help if called by a specific liaison person. Otherwise it will be difficult to keep them at home, and they will leave behind yet another back-up team – their own, or, worse, none.

In a border dispute arbitration, a friend of mine asked his client, a country, whether they were prepared to go to war with the neighboring country over the border dispute. Would they then set up headquarters? Would they have an army general making decisions? Would all this be done with appropriate safety measures to prevent any decisions or discussions leaking to the other side? The answer was, of course, yes to all of these questions. That is how they conducted the arbitration – from a well-protected underground fort. The other Party did not do this and could not protect its secrets.

## (c)   Settlement

**201.   Q: Instead of gearing up for arbitration, is this not the moment to try to settle?**

A: It is.[42] In fact the moment is good whenever the Parties are formally even. But settlement talks should always be conducted with care.

**202.   Q: Where is the danger?**

A: A front person should not simply muddle through, feeding wishful thinking to management. Hoping to achieve a settlement should not prevent a Party from preparing for the worst case, namely arbitration.

Above all, preserve your legal position in settlement negotiations. Do not give it up inadvertently. So write (do not just say): "This is written in the hope that we will reach an amicable solution going forward, but without prejudice to our legal position." "Thank you for your letter of .... As we understand you .... Or are we mistaken? Then, please advise promptly, so we may clear up this point."

Do not fall asleep.[43] Think of deadlines, time limits to present complaints and claims, the statute of limitations.

---

42. See questions 331 et seq.
43. See question 182.

**203.  Q: In settlement negotiations, should a Party disclose all it has up its sleeve?**

A: No. It may be strategically advantageous to keep the other Party guessing.

**204.  Q: Is settlement possible only before arbitration commences?**

A: No. One should also think of settlement during arbitration. Moreover, settlement negotiations should not necessarily be in the hands of Party Representatives.

**205.  Q: Once an arbitration is pending, is it not also in the Arbitral Tribunal's interest to achieve a settlement?**

A: It certainly should be.

**206.  Q: And the Parties themselves?**

A: Yes. However, there are Parties that simply cannot settle. For example, a country, or a Party that needs a particular outcome for political reasons beyond the dispute in arbitration.

In some cultures *saving face* is particularly important. This may in fact favor settlement, but must also be taken into account when designing the settlement itself.

**207.  Q: But let us assume that both Parties actually *would* prefer a settlement. How can an Arbitral Tribunal help them achieve this?**

A: The Parties and the Arbitral Tribunal may agree that it will be the Arbitral Tribunal's task to promote an amicable settlement.[44]

**208.  Q: This is easily written into an arbitration clause, the Arbitration Rules, a *lex arbitri,* or Procedural Order No. 1. But will it work?**

A: Not as well as some think.

In domestic litigation, the disputes are sometimes relatively simple, and finding an amicable solution is not that difficult between people who have much to share. But an international arbitration is different. It is not good enough for the Arbitral Tribunal to say at some point: "A settlement would be a good and cheap way to finish this arbitration. Would you like us to help?" After some shuffling, the Parties will answer, "Yes, but ..." Which normally means, "no."

---

44. See Annex (L), Procedural Order No. 1.

**209.   Q: At some point the Arbitral Tribunal may know how it is likely to decide the case. Should it give the Parties a hint?**

A: Some people think so, even though it is dangerous.[45] It may be preferable for the Parties to agree on a face-saving, amicable solution along the lines of what may otherwise become the Arbitral Tribunal's Award.

**210.   Q: An amicable solution only in name?**

A: Yes.

In some countries one also sees State Courts or Arbitral Tribunals that do not wish to be perceived as having made a decision. They propose a settlement so that they do not have to write an Award and stick their neck out. This is widely praised, but is not necessarily to the credit of a particular legal culture.

**211.   Q: Is there a good way that an Arbitral Tribunal can promote a truly amicable settlement without hinting at a possible decision?**

A: There was one arbitration where the Presiding Arbitrator, very famous, did absolutely nothing, and for a hefty fee. When the Parties saw this happening they settled truly amicably. The arbitrator thought himself a great arbitrator. Nobody else thought so.

Here is a better way: At the outset of an arbitration, the Parties take positions that are very far apart. When the positions diverge substantially, a settlement is harder to achieve than if they are close. Accordingly, the art of the Arbitral Tribunal will be to narrow down, step by step, with the Parties, the outcome that *they* may expect in the arbitration.

If that is done successfully, the Parties may foresee a narrower and narrower range of possible outcomes and, on this basis, settle by themselves, or with the help of the Arbitral Tribunal (if the *lex arbitri* or the applicable Arbitration Rules allow this and the Parties request it).

**212.   Q: Presumably one should focus on the big issues or the big claims?**

A: Indeed. If there are a number of issues or a number of separate claims, the Arbitral Tribunal should pick those that have the greatest impact, financial or perhaps political or psychological, or those issues that are easily resolved. It should deal with these first to get them out of the way.

---

45. See questions 216 and 217.

**213.   Q: How do you do this?**

A: There is no need to *completely* resolve all the most important issues. It may be possible to get the Parties to recognize the reduced range of possible outcomes. If they both assess this the same way, and the range is narrowed down, the Parties can at least find a partial settlement on these particular issues.

**214.   Q: What do you do about the small claims?**

A: Leave them to one side for the moment. Perhaps later it will be possible for the Parties to agree on what is sometimes called the *Pareto method*, that is, to resolve the small claims along the lines of the larger claims. Say the few larger claims are resolved one third in favor of Claimant, two thirds in favor of Respondent. You will then apply the same ratio to the many small claims, without even considering them in detail.

**215.   Q: Should the Arbitral Tribunal support the Pareto method?**

A: Yes.

**216.   Q: This presupposes that both sides were equally litigious from the start?**

A: Yes, but that may be presumed. You can also have each Party select a number of what it considers to be important claims or "Pareto" claims.

**217.   Q: Without Pareto agreement between the Parties, an Arbitral Tribunal could also render Partial Awards on some issues or claims, and hope that the Parties then settle the remaining issues?**

A: Yes, but once an Arbitral Tribunal has rendered decisions, or even just hinted at them, one Party may come to believe that future decisions will also be in favor of the Party that has been successful thus far.

**218.   Q: But that does not follow at all! May the further issues not be completely different?**

A: Yes, but Parties often have a tendency to think in terms of persons, while the Arbitral Tribunal believes that it is deciding in terms of issues. A Party that believes that the Arbitral Tribunal will go against it may start thinking of ways to get rid of it.

### 219. Q: If the Arbitral Tribunal is genuinely involved in settlement discussions, how should it proceed?

A: It should first help the Parties set the framework of a possible money settlement, dealing with the currency of the settlement, interest, all the various cost consequences, and enforcement. It should include an arbitration clause in the settlement agreement. It should determine whether it should issue a Consent Award.

In other words, the Arbitral Tribunal should help the Parties solve all peripheral problems, reducing the dispute to simple haggling over a Dollar figure. Once the Parties have agreed on that Dollar figure, there should be nothing left to discuss, and the dispute will not flare up again.

### 220. Q: Once the framework is agreed, how can one achieve a settlement on a figure?

A: Various "envelope" or "sealed offer" techniques may be used. The Arbitral Tribunal may announce its figure, after which the Parties may write anonymously "yes" or "no" on pieces of paper that they put into envelopes and seal. The Arbitral Tribunal itself, or even better, an assistant to the Arbitral Tribunal, may then open the envelopes and announce either: "We have two "yes". Congratulations on having settled." Or: "We do not have two "yes". Sorry, there is no settlement."

If there is no agreement, a Party that wrote "no," will of course know what it itself wrote, but it will not know whether the other Party would have accepted the figure proposed by the Arbitral Tribunal. A Party that wrote "yes" will know that the other Party wrote "no," but it can also be certain that the other Party will not know that it wrote "yes."

### 221. Q: Is there a method that does not involve the Arbitral Tribunal coming out with a figure?

A: The Arbitral Tribunal may ask the Parties to write down in their envelope a figure that they are ready to pay, or are ready to accept, in a settlement. (Example: Claimant 800, Respondent 300)

The Arbitral Tribunal must set, with the agreement of the Parties, the rules that will apply if the figures do not, by chance, coincide. One can, for instance, provide that the difference between the Parties will be split 50-50 (this would lead to 550), but perhaps only if the difference is no more than a particular amount (e.g., 400, so there would be no settlement in our 800:300 example). The Parties may gauge their up and downside.

Or one can provide that, at the same time as the Parties, the Arbitral Tribunal will itself also put a figure in a specially marked envelope. If the Arbitral Tribunal's figure (e.g., 600) is between the Parties' figures, the difference between its figure and the closer of the Parties' figures would then be split 50-50 (leading to 700 in our example). Alternatively, the closer Party figure could be taken (800).

**222.   Q: Is this flip-flop or baseball arbitration?**

A: Only the last suggestion is. Classical baseball arbitration simply provides that the figure of the Party that is closer to the figure of the Arbitral Tribunal (600 in our example) will apply. This way, the Parties will have an incentive to provide a figure with which they can live, but that they believe will be close to what looks reasonable to the Arbitral Tribunal (if the Claimant foolishly asks for 1,500, the result will be Respondent's 300 – a flop!).

**223.   Q: If a Party is approached with a settlement offer in the final phase of the arbitration, say, when the proceedings have been formally closed and the Arbitral Tribunal is preparing its Award, what should that Party do?**

A: It should ask itself whether the approach made by its opponent is inspired by a leak of information about the coming Award. The proposed settlement is then likely to be less favorable than the Award expected by the leaking arbitrator, and hence by the appointing Party. The approached Party should be wary of such late attempts to settle.

## (d)   Measures by State Courts

**224.   Q: Before one starts an arbitration, or before the other side starts an arbitration, are there measures that can be taken in the State Court system?**

A: Yes.

One is a freezing order[46] to seize assets of the opposite Party which could then be used to enforce a favorable Award. This can be done well ahead of an arbitration. You need a local lawyer to do this.

**225.   Q: Must the assets that are frozen be connected to the dispute that will be arbitrated?**

A: No. The assets need not be "traced."

**226.   Q: Could the assets also be receivables from a third Party?**

A: Yes. For instance, a bank account which is a receivable by the customer from the bank.

---

46. Formerly known as a Mareva injunction.

**227. Q: If the Award is immediately enforceable at the seat, is finding assets in the country of the seat a particularly attractive option for the Award creditor?**

A: It is, and if assets can be attached at the seat without establishing any connection with the dispute, then it is a particularly attractive option.

**228. Q: Still, the debtor might obtain a stay of execution at the seat?**

A: Yes, but this is very rarely granted. Besides, if the setting aside proceedings are swift, as they are in Switzerland, even a stay of execution will only postpone enforcement for the duration of the setting aside proceedings.

**229. Q: When does one start the arbitration?**

A: There is normally a short statutory deadline to "validate" the attachment, which can be done by starting arbitration. But one should know exactly what must be done to meet the deadline, or the attachment will be lost.

**230. Q: Presumably the Parties may also agree to postpone arbitration?**

A: Yes, or to replace the seized assets by a bank guarantee. There must be a full paper trail of all this.

**231. Q: Can one put a new attachment over assets that are already attached?**

A: Yes. Again, this must be studied with the help of lawyers from the attachment jurisdiction.

**232. Q: Are there other Provisional Measures that a State Court might grant to maintain the *status quo*?**

A: Yes, various orders to do or not to do certain things.

**233. Q: Which State Court should one use?**

A: One should consider a court at the seat of the future arbitration, which may need to issue a rogatory request to a court where the measure is required. One could also go directly before a State Court in the jurisdiction where the measure is required.

**234.  Q: This involves a complex analysis?**

A: Indeed, and consulting local lawyers in various jurisdictions.

**235.  Q: What about launching a "torpedo"? That is, go to a State Court which will accept jurisdiction over the case despite the existence of an arbitration agreement (which we will contest anyway). Then we should be able to argue before the Arbitral Tribunal that the case is *lis pendens,* so the Arbitral Tribunal should decline jurisdiction. Is this not a good idea?**

A: One sees this tactic from time to time. One should know exactly what one is doing.

**236.  Q: Are there countermeasures?**

A: Yes, but a precise analysis is required. If a torpedo is launched, it is important for decisions to be made fast, not by the local lawyers in the torpedo country, but by the international team leader.

**237.  Q: Are there anti-torpedo provisions?**

A: Not many. In Switzerland, Article 186 subsection 1bis Private International Law Statute is an anti-torpedo provision.

**238.  Q: A State Court could enjoin the other Party or its lawyers, or even its Party-appointed arbitrator, from proceeding in the arbitration (an anti-arbitration injunction). Surely then arbitration becomes difficult?**

A: Indeed. However, if one Party prevents the other from defending itself, the Arbitral Tribunal may draw the inference that the defense that the enjoined Party could not raise would have been successful. Otherwise, why was its opponent so determined to prevent the defense?

One can also imagine anti-anti arbitration injunctions.

# CHAPTER 3
# Setting Up the Arbitral Tribunal

## (a) One or Three Arbitrators, Party-Appointed?[47]

**239.  Q: Why do Parties prefer to nominate Party-appointed Co-arbitrators?**

A: Some Parties believe that they will enhance their chances of winning by nominating someone who will espouse their case as a super-advocate.

This is an illusion. The other arbitrators will easily detect bias, and the biased arbitrator will probably lose any influence over the Presiding Arbitrator. The appointing Party may then be left with nothing more than a virulent dissenting opinion.

**240.  Q: Still, would this not assist the appointing Party in preparing for setting aside proceedings at the seat, and for fighting enforcement (mostly) in its own country?**

A: Yes, but this will only be attractive to a Party that expects to lose in the arbitration.

**241.  Q: Will a Party-appointed arbitrator enhance the quality of the Award? By educating his or her Co-arbitrators, and moreover the Presiding Arbitrator, about the cultural and political conditions in his or her country?**

A: Yes, and this effect will be achieved even with a partisan Party-appointed arbitrator.

---

47. Earlier versions of this subchapter were published by the author under the title "One or three arbitrators – The more the merrier, or is less more?", Yearbook on International Arbitration, Volume 1, Salzburg, 2010; and "Backstage in Arbitral Tribunals", Croatian Arbitration Yearbook, Croatian Chamber of Economy, Zagreb, 2013. The author thanks both copyright owners for the permission to use their earlier publications.

**242.   Q: Does having three arbitrators rather than one lead to additional costs and delay?**

A: The additional cost is negligible in a large case.

**243.   Q: Where do the large cases start?**

A: Many Arbitration Rules still have a threshold of USD 1 million. This is far too low. Cases up to USD 20 million can easily be handled by a sole arbitrator, even one who is not the most experienced. From about USD 30 million having three arbitrators makes good sense.

**244.   Q: Is it true that, at the upper levels, the additional costs of having three arbitrators instead of one are negligible in comparison to the costs of Party Representation?**

A: Yes.

It is of course also true that having three arbitrators makes it more difficult to find dates when everybody is available. This, however, is only part of the difficulty. Even greater scheduling difficulties arise with Party Representatives and the Parties themselves. In a recent arbitration, three busy arbitrators had several dates and times available for a telephone Case Management Conference, and had already deliberated on what to say at the conference. It took three months, however, before the Parties were at long last simultaneously available. The telephone conference lasted 20 minutes.

**245.   Q: Are the advantages of Party-appointed arbitrators then more psychological than real?**

A: Yes, but psychology is also part of reality. Moreover, there are Parties that find it imperative to appoint a partisan arbitrator. The people who make the choice cannot be faulted if the case is lost, so long as "their" arbitrator argued in their favor. This includes not only some large corporations, but also entire countries ruled not by laws but by men. As long as these types of Parties exist, Parties will prefer selecting their own arbitrators. They will not entrust the task to an Arbitral Institution or, in *ad hoc* arbitration, some judge at a faraway seat.

**246.   Q: A Party-appointed arbitrator may develop "diplomatic" illnesses that delay the arbitration, or will simply be slow. Or, worse, leak information to the Party that appointed them. How do you fight such mischief?**

A: One should not throw out the baby with the bathwater. And there are specific ways to fight abuse.

**247.   Q: Why are partisan arbitrators often slow?**

A: If an arbitrator is a member of an Arbitral Tribunal purely to help the Party that appointed him or her, and the Presiding Arbitrator develops views that are favorable to the appointing Party, then the partisan Co-arbitrator will have no reason to work very hard.[48]

**248.   Q: Is there a possible compromise between having all Party-appointed arbitrators and having the Arbitral Institution make all the appointments?**

A: Yes, the Parties could agree to a shortlist-and-ranking system. The shortlist may be established either by the Co-arbitrators, when one is looking for a Presiding Arbitrator, or by the Arbitral Institution if one is looking for one or three arbitrators. The shortlist may be even more useful if, beforehand, the Parties specify their views about the requirements or profile that arbitrators should meet. But it is often difficult to find a common profile at an early stage of an arbitration, and at the beginning the profiles will be quite different. This once again shows that an Arbitral Tribunal with two Party-appointed Co-arbitrators, each fully meeting one of the Parties' requirements, will be preferable to one consisting exclusively of Arbitral Institution appointees.

**249.   Q: What is the most important decision in an arbitration?**

A: Choosing the presiding or sole arbitrator. It is true that the arbitration is worth what the arbitrator is worth. The choice must be made carefully, and it must be made at the beginning when, unfortunately, one knows but little of the case.

In a three-person Arbitral Tribunal, it is in the self-interest of the Co-arbitrators to have a competent person in the driver's seat. Appointing an inept Presiding Arbitrator will lead to long, boring hearing days in badly lit, windowless rooms, going hungry or eating unpleasant sandwiches, being crammed into low, uncomfortable chairs at narrow tables, and trying to hear a witness testifying at the other end of the room. Everybody will be trying to find a document "two thirds into the binder submitted with the reply to the rejoinder to the answer and looking like this." Afterwards the Parties will fight about the minutes because no proper verbatim Transcript was taken.

The choice of presiding or sole-arbitrator should not be left to others, neither a State Court nor the ICC Court (which is a court only in name).

---

48. See question 903.

**250. Q: Why not leave this to a State Court?**

A: Suppose a State Court must appoint an arbitrator, as must necessarily happen in an *ad hoc* arbitration when the Parties or the Party-appointed arbitrators cannot agree. A State Court is poorly equipped to make this choice. It is often too local in its outlook.

Especially in the civil law, State Court judges tend to be bureaucrats with limited knowledge and experience of the world. Languages and comparative law are not their daily concern.

In the common law, many judges have been distinguished practitioners. However, many speak only English, and may have only ever seen the English-speaking, cricket-playing parts of the world.

Moreover, judges everywhere will know many people, but mostly within their own jurisdiction, namely fellow judges and lawyers appearing before them.

Appointing a local practicing lawyer is tricky for a judge, because the judge will often consider an appointment to be a favor. To some judges, an arbitration appears to be a juicy plum. Favoring one lawyer within the jurisdiction over others is something a judge will often wish to avoid. Judges are more afraid of lawyers than lawyers are of judges.

State Courts will therefore tend to appoint former local State Court judges. Their idea will be that these are valued ex-colleagues who have vast experience. True, but experience in local court cases only, not in arbitration, and certainly not in international arbitration. They are real specialists, but in the wrong area.

**251. Q: So is this a reason why one should prefer institutional arbitration?**

A: Yes. Arbitral Institutions should know something about arbitration and arbitrators all over the world, and many do.

**252. Q: So why not leave it to the Arbitral Institution entirely?**

A: It is better than leaving it entirely to State Court judges, but it is still not the best solution. Consider the method by which the ICC picks Presiding Arbitrators in the absence of agreement by the Parties or the Party-appointed arbitrators. It relies heavily on proposals made by its national committees. Some national committees are knowledgeable and professional, but others are slow and unpredictable, and may well select unsuitable Presiding Arbitrators. This is known in the jargon as the "ICC Roulette."

**253. Q: At least the Arbitral Institution knows many people, does it not?**

A: Some officers of the Arbitral Institution, yes, but not all young trainees.

**254.  Q: Should one fear favoritism from some Arbitral Institutions?**

A: Consider this true story: There was a Chairman of a small Arbitral Institution who said: "I must appoint the best to preside, and I am the best."

Most Arbitral Institutions, such as the ICC, are rightly prevented from appointing their own people. At the ICC, this unfortunately rules out some of the most suitable people because they are court members. This is particularly unfortunate in countries where there are few suitable people in the first place.

Beware of any Arbitral Institution appointing recent staff members.

**255.  Q: Are Arbitral Institutions fast in picking a Presiding Arbitrator?**

A: Not always. Stockholm is particularly fast because it picks people in advance, just in case, and has a board of multinational specialists. The ICC is slower because it normally selects a national committee only if it has to, and some of these are slow.

**256.  Q: So should you do it yourself?**

A: Yes. "Shortlist and rank" is a good method that involves the Parties also.[49]

**257.  Q: Is it true that Parties prefer to nominate one arbitrator of a three-person Arbitral Tribunal, rather than having all arbitrators appointed by the Arbitral Institution?**

A: It is true.

Not always for the right reasons. Many Parties believe, often wrongly, that the arbitrator that they appointed will be biased in their favor. If that were true, decisions would hardly ever be unanimous, when in reality, most seemingly are,[50] and dissenting opinions are rare.

**258.  Q: Would an all-neutral Arbitral Tribunal not be preferable?**

A: No. The Parties regularly want to nominate "their" arbitrator, and who are we to tell them what would be good for them?

It is a fact that Parties hardly ever provide in their arbitration clause that *all* three arbitrators shall be nominated by the Arbitral Institution, which the Parties could perfectly well do.

---

49. See question 290.
50. See question 885.

Also, there is the experience of at least one Arbitral Institution, the Zurich Chamber of Commerce. For many years, it *had* a system of all-neutral arbitrators nominated by the Arbitral Institution. In that system, the Arbitral Institution would appoint the Presiding Arbitrator and nominate four potential Co-arbitrators, from whom the Presiding Arbitrator could choose two. This was a system that allowed an Arbitral Tribunal to be formed partly by lawyers and partly by experts, all neutral.

This sounds attractive, at least in small cases. However, when people had chosen the system, they were often surprised when they saw what it meant, which rightly struck them as unusual, though not necessarily bad. Incidentally, this shows that Parties often have little idea of what they are getting into when they make an arbitration agreement.

### 259. Q: Where did that system come from?

A: This was meant to replicate a Commercial Court which indeed had (and has to this day) a combination of professional judges and technical and business people sitting alongside them. But many people wanted more of a say in the composition of the Arbitral Tribunal, hence arbitration.

In any event, the all neutrals arbitration system did not spread and was finally abolished.

### 260. Q: How does somebody become an arbitrator, a professional international arbitrator?

A: It is a question that older arbitrators are asked time and again. There is a short answer. There is also a longer answer. First, here is the short answer:

It is a bit like the way you become an orchestra conductor.[51]

### 261. Q: Why do you say that?

A: Look at today's better known arbitrators – or conductors, for that matter. Many started out as assistants preparing the documentation, the score, helping organize, sitting in, and then started following in the footsteps of their mentor.

Some others started out as orchestra musicians, then started conducting early and did more and more conducting after that.

There are also some very exceptional types who had distinguished careers as opera singers or solo pianists and then suddenly took up conducting as a second career.

---

51. An earlier version of the matters discussed in questions 260 et seq. was published by the author under the title "So, you want to become an Arbitrator – A Roadmap", The Journal of World Investment, Vol. 4, No. 1, 2003, pp. 13–15. It was reprinted, with permission, in Newsletter of Chartered Institute of Arbitration, Malaysia Branch, Vol. 4, 2003. The author thanks the copyright owners for the permission to use the earlier publication.

Some others were asked to stand-in, quite unprepared, when the maestro caught a cold. That is what happened to me many years ago. When I first did it, I thought: "Hey, this is fun"; and people apparently said: "Well, it did not look promising, but it could have been worse. We might try him again."

And that is how you normally become an arbitrator – by good luck.

### 262. Q: Well, is it just good luck?

A: Here comes the longer answer. It is not only good luck. You have to ask yourself: "What are people looking for when they are looking for a good international arbitrator?"

You do not become a good international arbitrator overnight. You must have some basic skills, and those take a while to acquire.

### 263. Q: Such as?

A: You need to have independence of judgment, imagination, creativity, quickness of mind, and also a good memory. Good memory for the things that you learned at home, and those that you learned in school - yes, physics, biology, chemistry, history, all the things that you thought you would never need again. And above all, languages. This is the key to everything else.

### 264. Q: Anything else?

A: Yes, on that basis, a multicultural background, a multicultural life. You develop a liking for travel, for different lifestyles. Politicians show us the way to do it. When they are in China, they use chopsticks.

### 265. Q: In other words, you have to have an interest in people?

A: Yes.[52]

### 266. Q: More?

A: Apart from this mindset, you also just simply need to be organized as a professional. You need to know how to work with people. You do not have to be high-tech; you can also work low-tech and find your way. Some people in your office should be a bit more high-tech than you. The late Robert Briner liked to say: "Arbitration is mostly logistics."

---

52. See question 448.

**267.  Q: Still more?**

A: One last thing is that you must know how to relax. You must know how to manage stress and when to work and when not to work.

**268.  Q: Should one be a lawyer?**

A: It definitely helps. More about this later.

**269.  Q: What else?**

A: Once you discover that you really would like to be an arbitrator, and perhaps you have been one for the first time and a second time, you must *focus* your activities on this dispute resolution business early on.

Once that is the goal, you must find the time to do it (even if, at first, the money is not so good). You have to develop some specific arbitration knowledge, and you can learn this at many seminars and colloquia and so on. You must find the time to concentrate your mind on it and to gain experience. Experience is really learning from your own mistakes and preferably also from other peoples' mistakes. Perhaps even a book like this can help.

Get on with it. Answer at once. Never say no. If you cannot do something, just find somebody else who can, so at least you may be asked again.

**270.  Q: Do you have to be prominent?**

A: Prestige – symbolic capital, as it is somewhat pompously called – can help, but not much. If you are a partner in a well-known law firm, this will be seen as a sign of quality, but it will not help in any other way. What you really need is simply quality of judgment, and quality in the art of persuasion and presentation of your judgment. You must sell what you are saying.

**271.  Q: Is it important to get to know the good and the great members of the "mafia"?**

A: I would say, not really. They will soon know *you*.

How do you get appointed? You do not get appointed by the good and the great; you get appointed by your peers and those that are younger than you. These are the people whom you must persuade that you might be a candidate to sit as an arbitrator. So join the groups. If you are still able to, join the under-forty groups of the various associations in this world, and do something there. Get to work there. Participate in working parties, help draft a new statute – it is going to be fun – help draft new Arbitration Rules or new guidelines. Participate in the work of the IBA, of UNCITRAL, or of WIPO. By working with people, you get to know them, and they get to know you.

**272.  Q: Should you get on the lists of Arbitral Institutions?**

A: It is not that important, because that is not where the appointments come from. Many of these lists are just the lists of the ambitious who pestered the Arbitral Institution long enough to get listed. Then they think that they will get appointed. But instead they get disappointed.

**273.  Q: So you have to do your own marketing?**

A: Marketing is not a dirty word. Marketing an arbitrator is of course a bit different from developing a brand or selling a law firm like yours. However, even when you market your law firm you try to develop a consistent product, a recognizable name, a certain corporate culture, an image, and that is what you are selling.

As an arbitrator you are a bit removed from all that. You are yourself, and you have to develop your own individual brand. The simplest thing is to get your name out there as much as you can, and on all kinds of occasions. That is where lists come in and where vanity publications may be useful – things like the "Best Twenty" or whatever of this sort. If you can do a little more of that, that can be helpful. If it comes naturally to you, you can and should develop your personal style, beginning but not ending with, perhaps, the arbitrator who always wears a scarf around his neck. All these things are good, but never forget: Be yourself.

**274.  Q: For an arbitrator to be neutral, is it not a good idea to take this person from a neutral country?**

A: A popular choice, but this is another myth. The political neutrality of a country has nothing to do with the attitude of its citizens.

**275.  Q: In investment protection disputes, some arbitrators have the reputation of being sympathetic to host states, some others of favoring the investor. Is there any truth in this?**

A: There is, but this is investment arbitration. In international commercial arbitration, arbitrators are not so easily labeled.

**276. Q: Back to Party Representation. How do you select your arbitrator? Does it make sense to appoint somebody knowledgeable about the applicable law?**

A: This should not be the primary concern. Of course, sometimes the applicable law may be important. However, a lawyer familiar with a similar law should be able to understand a related system. Even the common law/civil law divide is not too difficult for a capable lawyer to bridge.

In one arbitration, the Parties apparently believed that Swiss substantive law would apply, and appointed three Swiss lawyers. Yet it turned out that Texan law was applicable to the merits, and the three Swiss arbitrators applied Texan substantive law. When, on enforcement in Texas, one Party argued that the arbitrators had misapplied Texan law, the Texan Court said that, on the contrary, they had got it exactly right.

In a panel of three, it is not likely that all three lawyers will be from the same jurisdiction. Arbitrators from other jurisdictions may be curious and eager for statements about the applicable law by the arbitrator from that jurisdiction. They may however be skeptical, and then the intended effect disappears.

**277. Q: Will somebody from our own jurisdiction not push in our favor?**

A: Perhaps, but appointing a partisan arbitrator is not a promising strategy.[53] It is a fallacy that one's own law always helps.[54]

**278. Q: To appoint an arbitrator who is an expert in the subject matter of the dispute should save money?**

A: This is a frequent misconception. We are looking for somebody who, in a team of three people, will be able to understand all the complexities of an international arbitration.

Yes, some of the questions will be technical, but many more questions will be completely different. There will be questions of law, questions of understanding business relationships, questions of language, psychological approach, and many more. Coal specialist Professor X may not be the best person for all these other things.

In any event, we should not be looking for somebody who knows everything already. Nobody does. And people who believe they do are downright dangerous.

Rather, we must look for somebody who has the curiosity and ability to learn. Even lawyers can, with adequate help, understand technical questions. Some technical people such as engineers may, it is conceded, also learn about the law.

---

53. See question 239.
54. See questions 693 et seq.

But beware of the elusive, rare bird of all feathers. Those who chase after such a bird may well find themselves in the swamps.

### 279.   Q: If we are to teach an Arbitral Tribunal technical things, how should we go about this?

A: It can be done with the help of Party-appointed Experts who are good communicators. As a Party Representative, you will need somebody like this on your team from the very start, first to teach *you* and the other team members. In many arbitrations this happens too late, if at all. One pays a high price for beating around the bush without understanding, let alone explaining, the technical aspects of the case.

### 280.   Q: Should we choose an arbitrator from the seat of the arbitration?

A: Again, this is only one factor. Think of who the Presiding Arbitrator might be. If you would prefer somebody from the seat in the chair, then picking somebody from the seat as your Party-appointed Co-arbitrator may defeat that preference.

### 281.   Q: So as one appoints a Party-appointed arbitrator, should one already be thinking about who the Presiding Arbitrator might be?

A: That was a special situation, but generally no. From time to time one sees some such attempt, but it will not always work, depending on the seat of the arbitration.

### 282.   Q: Where, for instance, will it not work?

A: One cannot predict who will be the Presiding Arbitrator with sufficient certainty. What can be done about this is limited. One can, for instance, *exclude* certain categories of arbitrators in the arbitration clause itself. But the Arbitral Institution is not likely to appoint such candidates anyway. It will definitely not appoint anybody from the country of one of the Parties. It is also unlikely to appoint anybody from the same country as one of the Co-arbitrators.[55] It will look for an equal distance between the Parties (and often their counsel), the Co-arbitrators, and the Presiding Arbitrator, also on cultural grounds.

By trying too hard to avoid trouble, the Arbitral Institution may occasionally exclude all tried and tested options and go for somebody totally unknown. This may lead to Arbitral Institutions making unsuitable appointments.

Take the case of a Belgian Party and a German Party, Paris seat, Swiss law applicable, Party-appointed arbitrators Swiss and Belgian. No Presiding Arbitrator from Germany, Belgium, Austria, the Netherlands, or Switzerland is likely to be appointed, nor

---

55. See question 280.

anybody from the Common Law. This will limit the candidates to French or Italians. Spaniards are already further remote from the applicable Swiss law. If one of the Parties says that it does not want anybody from France, the Presiding Arbitrator will definitely be an Italian, at the ICC upon proposal by the Italian National Committee.

Another example: The Parties are from the Philippines and the BVI, Manila seat, Philippine law applicable, the Party-appointed arbitrators are English and Swiss, the lawyers on both sides are from Hong Kong and the Philippines. The candidate to chair could be from Korea, Taiwan or Japan, or perhaps Singapore, Malaysia, Hong Kong, or even Australia.

### 283.  Q: Is this not giving too much weight to geographical proximity, and too little to comparative law?

A: Yes, a frequent mistake. Air travel costs time and money, but little in comparison to what you save by having a suitable person presiding. Frequently too little attention is also paid to civil law/common law aspects. Take the last example: The Philippines, Korea, Taiwan and Japan are civil law jurisdictions, the last four, Singapore, Malaysia, Hong Kong, and Australia, are common law jurisdictions, which do not fit the case particularly well.

### 284.  Q: Is somebody's passport really relevant?

A: Not normally, but many are fixed on citizenship. Citizenship is easy to ascertain and easy to handle.

Dual or plural citizenship can become an unnecessary obstacle. In Brazil, on cannot renounce one's citizenship. If you were born there, but left as a baby, you are *iure soli* a Brazilian for the rest of your life even if you never went back.

### 285.  Q: Will an arbitrator who speaks a particular language be biased in favor of the Party that speaks the same language?

A: Some Parties indeed think so. Normally Parties with limited language skills. Those who speak many languages have a more realistic understanding. To them, languages are just means of communication, not of identity and affinity.

In one case, a Party insisted on having a Presiding Arbitrator who would *not* know the languages of either Party, nor the language of the applicable law.

### 286.  Q: You found this silly?

A: Frankly, yes.

The idea should be to find somebody who is equally *close* to both Parties, not somebody equally *remote* from them. Those who understand both Parties easily are likely to be able to treat them on an equal footing. Those who are local in their outlook, and find it difficult to know and understand either of the Parties, may in the end be swayed by irrelevant considerations, such as a personal liking of one or the other of the Party Representatives. A person who objectively initially looks unbiased may later turn out to be the most subjectively biased.

### 287.  Q: How then can one influence the choice of an adequate Presiding Arbitrator?

A: One should pick a suitable Party-appointed arbitrator. Respondent should study the Party-appointed arbitrator proposed by Claimant. The idea should not be to mimic one's opponent's choice, but to counterbalance it, if needed.

One should definitely pick somebody very persuasive. There is then a better chance that this person will be able to persuade the other participants to agree on a suitable Presiding Arbitrator, or a shortlist of suitable people for the job. Suitable, not biased in the appointing Party's favor.

One also needs somebody who will be persuasive in the interaction with the Presiding Arbitrator. Substantial experience in international arbitration and with the Arbitral Institution in question can help.

Some say that you should pick the most persuasive lawyer you know as your arbitrator, and the second-most persuasive lawyer as your Party Representative.

### 288.  Q: If the Co-arbitrators come up with a common proposal for Presiding Arbitrator, or a common shortlist, should one accept this?

A: Yes, even if the arbitration agreement does not foresee this. One must assume that the Co-arbitrators knew what they were doing, and, in their own interest, picked a suitable selection process. If one picked the right Co-arbitrator, then one can also trust that he or she will be capable of picking wisely. The Co-arbitrators are selected precisely for this. A Party should follow its Co-arbitrators' choice. This is preferable to playing the ICC Roulette.[56]

### 289.  Q: By which process do Co-arbitrators select a Presiding Arbitrator?

A: There are various "shortlist and rank" processes.

---

56. See question 252.

**290. Q: Can you please describe one?**

A: This goes step by step.

It is recommended that the Party-appointed arbitrators first find agreement on the *process* as such, before they start talking about names. Otherwise, the "kiss-of-death" effect may eliminate a large number of suitable Presiding Arbitrators, merely because they were proposed by the other arbitrator.

Once the Parties have agreed on the profile that a suitable Presiding Arbitrator should meet, the Party-appointed arbitrators may submit this profile to the Parties that appointed them. This should be done in an even-handed way, avoiding direct contact between the Party-appointed arbitrator and the persons with whom he or she was originally in contact. The solution is to do it in writing. Even include a written statement to the effect that direct contact between a Party and a candidate would be improper.[57]

**291. Q: Will this prevent direct contact?**

A: One would hope so. The chosen candidate should be told about the selection process that was used, so any violation will become visible at that time – at least to the Presiding Arbitrator.

**292. Q: Once a profile has been agreed, how does one then proceed?**

A: The Co-arbitrators should each prepare a list of (say, five) candidates fitting the profile. Over the phone they can then together go down the alphabet to name candidates and discuss them briefly. About half the candidates may be acceptable to both Co-arbitrators, and each may have reservations about some of the others. This may result in a common shortlist, alphabetical only.

**293. Q: How long should the shortlist be?**

A: It should contain between four and ten names.

**294. Q: Why so many?**

A: One still needs a ranking. Some possible Presiding Arbitrators may be conflicted out or otherwise unavailable. A Party may rule out a candidate for reasons of its own that

---

57. See Annex (B), First Letter from Co-arbitratiors to Parties on Appointment of Presiding Arbitrator, for a diplomatic way of saying this.

it does not wish to disclose. A sufficient number of candidates should survive to give the Parties a choice.

### 295.   Q: Is it then not better to give the Parties the right to a peremptory challenge of such candidates?

A: If the shortlist is long enough, it is simpler and more elegant for the Party in question to rank such a candidate very low. The risk that this candidate will then emerge on top, or near the top, is then negligible.

### 296.   Q: Should the Arbitral Tribunal tell a candidate that he or she came out on top?

A: Yes, though of course only if it is true. Otherwise, you can just tell the candidates that they were ranked high up on the list. Either way, they will be flattered and normally accept.

### 297.   Q: Is it a good idea for the Parties to jointly ask the Arbitral Institution to set up a shortlist?

A: Not a particularly bad idea, but not ideal.

The process then becomes cumbersome. The ICC may ask some of its national committees for proposals.

Some busy arbitrators may not be particularly eager to do the necessary work (for free), just to be on a candidate *shortlist*. If picked from the list, a candidate will of course be pleased, but the other candidates may be unhappy if somebody else is preferred and they worked for nothing.

### 298.   Q: How does one pick the preferred candidate out of a shortlist drawn up by the Co-arbitrators?

A: The Co-arbitrators can ask the appointing Parties to rank the shortlisted candidates. The Co-arbitrators can also agree (internally) on what the Co-arbitrators will do if the Parties put more than one candidate in the same rank.[58]

Note that this is a ranking only, and the possible candidates will not yet have been contacted. The less successful candidates will not know of their initial luck in having been shortlisted and of their ultimate bad luck in not having been selected after all.

---

58. See Annex (B), First Letter from Co-arbitratiors to Parties on Appointment of Presiding Arbitrator, at the end.

### 299. Q: When will the candidates be contacted?

A: Only *after* they have been ranked by the Parties. The Party-appointed arbitrators (without the Parties), usually in common phone calls or letters "on behalf of both," will go down the list according to the established ranking. After all, not all candidates may be available.[59]

### 300. Q: Is this not a slow, protracted process?

A: Yes, but it has the advantage of being even-handed. A greater price is paid through the kiss-of-death method, an Arbitral Institution shortlist, or the ICC Roulette.

### 301. Q: How could the process be sped up?

A: The Co-arbitrators may not need to submit a profile to the Parties. The profile may be seen by analyzing the shortlist.

### 302. Q: Is it easy for the Co-arbitrators to draw up a shortlist?

A: If the Co-arbitrators know each other well, the process may be simple and short. Many decisions on Presiding Arbitrators have been made within 10 or 20 seconds. Even if the process takes longer it is time well spent.

### 303. Q: Another way for Co-arbitrators to save time?

A: Conflict checks by candidates in larger law firms can take some time. To avoid any delay, the Co-arbitrators could approach the candidates provisionally. Once the ranking is available they can straightaway pick the preferred available candidate. If the Co-arbitrators do this, they should tell the candidates exactly what the procedure is, without naming the Party Representatives. This way, if a candidate is eventually unsuccessful, the blame (if this is the right word) falls on the unidentified Party Representatives or their clients, not on the Co-arbitrators.

### 304. Q: What if a Party opposes a candidate from the start?

A: The situation is then similar to the challenge of an arbitrator, which happens much later, sometimes even towards the end of an arbitration. But we will discuss it now.

---

59. See Annex (C), Letter from Co-arbitrators to Parties after Having Found a Presiding Arbitrator Candidate.

## (b) Conflict of Interest, Misconduct, Challenge, Removal, Replacement of Arbitrators[60]

**305. Q: This differs from case to case, right?**

A: Yes. This is a wide and complex subject, and we will discuss it mostly from a challenged arbitrator's point of view.

Many well-known arbitrators once worked in large law firms, then changed firms, perhaps repeatedly, and may well now have their own boutique firm. The may know just about everybody in the hearing room one way or another. The key question is whether the arbitrator in question may be *biased*. *Dependence* (financial or psychological) normally leads to bias and is reasonably easy to identify. However, determining whether an arbitrator is biased in the absence of dependence is not straightforward and requires subtle analysis.

This book can only provide some practical advice, together with samples illustrating the tone that a challenged arbitrator should adopt.[61]

**306. Q: If an arbitrator or candidate is challenged personally, should he or she react promptly?**

A: Yes. Deal with the challenge early, but proceed with caution. Sleep on it three nights rather than two. Give the challenge attention and priority, but do not shoot from the hip. In fact, do not shoot at all. Take the high road, but do not look down your nose.

**307. Q: Do not take a belligerent stance, then?**

A: No. One should, as always, follow the maxim, *suaviter in modo, fortiter in re*. Never forget that, if the challenge is rejected, one should still be able to sit as an arbitrator as though the challenge had never been made. So write: "When I accepted my appointment, I declared that I was, and would continue to be, independent and unbiased. I have kept and will keep my promise. I have always been unbiased, remain unbiased, am not upset by the challenge, and have every intention to remain unbiased."

In practice, one sees challenges that at first glance seem unjustified, but then are answered in such a vitriolic way, that one has to say that the arbitrators in question have shown gratuitous bias and have shot themselves in the foot.

---

60. An earlier version of this subchapter was published by the author under the title "Don't be afraid – A pep talk", in Arbitration, the International Journal of Arbitration, Mediation and Dispute Management, Vol. 65 No. 1, London, 1999, pp. 24–25. The author thanks the copyright owners for the permission to use the earlier publication.
61. See Annex (M), Challenge of Arbitrators.

**308. Q: Does this mean that one should avoid conflict and simply step down whenever one is challenged?**

A: No. A Party-appointed arbitrator should respond in writing along the following lines: "In answering this challenge, I must consider the interests involved. It is entirely proper that a Party should be entitled to nominate an arbitrator who has its trust. That right should not be taken away from it for the pure convenience of the Arbitral Institution, let alone the arbitrator in question. One should keep in mind the interest of the nominating Party and of arbitration as a whole, which requires that unmeritorious challenges be seen as what they are and rejected, not side-stepped."

**309. Q: What do you write after that suave introduction?**

A: One should start with discussing whether the basis for the challenge is a procedural incident. One may have to write the following: "I note that the present challenge is based on the procedure followed in this arbitration by the Arbitral Tribunal as a whole. Whether the Award will be influenced by this procedure remains to be seen. This will be a matter for the ICC Court to consider when it scrutinizes a draft Award, and may come before the State Courts at the place of arbitration in setting-aside proceedings, or the State Courts at the place of enforcement. I do not believe that it is proper for a Party to use the challenge procedure against a particular arbitrator to prevent or correct an Award that has not yet been drafted, let alone finalized and issued. Moreover, it is always important to distinguish between the various members of an Arbitral Tribunal. A decision of the Arbitral Tribunal as a whole may not be attributed to its Presiding Arbitrator or to each of its members, even if, on the record, no dissent is apparent. A challenge should not be misused as a substitute for a potentially nonexistent, or now unavailable, remedy against a Procedural Order or an Award. This alone warrants the rejection of the present challenge."

**310. Q: Moreover, a procedural complaint must be raised properly and timely?**

A: Indeed. Many arbitration laws, and Article 39 ICC Rules, have a provision saying, in essence, "speak up or shut up." If a Party believes that it was treated unfairly in an arbitration, it should react promptly, though in measured tones. A complaint not timely made is deemed to have been waived. A Party cannot keep a grudge up its sleeve to be used later if needed. Nor can it preserve a grudge until further grudges have accumulated, and then try to say that they add up to something outrageous.

**311. Q: How should a Party complain in a hearing? Is it sufficient to point out that the procedural propriety is questionable?**

A: No. "Questionable" is not (bad) enough. One must say clearly that the Arbitral Tribunal is wrong.

According to the Swiss Federal Supreme Court, the challenging Party must even present a *motion* to the Arbitral Tribunal on how the mistake could be corrected.

**312.   Q: Is this not asking too much?**

A: It probably is.

**313.   Q: So, this is a second hurdle?**

A: Yes.

**314.   Q: If the challenge to the arbitrator is not really a masked procedural complaint (one that should have been made at once and therefore has been waived), what is the next hurdle that must be overcome?**

A: The challenge as such must be presented in time. In the ICC system, the time limit for challenges is 30 days after knowledge of the defect. In the Swiss Chambers system it is only 15 days.

**315.   Q: Is this not too short?**

A: Probably. Before presenting a formal challenge to the Arbitral Institution, it may be useful to directly request that the arbitrator in question step down, thereby avoiding cumbersome and bothersome proceedings. Fifteen days may not be sufficient time for this to take place.

**316.   Q: If there are multiple grounds for challenge?**

A: The challenged arbitrator must then deal with each ground separately. First, the arbitrator should ask whether each of the individual grounds was challenged within time. To conclude, write: "Many belated challenges do not combine into a timely challenge." "Many bad reasons do not add up to a good one."

However, a challenger may argue that the various individual incidents all have their *roots* in the *same* cause, and so does the challenge. The question is then *when* this one cause became sufficiently apparent to finally trigger the deadline for filing.

**317.   Q: If a challenge is late, as a challenged arbitrator do you simply stop there?**

A: No. Unfortunately, when they decide on challenges, many Arbitral Institutions do not proceed in an analytical way. As a subsidiary point you should therefore discuss the merits of each separate challenge. Do not summarize each challenge, just answer it.

Emphasize that the purpose of the challenge exercise is to make sure that the arbitrators have an open mind and thus will be *unbiased*. The challenged arbitrator should analyze whether the alleged circumstances might evidence *bias*, and argue that they do not prove *bias*.

### 318. Q: Should one discuss the IBA Guidelines on Conflicts of Interest?

A: One should say that they are not directly applicable by the Institution, but that, "for completeness' sake, let me point out that under the IBA Guidelines ..." Many Arbitral Institutions are adamant in saying that they do not adopt the IBA Guidelines, but in reality they often use them.

Read the IBA Guidelines well, not just the items on the traffic-light list. Many cases are not covered at all.

It is particularly important to understand the nature of the orange list. This deals with disclosure by arbitrators, not removal of arbitrators. The cases in the orange list are within the Arbitral Institution's discretion. They need to be discussed in detail.[62]

### 319. Q: What should be disclosed?

A: Some try to argue that "everything" must be disclosed, but this is not so. The criteria deserve close attention.

Moreover, failure to disclose is not *per se* a ground for removal. Hiding a fact *deliberately* may, however, lead to removal.

### 320. Q: What should one do if asked to comment on the challenge of one of one's Co-arbitrators?

A: Unless the challenge involves a particular incident, and *facts* that only the Co-arbitrators of the challenged arbitrator can either confirm or deny, they should avoid commenting. Normally the colleagues should simply write that they do not consider it necessary or proper to comment. They should not discuss the law and its application to the facts, nor describe the personality of the challenged colleague.

In any event, they should keep their comments short. They should not forget that, if the challenge is rejected, they will have to be able to work with the surviving Co-arbitrator.

---

62. See question 319.

**321.    Q: Can an arbitrator challenge a fellow arbitrator?**

A: No, and an arbitrator who attempts to do so may be removed. Rather, in cases of improper behavior by a Co-arbitrator, one should possibly disclose the fact to the Parties, who may then take the appropriate measures.

But think twice before you do this. A Co-arbitrator may consult with the Presiding Arbitrator and possibly the Arbitral Institution.

**322.    Q: What should an arbitrator do if a Co-arbitrator misbehaves?**

A: Think ahead. First, are you able to prove the misbehavior in question? If not, wait.

**323.    Q: Surely it is difficult to prove bias without documents?**

A: Yes, but consider this *true story:*

There was a case where the final deliberation went, by majority, against the Party that had appointed the minority arbitrator. Afterwards, the Presiding Arbitrator, as was his habit, checked the wastepaper baskets for secret documents that should not fall into the wrong hands. To his surprise, he found written instructions to the minority arbitrator written by the appointing Party. (Biased arbitrators are not always smart). A smoking gun.

**324.    Q: In that case did the Presiding Arbitrator send the tell-tale document to the Co-arbitrators? To the Institution? To the Parties?**

A: No, because the deliberation had already ended and had gone against the misbehaving Party. If removed, the misbehaving arbitrator would probably have been replaced by another person just as biased (though perhaps smarter). This would merely have delayed the Award, not changed it.[63]

**325.    Q: When in doubt, should a Party challenge?**

A: Challenge the Party-appointed Co-arbitrator of the other Party? Not necessarily.

**326.    Q: Challenge a Presiding Arbitrator?**

A: As a Party Representative, you probably have no choice. If a Party has good reasons to challenge a Presiding Arbitrator, it should go ahead, lest it lose the right to challenge through a deemed waiver.

---

63. See question 906.

Some say that if you shoot at a lion, you better kill it. True, if the challenge fails, then the Presiding Arbitrator, especially one who is biased or inept, may bear a grudge against the challenging Party. If that happens, things will get worse before they get better.

In the end there is a chance that the arbitrator in question will be removed after all, because the grudge will surface. With time, especially in a system such as the ICC that has scrutiny of draft Awards, the Arbitral Institution may come to understand the inner workings of the Arbitral Tribunal, and an inept Presiding Arbitrator's bias. Even if the biased arbitrator survives the challenge, the Award may, against expectations, turn out to be far more favorable than feared.

**327.   Q: Do Arbitral Tribunals have the power to exclude counsel from appearing if it would undermine the integrity of the process?**

A: This has happened on occasion, but the legal basis is doubtful.

An elegant solution to the problem is to include a provision to prevent maneuvers by which Parties seek to "shoot down" an arbitrator by creating a, usually last minute, conflict situation. A preventive text could be included in the signed ICC Terms of Reference, or the Arbitration Rules of the agreed Arbitral Institution (which are of course the agreement of the Parties). Once the Arbitral Tribunal has been formed, it must give its consent to any change of Party Representatives. This consent should not be unreasonably withheld by the Arbitral Tribunal.[64]

**328.   Q: Some arbitrators in large firms try to accept appointments under the proviso that, should their firm take on a new matter that would create a new conflict of interest, the Parties will let the arbitrator continue his or her mandate as arbitrator, provided "Chinese Walls" are installed within the firm. Is this proper?**

A: If the Parties agree to this *ex post*, there cannot be an objection, but *quaere* whether such an agreement can be validly given in advance.

---

64. See Annex (H), ICC Terms of Reference or Constitution Order, para. 1.

# CHAPTER 4
# Initial Steps in an Arbitration

## (a)  Request for Arbitration

### 329.  Q: How should you address an Arbitral Tribunal?

A: There are many good ways. You can say, "the Arbitral Tribunal" or "the honorable Arbitral Tribunal," "Sirs" or "Ladies and Gentlemen," "Madame Chair" or "Mr. Chairman," or, "Professor X" or "Dr. Y."

Avoid the second person "you," which some people find too direct or aggressive. Avoid the expressions "y'all" or "you guys," as used by Americans in the South or the West to say "you" in the plural. This may be misunderstood: "We are not guys," a dignified continental European professor once said.

Use the third person, it is less chummy.

### 330.  Q: How should you refer to the lawyers on the other side?

A: "Our eminent opponents," "our learned friends," "counsel for the other side," and the like.

### 331.  Q: How and when should Claimant commence arbitration?

A: Some Parties rush in with a short and perfunctory Request for Arbitration. They may hope to scare the other Party into a low cost settlement. However this is not the best opening move, unless the statute of limitations is about to run and you have no choice. A perfunctory Request for Arbitration will only elicit a perfunctory answer.

For Claimant, it is wiser to first spend as much time as necessary taking a hard look at the entire case, together with specialized counsel. The Party should think through the whole process of the arbitration on which it is now embarking, all the way through to enforcing an Award in various places.

Claimant should have a clear idea of its goal, and how the arbitration can help to achieve it.

**332. Q: Should a Party also think through its opponent's case?**

A: Yes. This may not be easy, but may lead to reasonable countermeasures.

**333. Q: Is Claimant's goal to win?**

A: Yes, but perfect "Justice" may come at a high price. Claimants normally realize this and just want a rough win.

There are cases where winning is not that simple. Claimant may hope to obtain a settlement, and then take the money and run. Or the goal may be to teach the breaching Party a lesson, and to discourage other Parties from breaching Contracts with this particular Claimant.

A Party may prefer to be Claimant, or it may prefer the role of Respondent, forcing the other Party into funding the arbitration.

A Party may be funded by an insurer. This may not be disclosed in the arbitration, but the insurer may have its own watchdog lawyer on the Party's team. The insurer may at some point think that enough money has been poured into the arbitration and close the spigot abruptly.

**334. Q: But one should nevertheless focus on deadlines, particularly the statute of limitations?**

A: Of course.

**335. Q: What should a Party do if it is unhappy with the arbitration agreement?**

A: The arbitration agreement may be "pathological."[65]

Perhaps some aspect of it may be remedied through innocent-sounding correspondence.

For instance, a Party may say that it recently looked at the Contract and the arbitration agreement, and it believes that the arbitration agreement must be understood in this or that way. Could the other side confirm its understanding? If the other side then agrees,

---

65. See questions 120 et seq.

or says nothing, then there is a good chance that the Party's understanding of the arbitration agreement will prevail. If the other side disagrees, the Party's position is no worse than it would have been had it not raised the point in the first place.

**336.   Q: Are there other things that a Claimant envisaging arbitration should do?**

A: Yes, now is the time to gather the evidence that, hopefully, one has already skillfully kept during the performance of the Contract. This may include pictures, addresses of potential witnesses (and former employees), contemporaneous Party-appointed Experts' Reports, the entire correspondence, a collection of site meeting minutes, and many other documents.[66]

**337.   Q: How does a Party provide a full statement of claim?**

A: If Claimant has put together the right team,[67] it should ask itself what it wants, and think hard about what to request in its Prayers for Relief, right down to questions of interest.

**338.   Q: Are there special aspects to consider in ICC arbitration?**

A: Yes. Beware of over-claiming, which, depending on the seat, may have expensive cost consequences. Do not be too afraid of trying to increase your claims in the course of the arbitration. This may require the Arbitral Tribunal's consent under Article 39 ICC Rules, but this will be gladly given.

In ICC arbitration there also is a very short deadline of 30 days to answer the Request for Arbitration. If Claimant has prepared a full statement of claim, Respondent will be hard pressed to answer it equally fully in 30 days. This will put Respondent at an initial tactical disadvantage.

This is another reason why you should not rush into filing an early, but perfunctory, Request for Arbitration, and then only afterwards get organized (or never). Get your opponents huffing and puffing, not yourself.

**339.   Q: But normally the goal is to obtain, at the end of the arbitration, as much money as possible for the client, is it not?**

A: Yes. One should therefore consider which currency to request in the Prayers for Relief, and what kind of interest.

---

66. See question 184.
67. See Annex (A), Our Arbitration Team, and Theirs, Internal Party Worksheet.

Of course, if the claim is contractual, it will be difficult to depart from the contractual currency. If, on the other hand, a claim is in *tort*, then one should ask oneself where the damage claimed arose, and in which currency. It may be a harder currency than the contractual currency, or more freely convertible. One might also try to show that, at some point, excess sums in a particular currency would have been converted to a different, more favorable currency. This analysis should be made with the development of exchange rates in mind.

**340.   Q: Do you also take into account interest rates?**

A: Yes, and the interest rates may differ from one currency to the other.

**341.   Q: This is not such an easy analysis, is it?**

A: No, but it may be worth doing.

In one arbitration, on the last day of hearings before deliberating, the Arbitral Tribunal asked the Parties when they could provide their final figures. One Party just sputtered. The other answered: "This morning, at eleven." These figures found their way into the Award.

**342.   Q: The Arbitral Tribunal has considerable freedom to shape the procedure. How should it exercise that freedom?**

A: This is a complex exercise.

First, the Arbitral Tribunal should be aware of the people involved in the arbitration. It will have to work with everybody in a professional way. For each participant, the Arbitral Tribunal should ask itself:

Who are these people? What kind of training do they have? Which universities did they attend? What are their language skills (do not just look at what they write – was it written by somebody else and merely signed by this person?) What is their experience? Have they published anything? What are this person's strengths and weaknesses?

Must these people observe particular festivals? Not eat certain foods? When is their weekend? (With precision: When is the onset of Sabbath, at this particular place? When does it end? When is Ramadan? Chinese New Year?) Ask about holidays in Procedural Order No. 1.[68]

**343.   Q: Do you look at the participants' websites?**

A: Yes. This way you may greet them by name the first time you meet them.

---

68. See Annex (L), Procedural Order No. 1, para. 5.

**344.  Q: Should an Arbitral Tribunal conduct an initial Case Management Conference in person?**

A: Preferably, yes. Case Management Conferences are usually time well spent.

Meeting everybody early, and a bit of small talk, may help with getting to know the protagonists.

A leisurely pace will build confidence. Frequent breaks, especially at the beginning, will make it possible for the lawyers to explain things to their clients and take instructions.

## (b)  ICC Terms of Reference or Constitution Order[69]

**345.  Q: What will be the focus of the initial Case Management Conference?**

A: The "Three Documents."

**346.  Q: What are the three documents?**

A: The ICC Terms of Reference or Constitution Order,[70] Procedural Order No. 1,[71] and the Procedural Timetable.[72]

**347.  Q: Terms of Reference are an ICC specialty, correct?**

A: Yes, but CEPANI has them also. What we say here applies *mutatis mutandis* to similar types of comprehensive, initial documents in other arbitration systems, such as Constitution Orders under the Swiss Rules.[73]

**348.  Q: Before drafting Terms of Reference, the Arbitral Tribunal could ask the Parties to explain in more detail what the dispute is all about. Is this a good idea?**

A: No. Do not rush into this. There will be plenty of time to do this in a structured and reasoned way. At the outset of an arbitration, it may be that one of the Parties, or even

---

69. Earlier versions of this subchapter were published by the author under the title "Pathological Arbitration Clauses – Malpractice, Diagnosis, and Therapy", Festschrift für Thomas Bär und Robert Karrer, Ed.Nedim Peter Vogt et al., 1997, pp 109–126; "Terms of Reference – A Practical Guide", The ICC International Court of Arbitration Bulletin, 1991, pp. 24-43. The author thanks the copyright owners for the permission to use the earlier publications.
70. See questions 347 et seq. and Annex (H), ICC Terms of Reference or Constitution Order.
71. See questions 380 et seq. and Annex (L), Procedural Order No. 1.
72. See questions 387 et seq. and Annex (J), Procedural Timetable.
73. See Annex (H), ICC Terms of Reference or Constitution Order.

both, do not really know yet what the arbitration is all about. Work with what they give you. Do not put the cart before the horse.

At the outset of the arbitration, the Arbitral Tribunal's primary goal is not yet to understand the dispute. It should simply get the process going. In ICC arbitration this presupposes having Terms of Reference and money in the till.

### 349. Q: Who should provide the first draft of the Terms of Reference?

A: The Arbitral Tribunal itself. Many suggest that it is easier to ask the Parties to contribute. But the Arbitral Tribunal's summary serves as a test of whether the Arbitral Tribunal has understood the case. Moreover, it will take the Parties a long time ("We must discuss this with our clients."). The alleged summary may turn out to be too long or too argumentative, or little more than what is already on record. The Parties may structure their contributions differently. Then it will be difficult to compare them. If the Arbitral Tribunal criticizes the structure chosen by one Party, that Party will be upset. If you now start criticizing *both* Parties' drafts, they will *both* dislike it. By contrast, if the Arbitral Tribunal prepares the first draft, the Parties may bend over backwards to accept it.

If the Arbitral Tribunal's first draft includes all that it has received from the Parties and this is skimpy, then the Parties cannot complain. They may expand the text if they find this necessary, but they will have to do so under time pressure. One should not forget that the Terms of Reference are not an occasion to present the first full brief.

### 350. Q: Should Terms of Reference be long or short?

A: This depends on the way the Parties have presented their cases.

In the Terms of Reference, there should be some balance in length between the presentation of Claimant's case and Respondent's case. Otherwise the Party whose submission receives less attention will feel short-changed. This sounds ridiculous, and it is, but some people are especially nervous at the beginning of an arbitration.

One has to make it very clear that by putting something into the Terms of Reference, whether at length or not, nobody is agreeing with that particular position. Not the Arbitral Tribunal, and definitely not the other side. Especially at the beginning of an arbitration, the suspicions of some Parties are great and need to be dispelled, even though, strictly speaking, it is quite unnecessary to emphasize that the Arbitral Tribunal takes no position (how could it?). Write several times, and in *italics*, that the Arbitral Tribunal does not endorse any Party's views.

You are better off having simple Terms of Reference that are signed on time, within 60 days of receiving the file, than more beautiful and elegant Terms of Reference that take longer to draft and are likely to be useless in any event.

The main purpose of having Terms of Reference is to get the arbitration going.

**351.   Q: So the length of the Terms of Reference is not important?**

A: No.

**352.   Q: In other words, the purpose of the Terms of Reference is to speed up the other two of the three documents - the Procedural Timetable and Procedural Order No. 1?**

A: Yes, even if this sounds facetious.

**353.   Q: What should the Arbitral Tribunal do if the Parties say: "Do not bother, we will draft the Terms of Reference ourselves"?**

A: Avoid it, if possible. It is far too slow, and often will not work.

**354.   Q: How can an Arbitral Tribunal defeat the Parties' attempts to do it themselves?**

A: If the Arbitral Tribunal has already prepared a draft, it should send it to the Parties as soon as possible.

If the Parties write that they will present a draft of their own, the Arbitral Tribunal should send its own anyway. "Crossing in the mail" is a trick that sometimes works. Or you can say: "Here is what we already have, for whatever it is worth, perhaps you may find it helpful."

Worst case, give the Parties a short deadline for their common draft, but get down to work and prepare your own draft anyway, and keep it ready. You can be sure that the Parties will not agree on a text within the deadline, at which time you can promptly send them *your* draft.

There was once a Party that, at the outset, did not believe that the young, unknown Presiding Arbitrator could prepare proper Terms of Reference. So it sent its own draft out of the blue. Immediately the young Presiding Arbitrator sent the Parties his own "rough" draft, as it was, just to show the Parties that he knew what he was doing. And that became the draft that was used.

**355.   Q: In the Terms of Reference, should the Arbitral Tribunal just cut and paste in the Parties' submissions, or should it shape them?**

A: Start by throwing together a cut-and-paste, but then straight away begin shaping and structuring. Give short names to the various claims or arguments. Use the same structure for both Parties' submissions as much as possible, one answering the other. Arbitration is structuring and shaping a dialogue.

87

**356.   Q: Do you send the first cut-and-paste to the Parties or the Co-arbitrators?**

A: No, this is just how *you* go about developing your draft. A Presiding Arbitrator should start with a reasonably well-written, shaped and structured draft. The Co-arbitrators may help with this. It is always preferable to take them on board.

**357.   Q: What do you do if one of the Parties has a threshold defense, such as a plea of lack of jurisdiction?**

A: Reproduce the threshold defense first, then the other Party's answer to the plea. There is no rule that Claimant should always go first with all its submissions.

**358.   Q: And if the other Party has not answered yet?**

A: Just write that it *reserved* its answer (even if it did not say even this). Soon the Arbitral Tribunal may receive an answer sufficient for inclusion in the Terms of Reference.

**359.   Q: Can the Arbitral Tribunal improve the Parties' Prayers for Relief?**

A: No. These must be reproduced *verbatim*, even if they are poorly worded. Yes, with all their typing errors and perhaps not-so-well-chosen abbreviations. But remind the Parties that the Terms of Reference are established "in the light of the Parties' latest submissions," and improvements are acceptable even as late as the Case Management Conference when the Terms of Reference are finalized. Perhaps the Parties will take the hint and improve their Prayers for Relief.

**360.   Q: What should be done if one of the Parties wishes to include a particular topic in the Terms of Reference, but the other does not?**

A: Simply include it and say that the other Party may respond in due course. If the Parties disagree on whether they disagree, they disagree.

**361.   Q: Suppose, one Party wishes the Arbitral Tribunal to make a stringent confidentiality order right from the start, and the other Party opposes this. Should such issues not be addressed straight away?**

A: In that case, the Terms of Reference may set out the positions of the Parties and state that the Arbitral Tribunal will deal with the matter promptly (to start with, provide for this in the Procedural Timetable).

Or you could deal with the issue in an oral exchange, when the arbitrators and the Parties meet for the initial Case Management Conference. That way you can issue an order as soon as the Terms of Reference are in place.

### 362. Q: Why not earlier?

A: First things first. Do not upset a Party if you still need its signature.

### 363. Q: Can the Party's signature be replaced by the ICC Court's approval of the Terms of Reference?

A: Yes, but this is a cumbersome process that one should avoid if possible.[74]

### 364. Q: Do you really need an initial Case Management Conference in person? Surely it is an unnecessary expense to bring people together from all over world just for a couple of hours.

A: A Case Management Conference in person is expensive, but it is often money well spent. You should even invite the Parties' management to attend. Sometimes, before the initial Case Management Conference, the executives have only heard their own people, and these people will understandably think of and depict themselves as the good guys, victims, or heroes. Now is the first occasion for management to see the opposite Party, and hear the other side of the story. Sometimes this may even lead to a settlement.

Experience also shows that people who have seen each other, even only briefly, take on a much friendlier tone than when they attack people who, to them, are mere names, and have been depicted to them as the villains in the piece.

### 365. Q: What should an Arbitral Tribunal do if a Party (usually Respondent) shows (or pretends) total ignorance of the arbitral process?

A: If in doubt, the Arbitral Tribunal should provide this Party with the entire documentation, possibly even background material.

### 366. Q: Such as the ICC Rules or the IBA Rules of Evidence?

A: Yes. However, the process of preparing and finalizing the Terms of Reference should not be held up in this way by Respondent.

---

74. See question 375.

**367.   Q: What do you do if a Party is poorly represented by local lawyers, with little knowledge of the arbitral process and indeed, of the English language?**

A: A Case Management Conference in person may help here. Insist that the Parties themselves (in other words, the clients) should be present. A client may then realize that a better team is required. In practice, this normally does the trick.

**368.   Q: Is all this not helping the initially ignorant or poorly represented Party?**

A: It is, and therefore one needs to be careful. It is essential to act completely above board so that the other Party can see what is happening. If the other Party has good lawyers, they will realize that having inept opponents will cause unnecessary delay and expense to their own client, which will be hard to recover in costs. For a Party Representative, having an opposite number who is competent, professional and trustworthy also serves the interest of one's own client.

**369.   Q: Has an Arbitral Tribunal ever expressly recommended to a Party to add a lawyer to its team who is conversant with international arbitration law?**

A: This once happened late in an arbitration. By that stage the Arbitral Tribunal had already assessed the lawyers for the other Party to be excellent professionals. They did not protest.

The end of the story is also interesting. The poorly represented Party initially followed the recommendation, and picked a lawyer knowledgeable in international arbitration. The new lawyer, however, stepped down very soon after having been appointed (no doubt because the required advance had not been made). The Party did not replace the new lawyer and continued with the old team. The Party in question promptly missed the deadline to request setting aside the Final Award. The Swiss Federal Supreme Court recounted the entire story (that the Arbitral Tribunal had providently set out in the Award), and refused to reinstate the missed deadline.

**370.   Q: What about the parts in the Terms of Reference that are the Arbitral Tribunal's own contribution?**

A: Some elements that require the signature of the Parties should be included.

**371.  Q: Do you have an example?**

A: One very special advantage of signed Terms of Reference concerns the New York Convention.[75] The Arbitration Agreement is usually found in the original Contract. However, no copy of the original Contract containing the Arbitration Agreement, signed by all Parties, is likely to be produced in the arbitration. This does not prevent the arbitration from taking place.

However, in the end, if the Arbitral Award is to be enforced (not necessarily by Claimant), the Award will have to be produced together with the *original of the Arbitration Agreement*, or "a duly certified copy thereof," whatever that means. This may well touch off a frantic search.

If the signed Terms of Reference say that, for the purposes of the New York Convention, they *themselves* serve as the original agreement to arbitrate, no Party needs to look any further than the Terms of Reference. These are usually easily found in the file of the arbitration. At the time of enforcing the Award this provision in the Terms of Reference can come in handy.

However, this is only possible if the Terms of Reference are *signed* by the Parties.

Any other contributions by the Arbitral Tribunal should preferably be short, because the whole document must in the end be signed by all Parties. It is much easier to add in details, say about procedure, into Procedural Order No. 1, which is simply issued by the Arbitral Tribunal without needing to be signed or endorsed by anybody else.

Plus, if a Party does not sign the Terms of Reference, the Arbitral Tribunal will have to pare down its text anyway, unfortunately excluding the elements that require the Parties' signature. If the Arbitral Tribunal expects a Party not to sign, then the draft should be minimal from the start. Travel light.[76]

**372.  Q: Should the Terms of Reference be signed at the initial Case Management Conference?**

A: Yes, and this is easily achieved provided people with authority to sign are present.[77]

However, if there is only a telephone hearing, one should make sure that the entire *text* of the Terms of Reference is agreed, in all its details, so that it can be signed without further discussions.

---

75. See Annex (H), ICC Terms of Reference or Constitution Order, at the end.
76. See questions 375 et seq. and Annex (H), ICC Terms of Reference or Constitution Order, para. 38.
77. See Annex (G), Cover Letter to Parties for the Arbitral Tribunal's First Draft Terms of Reference.

**373.   Q: Does dealing with every word of a long text in a telephone conference not take enormous time?**

A: Sometimes, one may indeed have to read out entire paragraphs, which is tedious. But a long telephone conference, or even two, is preferable to an angry exchange of emails once people are off the telephone. If you think of the travel time saved, even a long telephone conference seems short.

**374.   Q: Are there benefits in having the Terms of Reference signed by all Parties on the spot?**

A: It wastes less time.

**375.   Q: What should you do if one Party refuses to sign, or does not even appear?**

A: Then you must submit the Terms of Reference to the *ICC Court* for approval. Then pare them down and "travel light." That is, take out anything reflecting an agreement between the Parties (such as the New York Convention Special just mentioned), because there is no agreement.[78]

**376.   Q: What do you leave in?**

A: Only the bare minimum (the portions not marked by an asterisk in Annex J). Add a footnote where needed, saying: "This reflects orders by the Arbitral Tribunal, not an agreement by the Parties." One may send in an early draft to the ICC Secretariat and have it cleared in advance.

**377.   Q: The pared-down version is then submitted to the ICC Court for approval?**

A: Yes.

If a Party refuses to sign Terms of Reference, or worse, plays dead, the arbitration is delayed by several weeks. The next thing is often a fruitless attempt to have the Terms of Reference signed after all. In the end, the document goes to the ICC Court for approval.

---

78. See Annex (H), ICC Terms of Reference or Constitution Order.

**378.  Q: Are there other things the Arbitral Tribunal should do at the initial Case Management Conference in person?**

A: Yes, and it should still do these things even if the initial Case Management Conference is conducted via telephone, even if that makes it a long telephone conference.

Whatever the form of the initial Case Management Conference, the Arbitral Tribunal will want to prepare as thoroughly as it can. Often, an initial Case Management Conference will simply start with signing the already agreed Terms of Reference text.[79] For the rest it will be devoted to the other matters that should be discussed.

**379.  Q: What other matters?**

A: The other two documents, Procedural Order No. 1,[80] and the Procedural Timetable,[81] which requires that everybody come with their engagement calendars, or access to them ("You will have to call my clerk." "Do it yourself, please, and right now."), and whatever else the Parties would like to discuss.

## (c)  Procedural Order No. 1

**380.  Q: Should Procedural Order No. 1 be very detailed, or just contain the most necessary elements?**

A: There are different ideas about this. To be really useful, Procedural Order No. 1 should, in my view, be very detailed and proactively solve as many problems in advance as possible.[82]

**381.  Q: Why not simply say: "We will cross this bridge when we come to it," and hope for the best? In the end, many problems may not arise at all.**

A: True, but this will still leave many bridges to cross. If a problem is solved in advance, you will cross that bridge quietly.

Besides, once a problem arises everybody has an interest in one particular solution. Each Party will naturally assume that the other Party's solution is unfairly favorable to that Party. The Arbitral Tribunal will then be forced to make a decision and perhaps appear biased, at least to the Party that loses on that particular point. It is easier and cheaper to say: "We said something about this in Procedural Order No. 1." If Procedural Order No. 1 is based on extensive experience, totally unforeseen difficulties will hardly ever arise.

---

79. See Annex (H), ICC Terms of Reference or Constitution Order.
80. See Annex (L), Procedural Order No. 1.
81. See Annex (J), Procedural Timetable.
82. See Annex (J), Procedural Timetable.

### 382. Q: Do you have a standard full Procedural Order No. 1?

A: Yes, and it is Annex (L) herein. There you will also find references to these questions.

### 383. Q: Arbitration should be flexible, tailor-made. Is this text not mechanical and unnecessary?

A: A mantra heard each time an Arbitral Tribunal is proactive. Those who do not like a text will always also say that it is too long. But what do you do if you have no text at all? Extreme flexibility comes at a price. It often leaves you far worse off.

Even a standard full Procedural Order No. 1 can have sufficient flexibility built in.

The Parties can suggest a better text – but in practice they rarely do, which shows that the draft is not so bad after all.

### 384. Q: How do you make sure that a detailed Procedural Order No. 1, does not bind the Arbitral Tribunal's hands too much?

A: The necessary flexibility can already be provided in the *opening section of Procedural Order No. 1*.[83] This is good enough.

### 385. Q: Is it not sufficient to refer to the IBA Rules of Evidence, 2010, instead of issuing a Procedural Order No. 1?

A: To save copying the IBA Rules of Evidence, 2010? Yes, but not sufficient. You need to retain some flexibility especially concerning production of documents.[84]

Moreover, the IBA Rules do not deal with all problems, glossing over some for various political reasons.

One should also reserve the right to issue further Procedural Orders.[85]

### 386. Q: Should every Procedural Order be signed by the entire Arbitral Tribunal?

A: This should be resisted. The Terms of Reference must, however, take precedence over Procedural Orders issued by the Arbitral Tribunal, since they were signed by the Parties themselves (usually), or at least approved by the ICC Court. That is why it is preferable to have three documents, rather than cramming everything into the Terms

---

83. See Annex (L), Procedural Order No. 1, para. 3.
84. See Annex (L), Procedural Order No. 1, para. 4.
85. See Annex (L), Procedural Order No. 1, para. 3.

of Reference. Long term procedural aspects will find their place in Procedural Order No. 1 and later Procedural Orders, and the timing in the Procedural Timetable.[86]

It is not necessary to number all Procedural Orders, some of which are simple extensions of deadlines. It is perfectly acceptable to write casual letters to the Party Representatives which, legally, are of course orders, but sound friendly and not too much like what comes from a State Court.[87]

Keep track of deadlines in the Procedural Timetable,[88] which should always be updated.

## (d)  Provisional Procedural Timetable[89]

### 387.  Q: What is the legal nature of the Procedural Timetable?

A: It is an order. The Presiding Arbitrator can write at the bottom, "So ordered," and date and sign. It should be clear that the Procedural Timetable is binding upon the Parties, but is "provisional," and thus may be changed at any time. One should instill some discipline in the Parties in this respect.[90]

In an arbitration you cannot *force* the Parties to something, but you can persuade, cajole, charm, scare, trick, or shame them, or use any combination of these.

### 388.  Q: In the Procedural Timetable, do you map out the entire arbitration?

A: Yes, but it is still a *provisional* Procedural Timetable, and this should be emphasized in Procedural Order No. 1. One should not be over-optimistic. An inexperienced Presiding Arbitrator once drafted an initial Procedural Timetable that went to a Final Award in six months. One Party loved this, but was soon disappointed; that arbitration lasted more than five years.

It is wise to put some "give" into the Procedural Timetable, especially before a hearing. The Arbitral Tribunal can hardly *promise* that others will comply. The ICC Secretariat that deals directly with the Arbitral Tribunal does not welcome bad news (no bureaucracy does).[91]

---

86. See Annex (L), Procedural Order No. 1, para. 3.
87. See question 392. Examples of how to set deadlines in a friendly tone: See Annex (G), Cover Letter to Parties for the Arbitral Tribunal's First Draft Terms of Reference.
88. See Annex (J), Procedural Timetable.
89. See Annex (J), Procedural Timetable.
90. See Annex (L), Procedural Order No. 1, paras 5, 6 and 8.
91. See Annex (J), Procedural Timetable.

**389.   Q: Should the provisional Procedural Timetable include, well before the Evidentiary Hearing, a day or two set aside for possible argument, Provisional Measures to be issued by the Arbitral Tribunal, oral argument about a possible Preliminary Award, and the like?**

A: Yes, finding dates and times on short notice, even for a telephone conference, is often surprisingly difficult. A single day blocked for a hearing may in the end be used for a telephone conference only, or a deliberation, or internally by Party Representatives to work with their clients. Better to have a date that you do not need than to need one that you do not have. If the date is simply cancelled, nobody is likely to mind.

**390.   Q: What about integrating the Procedural Timetable into Procedural Order No. 1? Is this a good idea?**

A: This is not recommended. As the arbitration evolves, the Procedural Timetable will repeatedly change. Procedural Order No. 1 will remain.

**391.   Q: How do you set deadlines? The same way as a State Court?**

A: There are parts of the world where, for populist reasons, statutory deadlines are unreasonably short, but then routinely extended. An Arbitral Tribunal should avoid this.

The style in an arbitration should be as different as possible from that used in State Courts. State Courts usually set deadlines by a number of days and threaten what would happen if the deadline is not kept. By contrast, an Arbitral Tribunal should set deadlines by indicating the end date, and possibly even the time of day,[92] to treat the Parties equally, giving preference to the time zone at the seat of the arbitration.

Indeed, if the Arbitral Tribunal can avoid setting a formal deadline, it should do that. It could write something like: "If you could react to the present letter by, say, Friday, … the Arbitral Tribunal could produce a new draft on the following Monday, …, which would be early enough for you to comment in the course of that week before we meet, as planned, on the Tuesday of the following week." Good Party Representatives will take the hint.

**392.   Q: How do you drive the point home that decisions by Arbitral Tribunals are not just invitations, and should be taken seriously?**

A: To bring the point home that deadlines are to be taken seriously, and will not be extended routinely, Procedural Order No. 1 should provide for strict rules.[93]

---

92. See Annex (J), Procedural Timetable, at the end.
93. See Annex (L), Procedural Order No. 1, paras 6, 7 and 8.

However, an Arbitral Tribunal need not threaten any consequences if the deadline is not kept. For this, Procedural Order No. 1[94] is entirely sufficient.

**393.   Q: Why do State Courts then always threaten what they would do if a deadline is not kept?**

A: Because they have to deal with all manner of Party Representatives, and sometimes even Parties that have no representative at all. An emanation of the State cannot treat some citizens with more courtesy than others; it must treat all its users the same way. By contrast, the Arbitral Tribunal will know how skillful and experienced the Party Representatives are and can treat them accordingly, but always equally.

**394.   Q: Are there other time management tools?**

A: Yes, a Case Management Conference, via telephone, close to the Evidentiary Hearing,[95] witnesses conferencing,[96] and the chess clock.[97]

**395.   Q: Should Arbitral Tribunals be proactive? Should they ask questions?**

A: Yes, without revealing too much what they are thinking (if at all). One may need to ask some questions just as a smoke screen for the one decisive question.

**396.   Q: Are there areas where an Arbitral Tribunal should not be proactive?**

A: Yes, where a factual defense is waived if not raised timely. A plea of lack of jurisdiction must be raised timely by Respondent, or an unconditional appearance is entered. The Arbitral Tribunal should sit tight and not help a Party raise a possible defense.

---

94. See Annex (L), Procedural Order No. 1, para. 8.
95. See Annex (J), Procedural Timetable, and also see questions 607 et seq.
96. See questions 542 et seq.
97. See questions 552 et seq.

# CHAPTER 5

# Written Submissions, Evidence

## (a)   Written Submissions[98]

**397.   Q: The next thing after the Terms of Reference will be written submissions, right?**

A: Yes, and it is better for the Arbitral Tribunal to tell the Parties early on how it wants them to be presented, as anybody who has had to deal with voluminous and poorly presented first submissions will tell you.

Procedural Order No. 1[99] should deal with these matters, and also how the Arbitral Tribunal will deal with the problem of Parties missing the deadline for submissions.

**398.   Q: The Arbitral Tribunal could tell the Parties these things orally. Why write about them and appear unnecessarily petty?**

A: True, but consider this: Written submissions are normally first prepared by more junior lawyers. These people may not have been present at the initial Case Management Conference leading to the Terms of Reference, though they will probably appear later. Ideally, these junior lawyers should take Procedural Order No. 1 and draft their written submissions (or memorials as they are sometimes called) accordingly.

---

98. An earlier version of this subchapter was published by the author under the title "Awards and Orders – Labels Matter After All", Tijdschrift voor Arbitrage, 2004/2 Art. No. 20, pp. 57–62. The author thanks the copyright owners for the permission to use the earlier publication.
99. See Annex (L), Procedural Order No. 1, paras 17 to 24.

**399.   Q: Surely large law firms should know how to do these things anyway?**

A: They should. But even in large law firms there are beginners who need to be told mundane things. Everybody was once a beginner.

Moreover, not all partners in a law firm have the time and inclination to teach. It is convenient for a partner to be able to say: "By the way, please make sure that we comply with Procedural Order No. 1. We have this pedantic Arbitral Tribunal. Better not upset them unnecessarily."

**400.   Q: How many written submissions/memorials should each Party submit? Does this depend on the *lex arbitri*?**

A: No, it depends on the lawyers that appear for the Parties. In the common law tradition, there are normally two written submissions by Claimant, one by Respondent. In the civil law tradition there are two submissions from each Party, so Respondent has the last word. Same thing for a counterclaim. It is possible to use either system, irrespective of the *lex arbitri*. The same system should then also be applied to other submissions, and to the way the evidence is presented.

**401.   Q: So this does not depend on the seat of the arbitration?**

A: No. Nor on the arbitrators. It should depend on the people appearing on behalf of the Parties.[100]

**402.   Q: What do you do if the Parties or their lawyers come from *different* traditions? The civil lawyers will find it odd, or even unfair, if Respondent does not have the last word. What do you do then?**

A: In such cases, you err on the safe side and give Respondent or counter-Respondent the last word.[101] However, you must make sure that the last submission is not misused.[102]

**403.   Q: Surely on the counterclaim the last word must be with the counter-Respondent/Claimant, in a last, extra, submission?**

A: Yes. The same rules must apply as for the main claims. The Procedural Timetable should take that into account, and provide for that extra submission, usually[103] Claimant's rejoinder on the counterclaim.[104]

---

100. See question 402.
101. See Annex (J), Procedural Timetable.
102. See question 403.
103. See question 402.
104. See Annex (J), Procedural Timetable.

Here there is a special pitfall of which one must be wary. The temptation is great for a Party to present new arguments and new evidence on the main claim, under the guise of a last submission on a counterclaim. An Arbitral Tribunal is well advised to caution the Parties against such foul play, and to take precautionary measures against this.[105]

### 404. Q: Until which time should Parties be permitted to bring counterclaims?

A: Counterclaims must normally be brought with Respondent's first (and, depending on the Procedural Timetable, only) submission on the merits of the main claim. Specify this in the Procedural Timetable.[106]

However, there are exceptions. For instance, Respondent may repeatedly request and receive extensions for the filing of its submissions on the main claim. This should not automatically lead to equivalent extensions of the time for a counterclaim to be filed. The link may then be broken, and procedure on the counterclaim sped up so it does not lag behind as it normally does.

### 405. Q: Is it a good idea for Respondent to raise a counterclaim in the first place?

A: Sometimes, yes. If Respondent believes that it really has a counterclaim it should go ahead with it. Perhaps it was already preparing to launch it as its main claim, but was beaten to the punch by Claimant in filing the Request for Arbitration.

### 406. Q: Is it better to present a main claim or a counterclaim?

A: Both should receive the same attention, and the procedure chosen should ensure this.

### 407. Q: Will a counterclaim reinforce the defense against the main claim?

A: Some believe that, by raising a counterclaim for a little more than the main claim, one counterbalances the main claim. If there is a settlement providing that each Party retains what it has, giving up the main claims and the counterclaims as the case may be, this course appears attractive, but this is just one possible settlement.

---

105. See Annex (L), Procedural Order No. 1, para. 40, para. 8. See questions 107, 755.
106. See Annex (J), Procedural Timetable.

**408.  Q: Why should the mere fact that a counterclaim is raised lead to a settlement?**

A: Indeed, this may be wishful thinking. One should also think of the cost conse-quences. Separate advances may be called in for the counterclaim, which will have to be funded by Counterclaimant/Respondent. Moreover, if the counterclaim is ulti-mately rejected, and costs follow the event, an excessively eager Counterclaimant may be left with the bill.

**409.  Q: Not all counterclaims have a link with the main claim, correct?**

A: Yes. The practical considerations are then different.

**410.  Q: A counterclaim will complicate the proceedings. Is that an advantage to Respondent? A counterclaim as a delaying tactic?**

A: Delaying tactics are usually not a good idea. Besides, if one wants to delay, there are easier and cheaper ways to do it than raising a counterclaim, with the risk that it may be rejected, with costs.

**411.  Q: While the main submissions are prepared and presented, are there other things that an Arbitral Tribunal could ask the Parties to do?**

A: Yes. The Arbitral Tribunal should ask itself whether there are preliminary or threshold issues that should be resolved up front ("bifurcated"). There may be special problems regarding the proper constitution of the Arbitral Tribunal, its jurisdiction, *res iudicata,* and other threshold issues that can be bifurcated.

**412.  Q: If there are such threshold issues, what should a Party Representative do?**

A: A Party is well advised to raise them promptly, completely and separately, not in the same submission as the defense on the merits. Otherwise the Arbitral Tribunal may overlook them, not treat them seriously, or routinely lump them together with the substantive issues.

**413.  Q: This means there will be other submissions, apart from the main submission?**

A: Yes. A Party that wishes to raise threshold questions should voice its desire at the initial Case Management Conference, and insist that those questions be "bifurcated" and briefed first. A Party should hold back its answer on the merits even if bifurcation was not (yet) foreseen by the Arbitral Tribunal.

**414.   Q: Does this hold up the entire process?**

A: Not necessarily. The Arbitral Tribunal can squeeze in shorter deadlines for such threshold defenses, and perhaps only one exchange of submissions, followed by a hearing which will deal with the defenses orally and lead to an interim decision. The "main" submissions on the merits may run as originally foreseen, more slowly, in parallel.

**415.   Q: Is this not a waste of time, if one of the threshold defenses ultimately succeeds?**

A: True, but in arbitration going fast is often preferable, at least for the Arbitral Tribunal, even if the Parties must do some (potentially) unnecessary work. In any event, Claimant usually will not mind pushing ahead with its main claims, and should be ready for this. By the time Respondent is due to answer the main claim on the merits, the Arbitral Tribunal may already have rendered its decision on Respondent's preliminary defenses.

**416.   Q: The decision. Do you mean an Award or an order?**

A: It could be either one. Many preliminary defenses, such as a plea of lack of jurisdiction, must indeed be decided in an Award.

**417.   Q: In ICC arbitration does this mean that the draft Award must be submitted to *scrutiny* by the ICC Court?**

A: Yes, and unfortunately this takes time.

**418.   Q: Can an Arbitral Tribunal ask the Arbitral Institution to work fast?**

A: This is possible.

**419.   Q: Could an Arbitral Tribunal avoid ICC Scrutiny by issuing an order instead of an Award?**

A: That would be cheating. *In the ICC system, whenever* something *is called* an Award, it *must* be scrutinized.

**420.   Q: So you can avoid ICC Scrutiny just by calling your decision an order?**

A: This is unwise. As the Brasoil case showed, the distinction between orders and Awards is one that must be made by the *lex arbitri*, and the State Courts at the seat.

There is no way to get away from that. As that particular Arbitral Tribunal learned to its peril, an order that should have been an Award may be *recharacterized* as such by the State Courts at the seat, and may be set aside by them.

**421.   Q: So, in ICC arbitration, the burden is on the Arbitral Tribunal to distinguish correctly between matters that should be decided in Awards and matters that can be decided by an order?**

A: Yes. Theoretically this is a distinction that the *lex arbitri* must make, but the burden is on the Arbitral Tribunal to follow and give effect to it in practice.

A commonsense method is to look at the Prayers for Relief. Any decision on a particular Prayer for Relief that may later need to be *enforced*, possibly in a country other than that of the seat, should be in the form of an Award. If there is a preliminary question *on the way* to the decision on such a matter, that preliminary decision should also be made in the form of an Award, a Preliminary Award to be precise.

**422.   Q: There is some confusion about adjectives that qualify Awards?**

A: Yes. Perhaps this is helpful: One should distinguish Awards according to three different criteria:

| Time | Interim Award | as opposed to | *Last Award* *(in ICC parlance, Final Award)* | The last Award is the last which is issued in this arbitration. An interim Award is an earlier Award. |
|---|---|---|---|---|
| Scope | Partial Award | as opposed to | *Full Award* *(in ICC parlance, Final Award)* | A partial Award decides some but not all Prayers for Relief in this arbitration. A full Award decides them all. |
| Stage | Preliminary Award *(in ICC parlance, Partial Award)* | as opposed to | *Final Award* | A final Award decides finally one of the Prayers for Relief. A preliminary Award decides just a preliminary question for one or several Prayers for Relief. |

Since these distinctions are made according to different criteria, they can be combined.[107]

**423.   Q: This makes for eight combinations?**

A: Yes.

**424.   Q: Why then does the ICC distinguish just three types of Awards: interim, partial, or final?**

A: This is indeed confusing. Still, an ICC Arbitral Tribunal must comply with the ICC Award Checklist, and pick one of the three available adjectives.

**425.   Q: Is a decision on the jurisdiction of the Arbitral Tribunal a Preliminary Award?**

A: An Award, yes, but which type of Award depends on its content.

If jurisdiction is *accepted* over all Prayers for Relief in a separate Award, this is a Preliminary, Interim, and Partial Award.

If jurisdiction over all Prayers for Relief is declined, the Award declining jurisdiction is a Final Award.

**426.   Q: What if jurisdiction on *ratione materiae* is declined only over parts of the Prayers for Relief? Or jurisdiction *ratione personae* declined only over some Parties, not all?**

A: This is more complicated.

If the Arbitral Tribunal declines jurisdiction over only a particular Prayer for Relief, that is the end of that particular Prayer for Relief, and the Award declining jurisdiction over that Prayer for Relief is a *Partial* Final Award. If the arbitration continues in respect of the other Prayers for Relief, the Award now issued declining jurisdiction on the one particular Prayer for Relief is an Interim Award, not the Final Award.

---

107. An earlier version of this table appeared in the author's country report "Switzerland", in Practitioner's Handbook on International Arbitration, Ed. Frank-Bernd Weigand, 2nd edition, London, 2009, pp. 815–876, © Oxford University Press. It is used here by permission of Oxford University Press.

**427.   Q: All of these are Awards that award nothing?**

A: Except possibly costs, yes. Some have difficulty with this, a difficulty stemming from the English language.[108]

**428.   Q: Surely Prayers for Relief rarely say that the Arbitral Tribunal should accept jurisdiction?**

A: True, not in so many words, but by necessary implication. If Claimant wants the Arbitral Tribunal to issue an Award on the merits, the Arbitral Tribunal must necessarily accept jurisdiction before it issues such an Award. And, if Claimant wins on this point, that, by definition, is a *preliminary* decision.[109]

**429.   Q: If Respondent enters an unconditional appearance, this is surely the end of the jurisdiction question?**

A: Indeed. Actually, the jurisdiction question has not even *begun*, because normally it may only be raised by a timely plea of lack of jurisdiction.

If there is no timely plea, and there is an unconditional appearance, this *in itself* confers jurisdiction upon the Arbitral Tribunal. So there is a new, independent basis, even if the original arbitration agreement would not have sufficed to confer on the Arbitral Tribunal jurisdiction *ratione materiae* and *ratione personae*.

**430.   Q: So the question whether the original arbitration agreement was valid is then moot?**

A: Yes.

**431.   Q: Then it is important to determine the deadline for a plea of lack of jurisdiction?**

A: Yes.

**432.   Q: Should one put this expressly into the provisional Procedural Timetable?**

A: No.[110] If a Party fails to enter a timely plea of lack of jurisdiction, that is the end of the matter. The Party's unconditional appearance confers jurisdiction as a matter of law.

One should not help a Party wishing to contest jurisdiction.

---

108. See question 84.
109. See questions 422 and 425.
110. See Annex (J), Procedural Timetable.

**433.   Q: If issuing an Award just on a preliminary question is such a cumbersome undertaking, is there no way around it for an Arbitral Tribunal?**

A: As we just saw,[111] issuing an order instead of an Award is not the right solution. But there is another solution, not necessarily a good one for the question of jurisdiction, but appropriate for such questions as the applicable law.

**434.   Q: How does that particular question come up?**

A: It often happens that, at the outset of an arbitration, the Parties get excited about the question of the applicable law. Each Party claims that a particular law is applicable, usually its own.

**435.   Q: But did you not say that one's own law is not necessarily better than the law of the other Party?[112]**

A: It frequently happens that the question of the applicable law has been studied in depth (but in the abstract) by some younger lawyers in a Party's team. All that work needs to be sold to the client, and the way to do this is to show off the research in a written submission on the applicable law.

**436.   Q: Is the Arbitral Tribunal then forced to take up the question with equal learning, and render a decision on the applicable law?**

A: No. There is no obligation for an Arbitral Tribunal to deal with irrelevant questions and unnecessary submissions, let alone to do so at once and in detail.

**437.   Q: Perhaps the Parties have done serious research, and perhaps they are on to something. How can an Arbitral Tribunal know at such an early stage whether submissions on the applicable law are relevant or unnecessary?**

A: Yes, this is possible, and is one of several reasons why it would be better for an Arbitral Tribunal not to render a decision on the matter right away. A decision, incidentally, that would have to be in the form of a Preliminary, Partial, and Interim Award. Once rendered in the form of an Award, it would bind the Arbitral Tribunal itself, even if it had second thoughts.

---

111. See question 409.
112. See question 276.

**438. Q: If there is a way around this for an Arbitral Tribunal, what is it?**

A: The Arbitral Tribunal can tell the Parties that the applicable law question will be decided *in due course,* perhaps after hearing further argument. *For the time being,* the Arbitral Tribunal requires no further submissions on this point, and the Parties are *ordered* to *assume* that the applicable law is the law of X.

**439. Q: Ordered?**

A: Yes, this is just a Procedural Order, and if the Arbitral Tribunal makes it clear that, at this stage, it renders no decision on the question of the applicable law, this is entirely proper.

In due course, presumably in an Award on the merits, possibly the last Award, the Arbitral Tribunal will have to revert to and decide the question of the applicable law, along with, or rather ahead of, all the substantive questions. But not by itself in a Preliminary (Partial Final and Interim) Award, with all the separate, cumbersome procedure that must then be followed. At the end, everything can be dealt with in one go.

**440. Q: In one go? That is, in the ICC system, all goes to ICC Scrutiny in one draft?**

A: Exactly, rather than going to scrutiny twice.

**441. Q: If they are "ordered to assume," will the Parties not know that the Arbitral Tribunal has made up its mind?**

A: They will not *know*, and there is nothing to *know*. All the Arbitral Tribunal is telling the Parties is to *assume*. The Arbitral Tribunal really should not make up its mind too early.

The Parties can then only guess, at their peril. One should keep them guessing. If they guess wrongly, so be it.

**442. Q: To what extent should the Arbitral Tribunal be informed about** *parallel proceedings*?

A: There, a balance must be struck. Usually the Parties say too much or too little about parallel proceedings. The Arbitral Tribunal should receive information that is likely to have an impact on the arbitration, but be spared receiving copies of entire proceedings before another *forum*. These will be of no help to the Arbitral Tribunal. The Arbitral Tribunal may have to take this into its own hands.[113]

---

113. See Annex (L), Procedural Order No. 1, para. 16.

**443. Q: Procedural Order No. 1 covers many more matters than those mentioned here so far. What are these?**

A: It will be easier to deal with these further points as they arise. Procedural Order No. 1[114] anticipates many problems that may or may not arise in the course of an arbitration, and tries to solve them in advance.

**444. Q: So one Procedural Order No. 1 fits all?**

A: In a way. It is a full toolbox, though many tools will remain unused.

**445. Q: At some point soon in the arbitration there may be a request for Provisional Measures, correct?**

A: Yes.

**446. Q: Most arbitration laws provide that the Arbitral Tribunal may issue Provisional Measures, or may do so if the Parties have agreed, which they do by agreeing to Arbitration Rules that say so. Is it really necessary to cover this point once again in Procedural Order No. 1?**

A: It may still be useful in *ad hoc* arbitration, depending on the *lex arbitri*. Besides, do Provisional Measures include orders for security for costs? Procedural Order No. 1 can answer this affirmatively for jurisdictions where this is not yet clear.[115]

The Arbitral Tribunal should be kept informed about non-compliance with its orders.[116]

**447. Q: What is an Arbitral Tribunal's focus in the middle phase of the arbitration, culminating in the Evidentiary Hearings?**

A: The procedural questions should, for the most part, already have been resolved in Procedural Order No. 1, and by further orders. At the Evidentiary Hearing an Arbitral Tribunal's focus can then shift to the *facts*.

**448. Q: Not yet the law?**

A: No. There is little point worrying about the law before the facts of the case have been established, all the facts. The Arbitral Tribunal must try to understand what happened, and to see the full picture in its true colors.

---

114. See Annex (L), Procedural Order No. 1.
115. See Annex (L), Procedural Order No. 1, para. 15.
116. See Annex (L), Procedural Order No. 1, para. 16.

In order to know what happened, the Arbitral Tribunal must understand why it happened. In the physical world, cause and effect reign supreme, but in human matters, people are often driven by goals. In business you must therefore understand the people and their dreams before you understand the facts

Accordingly, the Arbitral Tribunal should try to understand not only the external facts, but what made the Parties tick. What were the economics of their transaction? Why did they, at the time, write what they wrote? What were their hopes and fears? Did they trust each other? Did they like each other? How and when did the magic go out of their relationship? How do they feel about each other today?

### 449. Q: Surely it is irrelevant what the Parties thought?

A: Almost always. Establishing the facts is ultimately only a question of finding out what happened and who said what to whom. But in determining these matters it often helps to ask why.

### 450. Q: All this is from the perspective of the Arbitral Tribunal?

A: Yes.

For Party Representatives it is totally different. They will have thought about the legal conclusions from the very beginning of the arbitration. Which facts could be relevant for the legal consequences that they wish the Arbitral Tribunal to draw? Which facts are necessary for the factual conclusions that they would like the Arbitral Tribunal to draw? Other facts should be ignored, except to the extent that the other Party may wish to allege and prove them. Party Representatives should ask themselves about the relevance of these facts, if any, to their opponent's case, and then think how they could disprove them, and whether it is worth trying.

## (b) Documents and Production of Documents

### 451. Q: Contemporaneous documents should be submitted together with the main written submissions, not afterwards all in one go. Why is this?

A: The other Party should know about them early on, and the members of the Arbitral Tribunal.[117] In an international arbitration, the contemporaneous documents are, so-to-speak, the backbone of the factual case.

---

117. See Annex (L), Procedural Order No. 1, para. 22.

**452.   Q: The backbone?**

A: You may liken the work of an Arbitral Tribunal to that of a paleontologist or a historian. A paleontologist tries to reconstruct a dinosaur that walked the earth a long time ago. The starting point for the paleontologist will be the bones that somewhere have been preserved to this day. A historian will start with contemporary documents that are still around, and so will an Arbitral Tribunal.

**453.   Q: And the flesh will be put on the bones by the testimony of witnesses?**

A: Yes.

**454.   Q: Still, the documents are more important?**

A: More reliable in any event. The documents were written with a commercial goal, and normally not with a future arbitration in mind (not in the beginning anyway). What was written at the time is now difficult to explain away. There is no way around contemporaneous documents.

**455.   Q: Can a Party try to hide documents that it does not like?**

A: A Party can try to hide the truth, but if there is a process by which the truth will come out in the end, it is arbitration.

**456.   Q: But if a document is hidden from the other Party and the Arbitral Tribunal, it might take a long time to be revealed?**

A: Yes, it might, but once it comes to light, the effect can be devastating. A Party that is caught lying or cheating is not likely to win.

**457.   Q: If you represent a Party, you have professional ethical obligations. Should you ask your client to tell you the full truth and give you the full documentation?**

A: Yes, for practical reasons, if not for professional ethical ones. Even if you believe that you have no professional ethical obligation to hand in damaging documents, ask for them.

**458.   Q: Do you have the obligation to ask?**

A: Not in all systems. Obviously there is no jurisdiction where lawyers are allowed to lie. However, professional ethics may not require them to *volunteer* information damaging to their client, or to *request* that information from them. Still, in practice, it is very uncomfortable for a Party Representative to sit on a mine that may explode any moment, and a Party Representative may refuse to bear that risk.

### 459.   Q: What should an Arbitral Tribunal do as the file is growing?

A: In the lead up to the Evidentiary Hearing, the Arbitral Tribunal should organize the file as much as possible, so that during the hearing itself little time is lost on locating a particular document. This also helps arbitrators to understand the case.

The Parties should be encouraged in Procedural Order No. 1 to organize the file in a sensible way.[118]

The various types of documents should be kept apart in separate binders and numbered separately.

### 460.   Q: Which types?

A: This depends on the nature of the dispute.

Is the dispute about what the Parties said, wrote and signed? Within the factual documents, one should then distinguish between general correspondence, minutes of meetings, reports and contractual documents.

Or is it technical? Then one may distinguish between technical background materials, patent applications, research papers on technical questions, test reports, minutes of site meetings, requests for variations, variation orders and engineer's decisions.

Is the dispute essentially legal? The legal materials should always be kept separate from factual materials.[119] Among the legal materials, one should distinguish between various jurisdictions and even areas of the law (e.g.: United States Patent Law, Delaware Corporation Law, French Arbitration Law), and separate out decisions of State Courts rendered in parallel proceedings, submissions in parallel proceedings, etc.

### 461.   Q: All these should be presented in a separate series? Many separate series?

A: Yes. Special series are fine, but rather than split numbers, foresee a system of consecutive numbers starting "in the air" for each series.[120] This will be easier to handle even for people unfamiliar with the case. Moreover, it will group together documents that belong together, even if they come from opposite Parties, because they will bear similar numbers.

---

118. See Annex (L), Procedural Order No. 1, paras 22, 31 et seq.
119. See Annex (L), Procedural Order No. 1, para. 37.
120. See Annex (L), Procedural Order No. 1, para. 34.

**462. Q: How is that done?**

A: Materials on the substance of the applicable law on the merits may have numbers from, for example, 801 onwards for Claimant, and 1801 onwards for Respondent.

This way, whoever works with the file will easily find documents from both sides that are relevant for a particular legal question, and will not have to sift through volumes of irrelevant material. Say somebody is interested in a legal question within the applicable law. They will find it convenient if the legal materials from both sides dealing with this question can be easily located, put on a desk, and in the end put back where they came from.

**463. Q: Why start numbering "in the air"?**

A: A bit of redundancy will do no harm, even if the document numbers go into the thousands. By contrast, the names chosen by the Parties for the various series are not necessarily self-evident.[121] And if further documents are added to the file, there will be space for them.

**464. Q: Are there exceptions to the principle that each document should have its own number?**

A: A few. If the document is in one language and the translation is provided, the translation should have the same number as the original.[122] This ensures that the various language versions are found immediately. Also, the translation should be paginated the same way as the original. The pages in the two languages can then even be bound together facing each other (punching some holes on the right hand side).

Witness statements should not be numbered documents at all. They will not remain long in the midst of the factual documents. It is far simpler to organize them by Party, and then alphabetically by name. This way, a first and a second statement from the same witness will be next to each other. It may also be useful to have one separate binder for all the statements of each witness. There is no point carrying the Witness Statements for Thursday's hearing on Tuesday.[123]

**465. Q: What do you do if a document appears more than once in the file?**

A: Point that out and record it so the remark appears in the Transcript.

---

121. See Annex (L), Procedural Order No. 1, paras 34, 37.
122. See Annex (L), Procedural Order No. 1, para. 26.
123. All this is encouraged in Annex (L), Procedural Order No. 1, paras 26, 28, and 45.

**466.   Q: What do you do if new documents are presented at the hearing?**

A: First, one has to decide whether they should be admitted into the file. Only then should they be read and used.

If documents are admitted into the file at the hearing, the simplest way is to put them into a "hearing file." The Presiding Arbitrator announces: "This is the new document of 3 February 2014, 15:13, submitted by Claimant." Far simpler than people trying to figure out whether it should be called C517, or C518, and then giving it a flag and trying to insert it in the back of a binder, which may be difficult anyway.

If cross-bundles (files put together by a Party to facilitate cross-questioning of an opposite Party's witness, one file for each adverse witness) are presented (which is useful), make sure that they use the same numbering as in the main file.

**467.   Q: While the Parties are making their main submissions, you almost always have *production of documents,* as foreseen in the IBA Rules of Evidence. Is this simply cumbersome and time-consuming?[124]**

A: It should provide more bones, but often yields only limited benefits.

**468.   Q: Suppose you *have* Production of Documents. How does it start?**

A: Not always with a formal request accompanied by a Redfern schedule as provided in Procedural Order No. 1.[125] Some requests, particularly for production of documents, are unfortunately hidden within a written submission. These need to be spotted at once.

**469.   Q: So, as an arbitrator, you should read a written submission as soon as it comes in?**

A: Yes, but only very quickly, just to spot hidden requests and get a general idea of what the submission says. This is not yet the time for the members of the Arbitral Tribunal to study first submissions in detail. The Counterparty will study the submission and its exhibits carefully, and may soon provide comments that the Arbitral Tribunal may find helpful.

**470.   Q: Should you use an assistant to skim through a submission?**

A: This is a good idea.[126]

---

124. See Annex (L), Procedural Order No. 1, paras 41 et seq.
125. See Annex (L), Procedural Order No. 1.
126. See question 107.

**471.   Q: Once it sees a request for production of documents, what should an Arbitral Tribunal do?**

A: As always, the Arbitral Tribunal's first reaction should be to institute a dialogue. So institute a dialogue on a particular request, and insert this into the provisional Procedural Timetable.[127]

The Arbitral Tribunal may identify the request by some symbol, both in the file and in the Procedural Timetable,[128] and gather the correspondence on that request in a separate file using the same symbol.

If there is another request from the other side, that one will receive a different symbol.

*Playing card symbols* are easily available in your software, and have passed the test of time in badly lit inns.

**472.   Q: This system of symbols for bifurcated proceedings could also be used on a bifurcated exchange, for instance on jurisdiction?**

A: Yes, and other bifurcated exchanges.

**473.   Q: Have you ever run out of symbols?**

A: Out of playing card symbols? Yes, but of imagination, never.

**474.   Q: Could one structure the production of documents process in advance, putting it into the Procedural Timetable from the outset?**

A: This is sometimes attempted, and it may work. What is more important is to make it clear that production of documents should be *completed* by the time the main submissions have been made and the last documents have been submitted.

You can also enlist the help of a documents production master.[129]

**475.   Q: Does a draft Procedural Order No. 1 even suggest to the Parties to request production of documents?**

A: If giving bad ideas to the Parties worries the Arbitral Tribunal, it can provide in the first draft that, "There shall be no production of documents," and hope that the Parties will let that stand.

---

127. See Annex (J), Procedural Timetable.
128. See Annex (J), Procedural Timetable.
129. See question 170.

**476.   Q: Has this ever happened?**

A: Yes. In one case the Parties even suggested it themselves. Both American Parties using American lawyers!

**477.   Q: What do you do if a Party simply does not provide requested documents?**

A: The Arbitral Tribunal may then be asked to issue an order to produce. With or without such an order, if the Party still does not produce the requested documents, the Arbitral Tribunal will be left with drawing "adverse inferences," IBA Rules of Evidence, Article 9.

**478.   Q: Surely you cannot infer that the non-complying Party would have lost the arbitration had it complied with the request?**

A: No. You can only infer that a document that was withheld by a Party would have had the content that was alleged by the other side. Presumably a content adverse to the withholding Party's interests.

**479.   Q: Does this then presuppose that the requesting Party says precisely what it alleges the content of the requested document to be?**

A: Yes. Otherwise the request will be toothless anyhow.

**480.   Q: How can a Party and the Arbitral Tribunal know what a document says if they have not seen it?**

A: This is precisely the difficulty. One can, however, make allegations without knowing them to be true. But one must make the allegations and motivate them with an explanation as to why. If the request is just a shot in the dark, asking for "all documents relating to ...," then this is exactly the type of "fishing expedition" that is prohibited.

**481.   Q: Is there a role here for a confidentiality advisor?**

A: Yes.[130] The IBA Rules of Evidence, 2010, foresee this possibility.

---

130. See question 170.

**482. Q: What is the most important documentary evidence?**

A: The Contract. It is surprising how little the Contract is studied while it is being performed, and how, even in an arbitration, the Parties tend to lose sight of the Contract and its language.

**483. Q: But what counts is what the Contract *means*, and is that not a legal question?**

A: Yes it is. Some people say that what people *meant* is a factual question. True, but what *they* meant is irrelevant.[131] What counts is what their words must have meant to others, and what the words of the Contract meant. These are legal questions. And that is why the applicable law may be important right from the start.[132]

**484. Q: Is this true also at common law?**

A: Yes.[133]

**485. Q: Other important documents?**

A: Anything concerning the arbitration agreement. Amendments to the Contract. The termination letter.

Do not overlook any cautionary language: "This letter is without prejudice," "only to explore a possible settlement," "We understand your letter to mean .... If we are mistaken, please explain your position."

Also ask yourself what additional language would have been required to change the legal position. Remember the dog that did *not* bark in the Hound of the Baskervilles?

## (c) Witness Statements and Testimony[134]

**486. Q: In some State Courts, witnesses are hardly ever heard. How do they find the facts?**

A: Some State Courts, particularly in Germany, analyze the case on the basis of the written submissions. They determine which facts are disputed, and whether the dispute about these facts is relevant to the outcome of the case.

---

131. See Annex (L), Procedural Order No. 1, Appendix.
132. See questions 727, 697 et seq.
133. See questions 704 et seq.
134. An earlier version of this sub-chapter was published by the author under the title "Preparing Witnesses for Oral Testimony", The Vindobona Journal of International Commercial Law and Arbitration, 2006, pp. 207–214. The author thanks the copyright owners for the permission to use the earlier publication.

For each such relevant disputed fact, they determine which Party has the burden of proof.

Normally, they decide whether that burden of proof was met on the basis of the documents submitted by the Parties, together with their written submissions. Only in exceptional cases are witnesses heard about such facts.

This is influenced by modern Roman law civil procedure ("Gemeinrechtlicher Prozess"). The Germans call this "Relationstechnik." Many Germans are very proud of this. Some Germans would like to use this technique in international arbitration as well. They succeeded in inserting Article 2 Subsection 3 into the IBA Rules of Evidence. They claim that this endorses "Relationstechnik."

Few others think this a good idea for the majority of international arbitrations. The facts are often complex and not necessarily provable by documentary evidence. The legal questions are not yet sufficiently briefed and may also be complex, involving different laws in different areas of law. In most people's view, the facts need to be established in Evidentiary Hearings and the law should be argued later, often in Post-Hearing Briefs.

The initiative should not be preempted by the Arbitral Tribunal. The Parties should generally present their case as they think fit.

### 487. Q: As a Party Representative, how do you present the facts credibly? Should you use witnesses?

A: Use live testimony as much as you can, especially if the Arbitral Tribunal is worried that Witness Statements may have been written with the assistance of lawyers. For this reason, some Party Representatives try to avoid the system in which the only witnesses who testify are those whom the *opposite* Party wishes to cross-question (with all other written Witness Statements simply standing as confirmed).

### 488. Q: Hearing all witnesses means hearing more witnesses than is really necessary?

A: Yes. On balance the preferable system is therefore still: "These are our witnesses' statements, now you pick the witnesses that you wish to cross-question." This forces a Party to try and make its own Witness Statements readable and persuasive in and of themselves.

### 489. Q: To achieve this a Party should know the purpose of having a particular witness testify?

A: Yes. It is surprising how often witnesses are presented simply because (one suspects) they wished to testify, and they talk and talk without being properly led by their own side's counsel.

**490.  Q: How should one question one's own witness?**

A: On the basis of the Witness Statement. No leading questions on direct (if any) nor on re-direct.

As a Party Representative, you should ask your own witnesses the *w* questions, one at a time: *"Who?" "When?" "What?" "Where?" "Whom?" "Which?"*[135]

**491.  Q: And "why?"**

A: Normally this is not relevant, except to establish a state of mind.

**492.  Q: And how should one cross-question the opposite Party's witnesses?**

A: Never "preface" a question. Ask only leading questions, and ensure you already know the answer in advance, unless it does not matter.

A Party should use its own witnesses to make its case, not its opponent's. Sure, if a Party can bring its opponent's (for it, hostile) witness to say something that helps its case, that is a bonanza, but it happens more in novels and movies than in real life.

It is surprising how often witnesses are cross-questioned aimlessly, by questioners who just hope to discredit the witness, or to emphasize a point already on record.[136]

**493.  Q: All this presupposes that the Arbitral Tribunal is free to shape the proceedings. But the Parties have priority?**

A: Yes, they have priority, but a crafty Arbitral Tribunal gets what it wants anyway.

**494.  Q: How?**

A: By *hinting* at what it would like. At least one Party will agree, and the other may then chime in. Or the Parties may disagree, and then the Arbitral Tribunal is free to decide, and unsurprisingly it will then follow its own hint!

**495.  Q: What procedure must an Arbitral Tribunal follow to establish the facts?**

A: A question that is easier to answer than one might think. The *lex arbitri* leaves this to the Parties, and failing them, to the Arbitral Tribunal. This is simply a matter of applying the internal civil procedure applicable in the arbitration.

---

135. See Annex (L), Procedural Order No. 1, at the end.
136. See Annex L, Appendix.

**496. Q: Does this also apply to factual questions relevant to determining whether the Arbitral Tribunal was properly constituted or has jurisdiction?**

A: Yes. Judicial review of the Arbitral Tribunal's decision on these matters may be different, and follow more stringent criteria than judicial review of the decision on the merits. Otherwise, however, establishing the facts follows the same rules throughout.

**497. Q: Which means or types of proof should be permissible in an arbitration?**

A: Normally there is no restriction on the types of proof that are acceptable before an Arbitral Tribunal: documents and similar embodiments, testimony of witnesses and Experts, local inspection. Occasionally one encounters some limitations; the Parties may *stipulate* certain facts which are then binding on the Arbitral Tribunal, whether the Arbitral Tribunal considers them true or not. The Parties may also provide for *documents only arbitration.*

**498. Q: This is about which means of proof will be acceptable. But how about the standard of proof that must be met?**

A: That is a question that again must be answered by the internal procedural law of the arbitration.

**499. Q: Does this include a factual presumption of fact (*praesumptio hominis*)?**

A: Yes.

**500. Q: Suppose, however, that a fact is proven that is not directly the *relevant* fact, but by way of a legal presumption (*praesumptio legis*) one can then, based on the fact that is found, *presume* another fact to be present?**

A: The better view is that legal presumptions of fact are a matter of substantive law. The law is a system that attaches legal consequences to facts *as found*. In case of a factual presumption, the fact that it is found is the primary fact, and the presumed fact to which a legal consequence attaches is just a fiction, and a fiction instituted by the applicable law, not by civil procedure.

**501.   Q: Is a witness who has sworn to tell the truth more likely to do so than otherwise?**

A: No. Many people in the United States of America and some other countries believe in oaths. This may stem from the frontier, or perhaps from religious background. However, the belief is misplaced.

**502.   Q: Back to the standard of proof. When is a fact proven? Are the standards of "more likely than not," "balance of probabilities," and "preponderance of the evidence" all essentially the same thing?**

A: Probably.

**503.   Q: It is not a question for the Arbitral Tribunal to be persuaded one way or another? Is it decisive what the Arbitral Tribunal *intimately believes*?**

A: Some people think so, but think of criminal law. The "standard of proof" may well be different in criminal cases and in civil cases. In the United States of America, a distinction is made between persuading finders of fact 'beyond a reasonable doubt," which is required in criminal cases, and on "preponderance of the evidence," which is sufficient in private cases. This shows that the *standard of proof* depends on the law applicable to the question.

In the same legal system, that may differ for different aspects of the facts.

**504.   Q: How?**

A: One could imagine that, even in civil arbitration cases, a more stringent standard might apply to at least some aspects. With respect to allegations of criminal behavior, say fraud, "preponderance of the evidence" may not be sufficient. For this, one may need to meet the standard of "beyond a reasonable doubt."

**505.   Q: If the standards of evidence differ, which one should apply? Is this a question of the applicable law?**

A: Yes, but which applicable law? Probably not the law applicable to the merits. That deals with questions of substantive law. Here, however, we are in the realm of civil procedure. So the law that applies to the *standard of proof* should be the law applicable to the civil procedure before the Arbitral Tribunal. This in turn may depend on the *lex arbitri*, which will normally leave the standard of proof, as with any procedural question, to the discretion of the Arbitral Tribunal.[137] The civil procedure before the Arbitral Tribunal may be self-designed.[138]

**506.  Q: Suppose no sufficient proof is provided either way. Applying the relevant criteria of the law applicable to civil procedure before the Arbitral Tribunal, one cannot say either that an alleged fact did or did not occur. What do you do then?**

A: This is the *equipoise* situation. The law on *burden of proof* deals with the rare situation where the evidence is in balance, in equipoise. It says in which direction the balance must then tilt. In other words, to whose disadvantage it will be if a fact is neither proven nor disproven.

**507.  Q: And the Party that is disadvantaged is said to bear the burden of proof?**

A: Exactly.

However, in arbitration practice burden of proof is rarely decisive, except for the German "Relationstechnik" as used in German State Courts.

**508.  Q: Why?**

A: An Arbitral Tribunal will try to find the facts positively, and will not easily give up and decide just on the basis of the burden of proof.

**509.  Q: Unlike a State Court?**

A: Sometimes. State Courts must treat all those appearing before them alike. They do not have unlimited time. They will often be reluctant to administer proof, and especially reluctant to hear witnesses, which is cumbersome and expensive. State Court judges justify this by saying: "Witnesses lie anyway."

By contrast, an Arbitral Tribunal, at least one paid by the hour, will have the time necessary to ascertain the facts by all appropriate means, as it will be required to do. Therefore, the *non liquet* situation that is at the root of deciding according to the burden of proof will not arise in many cases.

---

137. See question 77.
138. See question 497.

**510.  Q: Rarely, but there will still be *non liquet* situations?**

A: Yes, particularly when it is unclear what was said over the telephone, or at a one-to-one meeting, and there is equally credible, but contradictory, testimony.

**511.  Q: Which law should apply to the burden of proof?**

A: The law applicable to the merits.

**512.  Q: Is it for psychological reasons that in Awards decisions appear to have been reached on the basis of the burden of proof?**

A: Yes, this way one avoids saying that one does not believe the testimony of a particular witness.

**513.  Q: Who should draft the Witness Statement?**

A: Ideally, the witness should prepare the first draft of the Witness Statement. If it is in another language, the Party Representative should take it the way it is and make sure that it is properly translated.[139]

**514.  Q: Is it proper to prepare a witness?**

A: Yes, Article 3 subs. 1 IBA Rules of Evidence. However, a Party Representative should repeatedly emphasize to the witness that his or her testimony must above all be *true*, and in all its parts truly *remembered*, not made up, surmised, or embellished.[140]

**515.  Q: Should Witness Statements be detailed?**

A: Yes, if a Witness Statement is unexpectedly brief or scant on detail, the Arbitral Tribunal will find it pared down and not authentic. A Witness Statement should sound true. Above all, it must be true.[141]

As a Party Representative, beware of the witness that embellishes his or her testimony. Do not worry about the relevance of details that are provided by a witness. A witness may well remember irrelevant details that, at the time, struck them in a particular way. Leave them in.

Unfortunately, sometimes your witness may *not* remember matters that *were* relevant. Take the details as they come, but do not push a witness for details that he or she does

---

139. See Annex (L), Procedural Order No. 1, para. 45.
140. See Annex (N), Instructions to Our Fact Witnesses.
141. See Annex (N), Instructions to Our Fact Witnesses.

not provide, unless you believe that the witness is deliberately withholding information. But then this is probably not the type of witness that you would like to field anyway.

Beware of the witness who recounts the same testimony *verbatim* several times. A witness should not sound like somebody who learned his or her lesson and now recites it, because this is not what is expected of the witness. Make sure that the witness understands the question and then honestly tries to answer it.

It is always a nice moment when a witness is asked whether he or she was told what to answer, and the witness responds: "Yes, the truth."[142]

### 516. Q: Should a witness be told what to wear for the hearing?

A: Yes. The Party Representative may tell the witness that the arbitration hearing is an important business gathering, or like an examination, and the witness should dress accordingly.[143]

It is also entirely proper to tell the witness to look at the Presiding Arbitrator and not at the questioner, even though the Party Representative is asking the questions. The witness should be told that the answers are for the Arbitral Tribunal, not the questioner.

As Party Representative, ask your own witness: "Please tell the *Arbitral Tribunal* whether . ...."

### 517. Q: Should a Party Representative explain to a witness about leading questions?

A: Normally, yes. Tell an intelligent witness about the role of the various questions, about the difference between open and leading questions, and about assumptions sometimes inadvertently or craftily made in questions, and how to react to these: "There, in your question, you assume ..., but I cannot confirm your assumption."

### 518. Q: How should a witness deal with a lengthy question?

A: The witness should answer as follows: "That was a long question. I no longer remember the beginning. Because of this, I am not sure that I understand the question at the end."

---

142. See Annex (N), Instructions to Our Fact Witnesses.
143. See Annex (N), Instructions to Our Fact Witnesses.

**519.  Q: At the hearing, is it effective for a Party Representative to ask an adverse witness how they are paid, in order to elicit the response that the witness is paid by the Party fielding the witness?**

A: This is a waste of time. It is obvious that the witness is paid, and the witness should be prepared for this type of question and answer the truth: "I am an employee of one of the Parties, but my Witness Statement is a true personal statement, and not influenced by my being paid by that Party."[144]

## (d)  Adverse Witnesses and Tribunal Witnesses

**520.  Q: How will an adverse witness be questioned?**

A: The Party calling that witness may prepare a questionnaire that the witness may or may not answer in writing in advance of the hearing. In any event, the witness that has provided neither a Witness Statement nor answers to the adverse Parties' questions may still be directly examined by that Party.

**521.  Q: If a witness has been called by one Party, can another Party also call that same witness?**

A: Yes. It is then even possible that the witness will prepare Witness Statements for both Parties. However, normally that witness may be a friendly witness to the first Party for which it will prepare a Witness Statement, and an adverse witness to the second, with no Witness Statement.

**522.  Q: Should the witness not be treated as a Tribunal Witness?**

A: If the Parties agree, this is a possibility. Otherwise, however, there is no need for the Arbitral Tribunal to intervene.

**523.  Q: Can a Party suggest that a particular witness be called as a Tribunal Witness?**

A: This sometimes happens when a potential witness says: "I will not testify for or against anybody, but if the Arbitral Tribunal wishes me to testify, I will." No matter what happens, when an Arbitral Tribunal calls a Tribunal Witness, the Arbitral Tribunal should tell the prospective witness of the precise circumstances. A Tribunal Witness should have trust in the Arbitral Tribunal.

---

144. See Annex (N), Instructions to Our Fact Witnesses.

**524.  Q: What if a tribunal or adverse witness has his or her own lawyer, and the lawyer wants to attend the hearing and question his or her client?**

A: There is no problem with the personal lawyer attending the hearing. However, the Arbitral Tribunal should resist any suggestion that the personal lawyer be allowed to question his or her client. The Tribunal Witness may, however, wish to consult with the personal lawyer, as to whether the witness should answer a particular question or "take the fifth."

**525.  Q: Plead the Fifth Amendment of the United States Federal Constitution against Self-incrimination?**

A: Yes.

**526.  Q: During the hearing? Do you then interrupt the hearing?**

A: No. In advance of the hearing the Arbitral Tribunal should establish the conditions of the possible testimony of the Tribunal Witness. The witness may ask whether the personal lawyer recommends answering a particular question. The personal lawyer may respond with a simple yes or no, whereupon the witness will normally follow the advice given by the lawyer.

Only yes or no. The consultation with the personal lawyer should not be about what the answer to the question should be, or why. Ahead of the hearing the Tribunal Witness and the lawyer may, of course, discuss all possible questions and all possible answers to them, but not while the witness is testifying.

**527.  Q: Should you then require the personal lawyer to sit *behind* the witness, to avoid the lawyer prompting the witness?**

A: Exactly.

**528.  Q: Can a Party call the other side's Party-appointed Expert as an adverse Expert witness?**

A: This is an unusual idea. A witness of fact is not "owned" by the calling Party, but a Party-appointed Expert is, well almost. Once the Expert has agreed to be appointed by one Party, the Expert is conflicted out for the other Party. It is conceivable, however, that a Party would wish to send a questionnaire of its own to an adverse Expert.

**529.  Q: Directly?**

A: No, through opposite counsel.

## (e)  Live Testimony

**530.  Q: How should the facts be presented to an Arbitral Tribunal?**

A: There should not be just one set of facts, but several. A subsidiary factual point may still bring your Party home, or close to home. Do not put all your eggs in one basket by having only one theory of your case.

At this stage there is no need to say which one of the facts one prefers, and which facts are presented only for good measure, to support a subsidiary position in case the main proof does not hold. This will be obvious to the Arbitral Tribunal anyway, and to the other lawyers in the room. In the Post-Hearing Briefs, it may be that one side will no longer pursue a particular allegation.

As a Party Representative, ask yourself how you can prove a particular fact. Are documents helpful? Do you need the testimony of a particular witness? Do you need a fall-back witness in case the first witness does not testify as you hope? What kinds of arguments can you make concerning the likelihood of a particular event?

**531.  Q: Should your witness be shown a key document in advance?**

A: Not necessarily. If the document is short, it may be effective to have your witness testify: "Oh yes, that is what I wrote at the time." Or: "This is the first time I see this document. It seems to me to confirm what I just said, that ..."

**532.  Q: One can be of the view that *direct* live testimony is time-consuming and not particularly useful if there are Witness Statements. But why exclude direct testimony altogether?**

A: There is a greater incentive for Party Representatives to put everything into a Witness Statement if there will not be any direct live testimony *at all*.[145]

Besides, experience shows that Party Representatives' so-called "warm-up" questions are usually no more than invitations to the witness to rehash what has already been said in the Witness Statement. The famous "three questions" are: "What do you have to say?" "Is there anything that you would like to add?" "Anything more to add?" This happens particularly with "big cheese" witnesses.

---

145. See Annex (L), Procedural Order No. 1, para. 62.

**533.  Q: What is a "big cheese" witness?**

A: A witness who is someone important at a client, the CEO for instance.

**534.  Q: Does the "big cheese" know the case?**

A: Often only on the basis of hearsay from the CEO's underlings.

**535.  Q: Then the "big cheese" testimony is not useful?**

A: Correct.

At that stage though, the Arbitral Tribunal will be reluctant to stop the witness and to appear nasty to one of the main sponsors of the show. Better to have the rule excluding direct testimony and not hear a witness unless the other Party requests to cross-question the witness. Attempts to cross-question a CEO just to embarrass that person are likely to backfire, because CEOs are usually very good at testifying.

Call a break after the "big cheese" has testified, so he or she can leave for more important things in a dignified way.

**536.  Q: Having to testify under cross-questioning can be hard on a witness. Should the witness be made comfortable first?**

A: Some witnesses may need it, but this is something that the Arbitral Tribunal should do. Nothing prohibits an Arbitral Tribunal greeting its guests in a friendly way and perhaps even engaging in some small talk.

**537.  Q: In front of everybody?**

A: Yes. The Arbitral Tribunal can also help with providing the witness with water. Have some cough drops ready in case a witness dries up, which is not so rare under stress.

The Arbitral Tribunal should protect a witness from excessively fierce or aggressive cross-questioning. You may have to remind Party Representatives that the witness is not a Party but a guest of the Arbitral Tribunal, and should be treated accordingly.

**538.  Q: Should cross-questioning be hostile in tone from the start?**

A: No. The tone should begin friendly and remain friendly as long as possible, *especially* if the testimony is dishonest.

Cross-questioning should start quietly with that particular witness' statement. How was it written? Sometimes amazing stories emerge. In a country where English is not widely spoken, all the witnesses of a Party were gathered in one room, and all their statements prepared, in English, with the help of the one person who spoke the local language *and* English.

Keep the tricky questions for the end, when the witness is off-guard.

**539. Q: Is a questioner required to "put it" to a witness that the witness is telling lies?**

A: Not in international arbitration.

**540. Q: If a barrister "puts it" to the witness, the witness will often be offended. How do you react?**

A: The Arbitral Tribunal should tell the witness at once that this is something that barristers sometimes believe they must do, and that it is not designed to anger and provoke the witness to see how the witness testifies once he or she loses composure.

**541. Q: Completely excluding live direct testimony seems a bit extreme. After witnesses have written their statements, some further evidence may come up. Should a witness not be allowed to comment on this? On direct?**

A: Certainly the witness should be allowed to comment on the further evidence *at some time*, but it need not be on direct. If there is no scope objection on re-direct,[146] it can be done then. The subject may already be brought up in cross, and if the witness is properly prepared, its testimony may be even more persuasive if elicited by the Counterparty, and it will then be on *that* Party's time!

## (f) Witness Conferencing

**542. Q: Does witness conferencing work?**

A: Yes. It is not true that it only works with Expert witnesses, and only two at a time, but it is more difficult to manage with several witnesses.

**543. Q: How should an Arbitral Tribunal manage witness conferencing?**

A: The Arbitral Tribunal should prepare several "baskets," that is, areas of questioning. It should then allocate each witness and each Expert to the appropriate basket, on the basis of their Witness Statements and Party-appointed Experts' Reports.

---

146. See Annex (L), Procedural Order No. 1, para. 65.

**544. Q: Should the Arbitral Tribunal get feed-back from the Parties on the allocation?**

A: Perhaps, it there is sufficient time.

**545. Q: Which seating arrangement works best for witness conferencing?**

A: Each Party's witnesses and Party-appointed Experts for a particular basket should be grouped together and seated on that Party's side, left or right. Name cards on their desks.

**546. Q: How do you manage witness conferencing with witnesses who do not testify in the language of the arbitration?**

A: You may well wind up with three relevant languages: the lingua franca of the arbitration, and one additional local language for each Party and some of its witnesses. For the sake of the Transcript, you need consecutive interpretation into and out of the language of the arbitration. For the other two, local, languages, you need whispered or simultaneous interpretation, with headphones for the benefit of those in the room relying on the interpretation.

Ideally, interpretation into a local language should be provided directly from the original, even if it is in the other local language, rather than going *through* the language of the arbitration.

This way, everyone can testify in the language of their choice, and everyone can understand the testimony in the original or one of the two other languages.

**547. Q: Who leads the witness conferencing?**

A: The Arbitral Tribunal. It will ask some questions of one witness, then probably ask one or more other witnesses to comment on the first witness' answers, or to answer the questions themselves. Then, the Party Representatives for one side, usually Claimant, will have an opportunity to ask further questions along that same line, then the Party Representatives for the other side. At the end, the witnesses may be asked whether anybody wishes to provide further comment.

This way, the Parties' right to be heard should be safeguarded, while concentrating first on one subject within the basket, then on the next.

**548. Q: Is it true that witness conferencing saves time?**

A: It is, but one should not rush through witness conferencing. Its benefits will be achieved only if it is conducted at a leisurely pace.

**549.   Q: Does witness conferencing take away the initiative from the Party Representative?**

A: Yes, to a large extent, but not unfairly so. It is a price worth paying.

**550.   Q: Still, should one discuss the process with the Parties in advance, and avoid it if any Party is adamantly opposed?**

A: Yes.

**551.   Q: Do you apply the chess-clock in witness conferencing?**

A: No. This would be extremely difficult. The Arbitral Tribunal should, however, make sure that no single witness, or Party Representative, monopolizes the process.

**552.   Q: By contrast, if witnesses are heard individually, a chess-clock system is applied?**

A: Yes.

## (g)   Assessing the Evidence

**553.   Q: Now, let us switch to the viewpoint of the Arbitral Tribunal. Do witnesses ever lie?**

A: Yes, but not as often as some cynically say.

One should be careful. Some people use the word "lie" too liberally. Lying means *knowingly* saying something that one *knows* not to be true. In other words, to pretend to have heard, seen, smelled, or said something that one *knows* one did not hear, see, and so on.

The testimony of an honest witness, however, is not necessarily true, because an honest person's memory is not infallible. But honest testimony that is objectively untrue is not a *lie*.

**554.   Q: Can you tell whether a witness is lying?**

A: This is difficult. It is easier to tell whether testimony is *subjectively truthful* or *honest*.

**555.   Q: How can you tell whether testimony is honest?**

A: Honest testimony accords with the witness' situation at the time in respect of the matters about which the witness is testifying. The witness may have been interested in a particular aspect, and will remember that aspect more than any other, even if that particular aspect is legally irrelevant. Honest witness memory may be vivid and perhaps reliable about that particular aspect, but fuzzy about the rest.

### 556.   Q: Do you have an example?

A: Some people pay particular attention to what they or others wear, and they will remember such details. In most cases, however, clothing is legally irrelevant. Good recollection about clothes does not mean that the witness has photographic memory about everything.

### 557.   Q: By contrast, a lying witness will be fuzzy?

A: Not necessarily. A lying witness was not there and makes up his or her testimony. The liar is well-prepared to lie. The liar's testimony will perfectly fit the present need of the Party fielding that particular witness. The witness will not deviate from the program of lies. The lying witness will even repeat him or herself and appear to recite a lesson which he or she has learned. Which is exactly what lying testimony is.

From the testimony it will remain unclear, however, *why* the witness should have been interested back then in these particular aspects of the case, and in nothing else. One would expect certain emotions, but the lying witness will not testify about emotions. The witness has none to testify about. He or she was not even there.

So lying testimony will lack signs of subjective truth.

### 558.   Q: An example?

A: Several pharmaceutical researchers once wrote in their Witness Statements, in identical words, that they were "outraged" by their opposite number's "unethical position." When asked about this incident, none of the witnesses showed any emotion. The Arbitral Tribunal concluded that the outrage had been supplied by the drafter of the Witness Statements.

### 559.   Q: Is consistency a sign of truth?

A: That is what laypeople, and (fortunately) lying lay witnesses, believe. In reality, consistency is a sign of a lie rather than a sign of honesty or truthfulness. Our memory is not necessarily consistent, particularly about aspects that at the time did not appear interesting or important.

Objective compatibility with contemporary documents, and possibly other testimony, is another matter.

**560.** **Q: If a witness claims to remember very well, and to be perfectly conscious that he or she must tell the truth, is this a sign of truthful testimony?**

A: Rather the opposite. Often it is those who are lying who protest too much that they are telling the truth. They want to be believed.

Those who subjectively tell the truth just do their best. They worry about remembering and telling the truth, not about being caught lying.

**561.** **Q: Is the demeanor of a witness useful to tell whether the witness is telling the truth?**

A: Not really. Demeanor is vastly overrated. Lying is, of course, stressful, but testifying is itself often stressful even for a witness who is honestly trying to tell the truth. The stress signs may be exactly the same. Moreover, signs of stress differ in different people. Some people sweat easily, some remain cool in all situations, even when they are lying. Some are even, one might say, professional liars. Think of actors and perhaps politicians.

**562.** **Q: Is this why an Arbitral Tribunal should not be particularly worried about having some people testify by video link, Skype or even by simple telephone link?**

A: Indeed, you do not miss much when people testify over a distance. Their testimony is as good or as bad as it would be in the hearing room.[147] A telephone line is often just as good as a video line.

**563.** **Q: Are there other ways to spot dishonest testimony?**

A: Not necessarily in the act, but once the Arbitral Tribunal and the Party Representatives receive the *verbatim* Transcript, they should analyze the *structure* of the testimony.

Just imagine the position of a lying witness. The liar feels uncomfortable. He or she must insert a program of lies into otherwise truthful testimony also rendered. This often shows at the seams in the Transcript.

**564.** **Q: In which way?**

A: The truthful testimony about peripheral matters will show signs of subjective truthfulness.

---

147. See Annex (L), Procedural Order No. 1, para. 71.

By contrast, the lying testimony about the core matters will simply reproduce the program of lies, and this portion of the testimony will show *no* signs of subjectively truthful testimony.

The structure of both parts may be different.

People who are not used to lying will try to lie as little as possible, and become careful about what they say when they are lying.

You often can observe in the Transcript that a lying witness first plays for time before lying. Sometimes one sees this pattern: Unwelcome question, procrastinating answer ("What do you mean exactly?" "Sorry, could you repeat?" "Do you mean, down to the last 10 centimeters?"), same question, lie. Next question. Same pattern again. Over pages of Transcript.

Lying witnesses may also worry about whether they have lied well enough. So, at the next occasion, they will revert and reinforce their original testimony ("As I testified, I recognized this person at this cocktail party. *I am sure of this. I was standing very close.*")

Once the subject is again outside the program of lies, the witness breathes visibly again, and may become prolific about irrelevant matters.

**565. Q: So the Transcript of testimony should be fully verbatim?**

A: Yes. Discuss this with the Court Reporter.

**566. Q: Are there parts of honest testimony that are particularly unreliable?**

A: Yes. People's honest memory of time and time periods is particularly poor. When did something happen? Five years ago or four? How much time elapsed? Three days, or a week, or two?

Sometimes people honestly lump two occurrences together, or even remember that something happened at different times, twice, when in fact it happened only once.

By contrast, a lying witness may claim an unusually good memory of time: "Why do you remember that this was on 6 August of that year?" "I just remember it that way." A more credible answer would be: "My birthday! Because of this stupid thing I was late for my own party."

**567. Q: How does an Arbitral Tribunal go about assessing the evidence?**

A: Remember that the documentary evidence is the backbone of the facts, and particularly of the dates. How does the testimony of fact witnesses fit with the documentary evidence? Might something about which testimony was given have in fact happened at another time? When?

**568.  Q: Does what we have just discussed about assessing the truth of the testimony of fact witnesses also apply to other types of evidence?**

A: Yes.

**569.  Q: If it is alleged that a document is a forgery, or if you suspect that it is a forgery, what do you do?**

A: You discuss it with the Parties.

If the suspicion comes from you, state the reasons for it. For instance, the photostat copy of a letter has paragraphs that are not properly aligned. Was the letter pasted together? Are there tell-tale-signs of sloppy photocopying? Or the letterhead does not fit the ostensible date of the document. Perhaps the telephone number on the letterhead is longer than it was when the document is supposed to have been written. Tell the Parties that this appears odd to you.

It has happened that such a document has then been withdrawn.

**570.  Q: Do you write about this withdrawal in the Award?**

A: Yes.

**571.  Q: Do you write in the Award that a particular witness lied?**

A: If you have to, write: "In the Arbitral Tribunal's view, this witness did not testify *ex propriis sensibus.*" "This testimony was surprising in view of documents ... and ...." But there are many occasions when you can simply say that the testimony of different witnesses diverged, that the evidence was at best in equipoise, and that the burden of proof was against this Party (the one that you think fielded a lying witness). This must of course be legally correct.

## (h)  Party-Appointed Experts

**572.  Q: Should Party Representatives submit models, primers, demonstrative exhibits, or even provide testimonials early in the arbitration?**

A: Yes. The arbitrators will be most grateful. They should ask for these things.

**573.  Q: Is the preparation of Expert Witness Statements different from the preparation of fact Witness Statements?**

A: No, except that Experts may be experienced in testifying.

Though some are not: "Why are you asking me such a stupid question? You know the answer, I am sure. Don't you know that I am a professor? I am here to give my opinion, not to answer stupid questions. I am not a criminal."


**574.  Q: What should an Arbitral Tribunal do with such an Expert?**

A: Call for a break to allow the lawyer for the Party that appointed the Expert to explain what the Expert's role is in the process. Fortunately, some Experts learn fast.


**575.  Q: Is it not a Party Representative's task to prepare the Expert?**

A: It is, but an Arbitral Tribunal must work with the people that appear before it.


**576.  Q: Many people say that a fact witness says what happened whereas an Expert says what is his or her *opinion*. Is this true?**

A: No, this is not the real difference. An Expert says what *normally* happens, and what *is* the opinion of colleagues, and what *is* his or her own opinion, and why. Thus, an Expert testifies about *facts*, but often they are facts *about opinions*.

It is particularly important for a Party Representative to work together with the Expert witness, so that the Expert Report and testimony will be easily *understood* by the Arbitral Tribunal.

The Expert witness should readily concede that his or her testimony proceeds from information received from a Party Representative, if that is so.


**577.  Q: How many documents should a Party Representative give the Expert?**

A: As many as possible, and all the documents that the Expert requests. The Expert should also be allowed a site visit if at all possible. This should come out in the report and in the testimony.

In one case, one of the Parties tried to make its case almost entirely by presenting a Party-appointed Expert with highly sophisticated computer simulations. When asked about the assumptions on which these simulations were based, the Expert said, unsurprisingly, that they had been given to him by his client. Nothing wrong with this. But he had never been anywhere near the site. Sophisticated as it was, this type of presentation did not persuade the Arbitral Tribunal, which was interested in what *really* happened.

The Expert Report should list the *basis* from which the Expert proceeds, that is, all the exhibits that the Expert had at his or her disposal.

**578.   Q: And then?**

A: The Expert's Report should then discuss, very didactically, the *technique* that was used to reach the Expert's conclusions. After all, the factual basis is what it is, and nobody can fault the Expert for this. The technique applied by the Expert may be good or faulty.

**579.   Q: Opposing counsel frequently tries to create the impression that the Expert was sloppy or inaccurate in drawing conclusions, and should have worked down to more decimal figures. How do you counteract this?**

A: An Expert should be prepared for this line of questioning, and be able to answer why certain shortcuts were taken and why it was proper to take them.

In doubt, it is often better to go the extra mile.

At the end, the *conclusions* should be stated clearly. They must of course fit with the position taken by the Party presenting the Expert Report.

**580.   Q: Is this a requirement?**

A: No, but presenting a report that takes a different position to that taken by the Party is not going to be effective. Quite the opposite. One must assume that what the Expert says is *endorsed* in full by the Party that presents that particular Expert.[148]

**581.   Q: What if the Expert could support *more* than the Party claims?**

A: Say your Expert is prepared to support a claim of 800 by the client, but for cost-cutting reasons, or because of another Expert, the Party is claiming only 550. In such a situation, ask the Expert to say, "at least 550." If asked how the figure of 550 was reached, the Expert should tell the true story, namely that he or she came to 800, but the Party's lawyers, for reasons of their own, asked to replace 800 with "at least 550," which was no problem for the Expert.

**582.   Q: How should one handle a hostile Expert?**

A: As a Party Representative, it is unwise to antagonize a hostile Expert. One will not win.

---

148. See Annex (L), Procedural Order No. 1, para. 47.

If one believes that it will shake credibility, one can question the Expert about his or her qualifications, preferably on the basis of the CV that Experts should provide together with the Expert's Report.[149]

In one arbitration, a Party-appointed Expert had a CV that listed many specialities. He was asked whether he was a specialist of one thing, another, and so on. In the end, the Party Representative had made the point that the Expert claimed expertise in many fields, but had no real expertise in *any* field, and certainly none in the relevant field. The Party Representative then simply said, "No further questions," not having asked a single technical question.

One may also ask questions about the factual basis on which the report is made, and about the technique that was used to come to conclusions. Otherwise, wait for the final argument or the Post-Hearing Briefs.

In international arbitration, there is no requirement to "put it" to an Expert that he or she is wrong.

### 583. Q: Procedural Order No. 1 also says that Expert Reports from legal Experts are not encouraged. [150] Does this mean that they are discouraged?

A: Yes.

If a Party wishes to make a legal argument it should by all means do so, but it should preferably submit this as its own legal argument, and in writing. This way, it will not use up its chess-clock time unnecessarily.[151]

### 584. Q: Should a Party argue the law in the principal submissions?

A: Yes, if the Party is ready, or in the Post-Hearing Brief. A Party can have that particular submission co-signed by the (foreign) lawyer in question if it (normally, wrongly) believes that this will add credence to the argument, or have each part signed separately by its author.

However, it is not an effective tactic to come before an Arbitral Tribunal with one of the Arbitral Tribunal's well-known colleagues, or a professor, to teach it the law, even if it is the applicable law in a jurisdiction that is not one of the Arbitral Tribunal's. Most arbitrators will just resent this.

Another reason why using legal Experts as witnesses should be discouraged, is that it takes excessive time to cross-question and question them, and in the end the Arbitral Tribunal will have little choice but to confront the legal Experts using more time still. If everything is done on paper, far less time will be wasted.

---

149. See Annex (L), Procedural Order No. 1, para. 45.
150. See Annex (L), Procedural Order No. 1, para. 48.
151. See Annex (L), Procedural Order No. 1, para. 49.

A Party Representative should not overlook the initial applicable law question. Many legal opinions are very learned, but about an irrelevant law or area of the law.

**585. Q: Example?**

A: A legal opinion about the law of civil procedure in the State Courts of Norway will not be helpful in an arbitration in Paris.

**586. Q: Experts in some countries have specific ethical rules that are designed to ensure the Experts' objectivity, and dispel the impression that they are mere "hired guns." What is the practical impact of such rules of ethics?**

A: None. The Arbitral Tribunal should not blindly follow opinions, even those of Experts. It must form its *own* opinion. Remember, Experts testify about facts.[152] Even a biased Expert can be useful.

Any Expert has a reputation to defend. This will provide a much better guarantee of neutrality than any formal test. Besides, a Party will not field a Party-appointed Expert without being reasonably sure that this Expert's honest testimony will help its case.

**587. Q: Should an Arbitral Tribunal encourage meetings between Party-appointed Experts, to limit the scope of their disagreement (hot-tubbing)?**

A: This is a much-touted technique, but is effective mostly *during* the Evidentiary Hearing, once the Party-appointed Experts have already testified individually. The rules of the game must be set beforehand.

## (i) Tribunal-Appointed Experts

**588. Q: Should an Arbitral Tribunal appoint Experts of its own?**

A: Preferably not. It leads to a cumbersome process, but is sometimes unavoidable.

**589. Q: How does an Arbitral Tribunal go about instructing a Tribunal-appointed Expert?**

A: You must proceed step-by-step. First, ask the Parties which questions the Tribunal-appointed Expert should report on.[153] These *questions* should be numbered and may be

---

152. See question 576.
153. See Annex (L), Procedural Order No. 1, para. 49.

couched in technical language that the Arbitral Tribunal may not (yet) understand, but any candidate for Tribunal-appointed Expert should.

The Parties should each provide the Arbitral Tribunal with a description of the *profile* that they argue the Tribunal-appointed Expert should meet.[154]

These profiles are likely to be similar, but not identical. It will then be the Arbitral Tribunal's task to harmonize them and come up with its own profile, or perhaps more than one, for different Experts.

**590. Q: The next step is that the Parties nominate candidates?**

A: Yes. The candidates should match the profile established by the Arbitral Tribunal. Perhaps the Arbitral Tribunal will have found some possible candidates on its own, it should add these to the list.

**591. Q: On this basis you establish a shortlist?**

A: Yes. The Arbitral Tribunal may then ask the Parties to comment on the candidates, or at least raise objections to one or more of them. Is one of the candidates too close to the other Party, for instance?

**592. Q: Next the Arbitral Tribunal should interview candidates?**

A: Yes. Once the Arbitral Tribunal has a *shortlist*, it must interview candidates.

**593. Q: How?**

A: This will be done, at least at first, only by the Presiding Arbitrator, after a first telephone conversation with the candidate. Normally the meeting will happen at an airport near the candidate's base. The candidate can drive to the airport and park there, and the Presiding Arbitrator can fly.

The Presiding Arbitrator should bring a draft appointment letter to the first meeting. The instruction letter could follow Annex (O). At the meeting, discuss this with the candidate(s).

Show the candidate the documentation that you have brought along and ask whether it is sufficient to answer the questions, or whether further documents should be asked of the Parties.

If the meeting goes well, an agreement on the appointment letter will be reached. The attached questionnaire may be supplemented if necessary. An agreement will be

---

154. See Annex (L), Procedural Order No. 1, para. 49.

reached on the documents that the Tribunal-appointed Expert will still need to receive from the Arbitral Tribunal.

If the Arbitral Tribunal has received the documents in duplicate with the main written submissions, these can be flagged during the interview, and need not even be copied. In the end, the flagged documents can be listed in dictation, handed over to the candidate on the spot, and put in the candidate's car at the parking garage (normally, a Mercedes or Jaguar). The Presiding Arbitrator can then fly home much lighter and relieved.

### 594. Q: What about additional documents?

A: These will have to be produced to the Arbitral Tribunal by the Parties on request. Another dictation on the spot.[155]

### 595. Q: When will the other participants in the arbitration be brought into the process?

A: There will then be a meeting between the entire Arbitral Tribunal and the favored candidate. The decision on a Tribunal-appointed Expert is an important decision, and should be made by the entire Arbitral Tribunal, not just the Presiding Arbitrator. Moreover, one still needs to finalize arrangements.

### 596. Q: What else is there to finalize?

A: Various decisions still need to be made about the additional documents to be submitted to the Tribunal-appointed Expert, and about advances, rates, and the timing of the report. These matters need to be prepared ahead of the meeting with the full Arbitral Tribunal.

### 597. Q: Should the Parties be present at this first "instruction" meeting with the candidate?

A: Preferably not, or the Parties will inevitably try to influence the candidate right from the start.

### 598. Q: With one Tribunal-appointed Expert you will not need two Party-appointed Experts. Does this not save costs?

A: Unfortunately not. Instead of having two Experts, one typically winds up with three, and the process just described costs time and money.

---

155. See Annex (L), Procedural Order No. 1, para. 42.

**599.  Q: Is it possible to appoint two different Tribunal-appointed Experts to answer the same question?**

A: It is possible, but it is not recommended to approach the matter so squarely. One may have two Experts in different fields. If there is some overlap between these different Experts with different specializations, this is even more useful, and will give the Arbitral Tribunal an opportunity to explore the reasons for the differences.

**600.  Q: If a Tribunal-appointed Expert has to go to the plant of one of the Parties, which measures do you take as an arbitrator to ensure the integrity of the process?**

A: This is always tricky. First, the equality between the Parties must be ensured. A representative of the other Party must be present at all times, and make sure that there is no attempt by the host Party to influence the Tribunal-appointed Expert. Sometimes the Arbitral Tribunal will have to send along a "watchdog." The Tribunal-appointed Expert must have free access and be allowed to see whatever the Expert wishes to see, or the Expert will report that he or she was denied access to ... whatever it was.

Such a visit may presuppose that the plant is shut down, which often happens during an annual shutdown, mostly in the summer.

It should also be clear whether the Expert may take pictures locally, or even ask questions. If this is allowed the process is even more difficult, because a record of the entire process must be kept.

There must be a full detailed report of such a visit.

**601.  Q: Can the Arbitral Tribunal discuss the draft report with the Tribunal-appointed Expert before the draft is submitted to the Parties?**

A: This is dangerous. However, you want to ensure the quality of the report. Therefore, it is important that the first draft already be presentable. Most Experts have experience with court or arbitral cases. Some still need to learn. The Arbitral Tribunal may discuss this with the Expert in advance, before he or she even puts pen to paper.

The entire process must in any event be entirely transparent. That is why exchanges between the Arbitral Tribunal and the Tribunal-appointed Expert should be in writing whenever possible.

**602.  Q: Can a Tribunal-appointed Expert participate in the deliberations of the Arbitral Tribunal? In the drafting of the Award?**

A: The answer is no. The Expert should not become an extra arbitrator.

The Parties would have to agree specifically to anything else.

**603.   Q: Has it ever happened?**

A: Yes.

**604.   Q: May an Arbitral Tribunal depart from the findings of the Tribunal-appointed Expert?**

A: Yes, but the Arbitral Tribunal must explain its own findings.

**605.   Q: How should Tribunal-appointed Experts be paid?**

A: Do not involve the Arbitral Institution, do it yourself. Why? Because if you go through the ICC, the money will go out of the advances, and these may be insufficient and slow to come.

**606.   Q: What about VAT on the Experts' fees?**

A: The Arbitral Tribunal should discuss this with the Expert and the Parties. If the Arbitral Tribunal pays VAT on the Expert's fees, that VAT will not be recoverable. If VAT is paid by the Parties themselves, they may be able to obtain tax credit for this.

Same thing for Court Reporters, interpreters, hearing rooms.

## (j)   Pre-hearing Case Management Conference

**607.   Q: In the Procedural Timetable,[156] one often sees a time set aside for a Case Management Conference soon after the main submissions and the Witness Statements are on the table, at least the first round. Is this useful?**

A: It is. This should be a call-in telephone conference, and the time, not just the date, should be set well in advance. People may not know where they will be months in advance, but they will have cell phones. Setting up a telephone conference between numerous participants on short notice is inefficient. It may require dozens of e-mails.

**608.   Q: What does the Arbitral Tribunal do at the pre-hearing Case Management Conference?**

A: It should get organized for the hearing. Mundane details mostly.

The Arbitral Tribunal may still have to make sure that the necessary interpreters and Court Reporters will be present and will have been adequately funded.[157] The Parties

---

156. See Annex (J), Procedural Timetable.
157. See Annex (L), Procedural Order No. 1, paras 30 and 51.

should remember that the good ones specialized in international arbitration have busy schedules.

There may also be some details about the file for the hearing. Who should bring what and so on.

### 609.   Q: Should a hearing file be prepared?

A: Some law firms like to do this and charge for it, but hearing files are rarely useful.

### 610.   Q: Other subjects?

A: The details for the hearing room or the retiring rooms for Parties may still need to be sorted out.[158] The Parties should pay directly for their own retiring rooms, lavish or more sparse.

But the most important aspect is the testimony of factual witnesses and Expert witnesses, to which the Evidentiary Hearing will be essentially devoted.

Who will testify? It may still be possible to *trade off* the testimony of one witness against another, and so reduce the number of witnesses who will actually attend. It may also be that a Party waives its right to cross-question a particular witness, in which case that witness will not come to the hearing.[159] This is actually another incentive for the Parties to present full Witness Statements. Prospective witnesses should be warned that their testimony may be called off at short notice. Some relish the idea of a trip, so dampen their expectations.

One thing that will often be discussed during the conference is the sequence of the testimony, and the presence or absence of witnesses in the hearing room. The Parties may have different views about this, often influenced by their legal traditions. German lawyers are keen on "witness sequestration or witness purdah."[160]

### 611.   Q: As an arbitrator, you do not seem very excited about "witness purdah"?

A: No, if each witness hears the other witnesses, as they often wish to, the testimony will be more useful. To begin with, a witness who has seen others testify is less nervous and needs less "warming up." They may also have a better understanding of the process.[161]

---

158. See Annex (Q) Checklist for Hearing Rooms.
159. See Annex (L), Procedural Order No. 1, para. 64.
160. See Annex (L), Procedural Order No. 1, para. 59.
161. See Annex (N), Instructions to Our Fact Witnesses.

**612.   Q: Is the testimony not likely to be warped if the witness has heard others testify?**

A: This is mostly a myth. Moreover, a witness that is not in the room may be told about the testimony given by other witnesses (or perhaps even given the Transcript). Outside the room, the witness may be prepared even more easily and skillfully by people who really know the case.

**613.   Q: What is the most important subject at the pre-hearing Case Management Conference?**

A: The chess-clock. This often must be "sold" to the Parties by the Arbitral Tribunal.[162] This is why Procedural Order No. 1, paragraph 60, goes easy on the chess-clock.

**614.   Q: Other pre-hearing points?**

A: The Parties' travel arrangements, hotels, so the Parties can be contacted last-minute.

**615.   Q: Could one provide for a week's moratorium before the hearing?**

A: This sounds good, but does not work well in practice. On occasion, one sees an arrangement whereby one Party may write on the even days, the other on the uneven days. These types of arrangements may simply trigger an avalanche of motions at the start of the hearing once the moratorium has ended, which is even worse for the Arbitral Tribunal.

The Arbitral Tribunal may ask that it not be bombarded by last-minute requests once it is already travelling. Instead, if the Party Representatives are really eager (which may be prompted by the clients), they may provide the arbitrators with documents "to await arrival" at their hotels.

Beware of skeleton arguments that have plenty of flesh.[163]

**616.   Q: Do you summarize what was discussed and decided during the telephone conference?**

A: Yes, for those who did not listen in, including the Court Reporters. A letter is sufficient.

---

162. See questions 624 et seq.
163. See Annex (L), Procedural Order No. 1, para. 31.

# CHAPTER 6
# Hearing

## (a)  Before the Hearing

**617.   Q: As an arbitrator, what do you do when you first arrive at the site of the hearing?**

A: As soon as you reach the venue, perhaps even on the eve of the hearing, go and inspect the hearing room. Is everything ready? Corrective action may be required. A basic rule of management is *c-c-c*: "*c*ommand, *c*heck, and *c*orrect."

**618.   Q: On the hearing day, is it that important to start on time?**

A: Yes, for everybody. Much of what we are about to discuss also applies to call-in telephone conferences. Waiting on the telephone is particularly tedious and may force people to listen to obnoxious music.

**619.   Q: How early should the Party Representatives be at the hearing venue?**

A: A Party Representative is well advised to arrive early and to have everything in the hearing room prepared and tested out: the seating arrangements,[164] the computers, the files, etc. Put away water bottles (if something can spill, it will). Do not build up files like a rampart in front of you; you will have to communicate with the witnesses, the Arbitral Tribunal, and opposing counsel. Look open and friendly, not defensive.

---

164. See Annex (L), Procedural Order No. 1, para. 50 and its Appendix.

Where is a photocopier, do you need a code? Where is the bathroom? How will you reach the next witnesses, by cellphone? Who will greet your witnesses when they arrive?

A Party should be completely ready to go perhaps 20 minutes before the hearing is supposed to start. Then there is still time to solve any unexpected problems that may come up – say, if a witness missed a plane. Everybody will have ample time to greet one another, get familiar with the facilities, drink a cup of coffee, and perhaps also catch up with the latest news and emails.

### 620.   Q: And the Arbitral Tribunal?

A: The Arbitral Tribunal should also be in the hearing room well on time.

Yes, even the Co-arbitrators. Do not let the Presiding Arbitrator get worried about your whereabouts. If the Arbitral Tribunal is incomplete you will need the Parties' consent to proceed, and this must be on record.

The Arbitral Tribunal needs to prepare its desk and its file.

The Arbitral Tribunal may circulate a "topographical" list of persons present, and arrange for it to be copied and distributed, preferably before the hearing starts. The names should be legible. Insist on having every person present listed, including administrative assistants and trainees. Do not forget to put in the date and the case number.

The Arbitral Tribunal may also have things it needs to sort out internally. Did all arbitrators receive – though perhaps not read – that last-minute submission?

Is there something that the Arbitral Tribunal wishes to discuss? It should not do this in front of everybody. Instead, it may go into a huddle nearby.

Talk with Court Reporters and interpreters.[165]

Many well-organized hearings start a few minutes early.

### 621.   Q: Before the hearing, what can the Arbitral Tribunal do to help the Court Reporters?

A: The Court Reporters need to prepare in advance. Ahead of the hearing, the Arbitral Tribunal should send the Court Reporters the Terms of Reference or a similar document, a copy of the letter summarizing the pre-hearing Case Management

---

165. See questions 621 and 623.

Conference,[166] a list of people expected to attend (perhaps the *Dramatis Personae*)[167] and the Witness Statements.

Ask everyone present at the hearing to give their business cards to the Court Reporters.

Just before the hearing, speak with the Court Reporters in confidence and tell them what the arbitration is all about.

### 622. Q: And during the hearing?

A: During the hearing, it is useful for the Court Reporters (and the Arbitral Tribunal itself) if the Arbitral Tribunal flags all documents that are mentioned, exactly where the relevant text portion appears, with the date *and time* when the document was mentioned (easy with a digital clock). Some even color-code the flags (green for Claimant, red for Respondent). Ask the Court Reporter to put the date and time (coordinate the clocks) into the Transcript at least once every page. Later on this will make it easy to bring together a document and what was said about it. Somebody once said: "In every arbitration, only some twenty documents in the file are relevant, but the whole question is, which twenty." The flags can help to find them.

Some move every document that is mentioned during the hearing into a special "core" file, which is easy to take away and study separately. But how do you find a document again once it has been moved? Leaving the documents in place and flagging them is normally more convenient.

Flags will also be useful for the Court Reporters if part of a document is read out loud, and, as is often the case, too quickly. Later in the day, the Court Reporters can go back to the original and improve the Transcript on this basis. You do not want a Transcript repeatedly saying, "inaudible."

Court Reporters should be encouraged to ask speakers to slow down and to help them during intermissions. The Transcript will be better if passages in other languages are transcribed correctly, rather than simply mentioning, "French spoken." Help the Court Reporters with this by slipping them notes at once. Yes, again with the date and time indicated.

### 623. Q: Before the hearing, what can the Arbitral Tribunal do to help the interpreters?

A: Talk to the interpreters. Find out their experience with law, with court cases, with arbitration. Discuss their role with them.[168]

---

166. See question 616.
167. See question 786.
168. See question 159.

## (b) Time Management[169]

### 624. Q: Why is time management important?

A: Because arbitration is a service. The Parties have every right to expect a cost-effective procedure. It is simply unethical for lawyers or arbitrators to drag out cases just so they can charge more hours.

Time is the most important cost factor. The real costs in arbitration are not air tickets, hotels and restaurants, not interpreters and Court Reporters, not even arbitrators and Arbitral Institutions. The real cost is time spent by lawyers and management.

Time management is the art of keeping costs down. Time and costs will be saved mostly by keeping Evidentiary Hearings short.

### 625. Q: What can the Party Representatives do?

A: Put together an efficient team. This will save time and costs.[170]

Concentrate on the bottom line. Ask yourself which points are worth making, and how you can make them in a short and memorable way, using which witness. And watch the clock!

### 626. Q: And what can the Arbitral Tribunal do?

A: Help the Party Representatives to structure their case from the start. Provide structure early in the Terms of Reference.[171] Refer, generally, to the IBA Rules of Evidence[172] and add, after consultation with the Parties, a detailed Procedural Order No. 1,[173] and a Procedural Timetable, including hearing dates *and start times* (which people need to make travel arrangements).[174]

---

169. Earlier versions of this subchapter were published by the author under the titles "Why speed is good for arbitrators", Liber Amicorum Michel Gaudet, 1998, pp. 135–136; extract from the ICC Publication Improving International Arbitration, ISBN 92-842-1255-3, copyright © 1998 International Chamber of Commerce; "We need Speed: Time Management in International Arbitration", The Vindobona Journal of International Commercial Law and Arbitration, 2008, pp. 271–278; "Chess Clock Arbitration – Questions and Answers about Time Management in International Arbitration", Liber Amicorum Tadeusz Szursky, 2008, pp. 41–47, copyright © Wydawnictwo C. H. Beck sp; Article with Andrew Burr: "Chess Clock Arbitration and Time Management – from the Perspective of the Arbitrator and Counsel", in Construction Law Journal, Vol. 26, No. 2, 2010, pp. 53–76, copyright © Sweet & Maxwell. The author thanks all the copyright owners for their permission to use their earlier publications.
170. See Annex (A), Our Arbitration Team, and Theirs, Internal Party Worksheet.
171. See question 349.
172. See Annex (L), Procedural Order No. 1, para. 4.
173. See see Annex (L), Procedural Order No. 1.
174. See Annex (J), Procedural Timetable.

Ask the Parties for a simple primer on the relevant technical aspects.[175] Study the file well, but only in the days leading up to the hearing. We learn fast, but unfortunately forget fast also.

### 627.   Q: How short should the Evidentiary Hearing be, and how do you keep it short?

A: It is not efficient to schedule hearings lasting more than a week. A week is sufficient for most arbitrations. Any suggestion to sit on weekends should be resisted.

Nor is it efficient to sit for more than six hours, net, per day (i.e., not counting frequent breaks). Give people sufficient time for lunch. Being time-pressed and fighting with the waiter for the check will spoil the best meal. Do not sit into the evening.

Long hearings make people hungry, inattentive, bored, unfriendly, and aggressive.

### 628.   Q: All this presupposes that everything that can be done in writing before and after hearings should be done in writing?

A: Yes. And what has been done in writing should not be repeated in live hearings.[176]

### 629.   Q: Should one have oral opening statements?

A: No need, they may be replaced entirely by written (skeleton) submissions.[177] If the Parties insist, then oral opening statements should be limited to no more than half an hour each.

### 630.   Q: How do you reduce the number of witnesses?

A: The number of witnesses and Experts to be heard live should be reduced through various means, particularly at a pre–hearing Case Management Conference.[178] Try hard to avoid live testimony from *Expert witnesses on law*.[179]

### 631.   Q: How do you manage the volume of oral evidence?

A: By side (not snide) remarks on doubtful relevance, and by using the chess-clock system.

---

175. See question 572.
176. See questions 532 et seq.
177. See Annex (L), Procedural Order No. 1, para. 54.
178. See question 608.
179. See Annex (L), Procedural Order No. 1, para. 48, and question 583.

**632. Q: How does the chess-clock system work? Do you use a real chess-clock?**

A: No, not a real chess-clock as used in chess tournaments to ensure that players have equal time. Good for chess champions, and not many buttons. But still too many buttons for lawyers. If you hit the wrong button, that mistake is hard to correct. Some arbitrators enlist the help of one team member from each side; others just do it on their own with a simple digital clock, a calculator and a writing-pad. Easy.

**633. Q: How do you allocate time to the Parties?**

A: Normally an equal number of minutes for a stretch of hearings.

**634. Q: How many minutes?**

A: A rule of thumb is to give each Party an overall amount based on an average of one hour per half day. Include oral opening statements, if any. This will be an incentive to keep them short.

**635. Q: What counts against allocated time?**

A: Time for questions to witnesses and receiving their answers, including normal interpretation.[180]

**636. Q: Each Party has just one hour in the morning and one in the afternoon?**

A: No. This is just the method to calculate how many minutes to allocate *overall*. Say the hearings are planned for four full days, all for hearing witnesses individually. Eight half days works out to eight hours for each Party, thus, a total of 480 minutes allocated to each Party. But this does not mean that on each of the four days each Party must use exactly 120 minutes or less. This is just the average. Each Party may use its 480 minutes whichever way it wishes; more minutes on one day and fewer on another, more time for a particular witness, less for others.

**637. Q: An average of only four hours per day for the Parties? This leaves plenty of time – for what?**

A: To give the Arbitral Tribunal sufficient time for sundry procedural matters, such as admonishing witnesses to tell the truth and having them confirm their Witness Statements, questions from the Arbitral Tribunal, interpretation incidents, procedural

---

180. See Annex (L), Procedural Order No. 1, para. 60.

incidents such as decisions having to be taken about new documents and recalling witnesses, and various other rare and unforeseen problems.

### 638.   Q: What kind of rare problems?

A: The fire alarm goes off. A participant passes out. Witnesses are stuck in an airport somewhere because of terrorism. All these things have happened. One needs time to solve such problems.

The chess-clock should reserve for the Arbitral Tribunal an average of about one hour per half day for these matters. This is normally ample time if one has a full Procedural Order No. 1[181] in place.

This makes it possible to sit for no more than about six net hearing hours per day. Six hours is about right. It is tiring for all those present (some non-native speakers of English) to hear people trying to make themselves understood in a language that may not be their first, with unusual accents, and to deal with complex facts and technical matters.

One also needs time to prepare for the next hearing day.

### 639.   Q: Is it not unfair to give each Party the same number of hours regardless of how many witnesses it will present?

A: It is erroneous to believe that the more witnesses one presents the more time it will take to hear them.

If anything, the time spent with a Party's witness is mostly spent on cross–questioning, which is time spent by the *other* Party, that is, the Party that does *not* present the witness.

Sometimes one Party will make its case with few witnesses while the other Party will have more. This may reflect the way the Parties are organized internally. A Party organized in a more specialized way will have more specialist witnesses than a Party that uses generalists. But even so, the testimony will cover roughly the same ground and will take roughly the same time.

### 640.   Q: Claimants usually say that their case is simple, and Respondents say that the case is complicated. Does that not mean that Respondents will have more ground to cover than Claimants?

A: This is another fallacy when considered in the long run. To be sure, a Request for Arbitration is often shorter than the answer. Things will, however, even out with the reply.

---

181. See Annex (L), Procedural Order No. 1, para. 60.

### 641. Q: Why will the time used even out?

A: Because the more defenses that are raised by Respondent, the more Claimant will have to reply to. It is likely that the time spent on a particular claim will be about the same for both Claimant and Respondent, as will be the time spent on a particular defense. The overall time spent by each Party will accordingly tend to be the same.

### 642. Q: Surely there is a disadvantage to the Party that must question a long-winded witness?

A: At first glance this appears correct. However, this also tends to even out over the course of the testimony of a larger number of witnesses.

If it appears that a witness is *deliberately* long-winded, the Arbitral Tribunal should intervene and show its impatience. In practice, such situations are rare because most witnesses are not particularly devious or crafty. For them, testifying is unusual and difficult. Some are not particularly good at it. It is unlikely that they will deliberately play games under stress.

Those who complain about long answers often only have themselves to blame. Good short questions lead to short answers that go to the point.[182]

Those who make long prefaces and ask long open-ended questions, even on cross, do not use their time wisely.

### 643. Q: What about interpretation? If a witness' testimony must be interpreted consecutively, does this not double the time?

A: Of course, consecutive interpretation takes time, but not nearly as much as the original testimony in the original language. This is because interpreters know what to interpret. They have just heard the testimony, while a witness must develop his or her answer and search for words, often in a language that is not the witness' first. Interpreters are eloquent professionals. The same cannot be said of all witnesses.

Moreover, it often happens that the questioner already understands the gist of the witness' testimony when given in the original language, or even every word. With this provisional understanding, the questioner will understand the full interpretation straight away, and be ready for the next pre-drafted question.

If a witness testifies through an interpreter, the witness, and the questioner, will also have a little more time to think about the answer and the next question. Thus, some of the time lost through consecutive interpretation will be gained in efficiency.

---

182. See Annex (L), Procedural Order No. 1, in the end, and questions 490 et seq.

Experience shows that, because of all these factors, consecutive interpretation does not typically slow down the testimony of a witness in any significant way.[183]

**644.   Q: But all this presupposes that the interpreters are good, correct?**

A: Absolutely, and an Arbitral Tribunal should take every measure to ensure that this is the case.[184] The interpreters may perfectly well come from the Parties themselves, as long as there is an interpretation-checker on the other side. Interpretation incidents must be addressed on the spot.

**645.   Q: Can one not save time by using simultaneous interpretation rather than consecutive?**

A: Yes, but one must then be certain that it is done flawlessly. With simultaneous interpretation errors will be difficult to spot and to correct. Simultaneous interpretation is also costly and may not be worth the extra expense.

**646.   Q: Should the Arbitral Tribunal have float time that it can distribute if it appears that a Party needs more time to make its case, perhaps because of a lesser command of the English language?**

A: Never say never. Something very unusual may happen in a hearing, and one must then be flexible.

But float time is generally a dangerous idea. If it is given to a Party under normal circumstances, the other Party will protest that the Arbitral Tribunal is treating the Parties unequally, and is blatantly helping the Party receiving additional time.

The second Party may be unhappy even if *both* sides receive equal *extra* time. It will argue that it did its best to present its case within the available time. Its opponent should have done the same and only has itself to blame.

Instead of distributing float time, the Arbitral Tribunal can ask its own questions on its *own* time. This is easy for the Arbitral Tribunal and difficult for a Party to oppose.

**647.   Q: So equal time to treat the Parties equally?**

A: Not really. The chess-clock is just a tool that helps manage time efficiently. The Arbitral Tribunal should make it clear from the outset that it does not believe that giving both Parties *exactly* the same number of minutes will automatically result in treating them equally. Equal treatment is a much more difficult concept, as we all know from the days of Aristotle. However, in practice equal time comes closer to equal

---

183. See question 155.
184. See question 156.

treatment than one may think. This is borne out if one analyzes the time spent by Parties in the vast majority of cases, those where neither Party exhausted its allocated time. By the time both Parties have made their case, one often sees that they have spent a similar number of minutes.

**648.    Q: Should an Arbitral Tribunal put time pressure on the Party Representatives from the outset? Or should ample time be distributed to them?**

A: Definitely the latter. The Arbitral Tribunal should help the Party Representatives do a good job. Do not put them under unnecessary stress. If, at the end of a stretch of hearings (say Thursday late afternoon), both Parties still have time on the clock but no more questions to ask, they will go home with a smile on their face. And the Arbitral Tribunal will not have to worry about a Party complaining in the end that it was denied a fair opportunity to present its case, especially a Party that reserved its rights about the chess-clock (which happens, but rarely).

**649.    Q: Sometimes one sees precise Procedural Timetables specifying who shall testify, when, and for how long. This looks well-organized. Is this not useful?**

A: This should be resisted. It is inefficient and illusory. One simply does not know how any particular witness' testimony will go, and one's Counterparty may be eager to spring a surprise.

The *sequence* in which the witnesses will be heard is more easily predicted, and will reduce the number of witnesses waiting in the wings for their moment on stage.

**650.    Q: Is the chess-clock really compatible with the Arbitral Tribunal's obligation to give the Parties a full opportunity to present their case?**

A: Full opportunity does not mean an unlimited opportunity to churn and filibuster. Indeed, the *lex arbitri* will often only say that only a *reasonable* or *fair* opportunity must be provided. This must be the case even where the expression "full" is used.

If the Parties wisely choose Arbitration Rules that say "reasonable," or if they expressly agree to the chess-clock outright, then there should be no problem anyway because that is their agreement.

In any event, to be on the safe side, from the start one should give the Parties a bit more time than they really need or overoptimistically estimate (which happens often). If some is left in the end, all the better.[185]

---

185. See question 648.

**651. Q: So one should be generous with time?**

A: Yes, but only with the number of days, not with the hours per day. The Parties will easily understand that the Arbitral Tribunal cannot distribute more days than there are. On occasion however, the Parties will request at the outset that each side be allocated significantly more time than one hour per half day. This should be resisted.

**652. Q: Even if people have traveled far? Would they not wish to make good use of their time?**

A: Good use yes, but there are limits.

Besides, the Parties need time to prepare for the next day. That preparation time will help keep the next day's hearing short and to the point.

It is also important that the Arbitral Tribunal have enough time of its own.

Occasionally the Arbitral Tribunal may wish to explore, on its own time, points that do not appear to have been covered adequately in the testimony. This is proper and hard to challenge.

**653. Q: What do you do if one side does not use its time wisely?**

A: If time appears to be wasted on points that appear irrelevant, the Arbitral Tribunal should intervene. The Arbitral Tribunal should also help speed up the testimony of a witness who struggles with language or is difficult to understand (perhaps difficult just for some in the back of the room, but *everyone* should be able to follow what is happening).

A live Transcript appearing on computer screens often helps participants who are not used to hearing unusual accents but that can read English well.

The Arbitral Tribunal should frequently tell the Parties how much time is still available – at least every half day but preferably at each break. From time to time it should also assess the situation with the Party Representatives, by asking: "How are we doing on time?"

**654. Q: Has a Party ever run out of time?**

A: Rarely. There was a case where a Party was about to run out of time, and tried to cram as much as possible into the record by talking fast. A rather ineffective method that simply made counsel look foolish.

In another case, counsel never raised the subject until late on Friday afternoon, when, after a full week of generously scheduled hearings, he requested another full week. The Arbitral Tribunal refused – it simply had not reserved the next week and had no time available until many months later.

The Party lost. But it had been given more than a fair opportunity to present its case. Its lawyer had squandered its time, and the Arbitral Tribunal had intervened repeatedly to speed up the proceedings.[186]

The case led to a malpractice suit against the counsel who had run out of time. This was an experienced American corporate counsel in a large firm, but he had little experience in litigation or arbitration. He should have known better than to take on a case that he simply could not handle properly.

### 655. Q: Should one use the chess-clock also for oral argument, such as closing statements?

A: Not necessarily, but the lawyers should at least know how much time they can use.

Whether the chess-clock is used or not, one should make it clear that it is not possible for a Party to "reserve time for rebuttal."

## (c) Hearing Incidents

### 656. Q: Procedural incidents may arise during the hearing. As a Party Representative, how do you prepare your witness for this?

A: Tell the witness that if somebody raises an objection against a question, the witness should remain quiet until the objection has been dealt with, and the Arbitral Tribunal instructs the witness to answer.

Tell the witness to remain cool, to take his or her time (also for a better Transcript), and to talk slowly. The witness should be told not to try to argue the case and do the job for which the lawyers were hired.[187]

### 657. Q: How can an Arbitral Tribunal help a witness?

A: The Arbitral Tribunal may say the following: "We arbitrators would have been very interested to be present at that meeting that you are telling us about. We would have opened our eyes and ears. Unfortunately, we were not there. But fortunately *you* were there. So could you help us by telling us, as precisely as you can, what you *saw*, what you *heard*, *smelled*, *tasted*, etc. The lawyers will no doubt tell you what to make of it."

### 658. Q: As an arbitrator, how do you handle a procedural incident?

A: Keep your cool. If a document surfaces that is not yet on file (allegedly it simply summarizes other documents, or "should not become controversial"), put it to one side

---

186. See question 654.
187. See Annex (N), Instructions to Our Fact Witnesses.

and possibly seal it, so that nobody – not even your curious Co-arbitrators – will be tempted to read it before the incident has been resolved. Then, at an appropriate moment, deal with the procedural incident. The chess-clock should leave enough time for this for the Arbitral Tribunal.

If the procedural incident concerns a witness that is testifying, ask the witness to leave the room, so that the lawyers can discuss the incident without influencing the witness. This is actually the equivalent of "approaching the bench."

Explain to the witness that being sent out of the room is not the same as what occasionally happens in school, and is no reflection on the witness' person or performance. Say to the witness: "Why are we sending you out? Lawyers sometimes fight, and we want to spare you this and give you a break. We will call you back soon."

If the Arbitral Tribunal does not know what to do, it should ask the other Party to comment. If it then still does not know what to do, it should take a break and discuss the matter internally. Leave the room to deliberate; the Arbitral Tribunal should never deliberate in front of the Parties.

### 659. Q: Should hearing incidents be recorded in the Transcript?

A: Yes. For instance, if the Arbitral Tribunal allows a witness to be present when another witness testifies, and a Party claims that this witness does not qualify as a permitted "client witness."[188] For procedural incidents such as this, you need a verbatim Transcript that establishes what happened and reflects any protest. The protester should be invited to dictate the text of the protest into the record (so that it can be reproduced in the Award, but do not dwell on this).

### 660. Q: What should an Arbitral Tribunal do if a Party walks out in protest?

A: While the Party is heading for the door the Arbitral Tribunal should immediately announce a break until a particular time. It should say that it will consider the situation *at that time*, but that for the time being the proceedings are merely interrupted.

By instituting a "cooling off period" in this way, the Arbitral Tribunal maximizes the chances that the Party that walked out will return without losing too much face.

### 661. Q: Has this ever happened?

A: Yes, and it worked. This was a case where one of the Party Representatives did everything he could to impress his client, and to prompt the Arbitral Tribunal to make

---

188. In the sense of Annex (L), Procedural Order No. 1, para. 69, (that allows two "client witnesses" to be present at all times).

a mistake, which, no doubt, he would then have exploited to derail the arbitration or delay it – one suspects, at least until he had done his homework. In such a situation, the Arbitral Tribunal should be particularly cool and cautious.

### 662.   Q: What do you do if a Party does not show up at a hearing?

A: This is another occasion where establishing a written record is important. State that the Party that did not show up had been properly invited, and exactly how this was done. Say that no reason for the Party's absence has *yet* been stated. Do not prejudge the reason; it may be perfectly innocent, and you should not be biased. In due course, deal with the problem. Keep the Party that did not show up informed.

All this should be presented painstakingly in the Award.

### 663.   Q: How do you go about improving the Transcript?

A: If the Presiding Arbitrator has a good rapport with the Court Reporter, the Transcript will be very good to begin with.[189]

You can then simply ask the participants for "Errata Sheets" (one for each day of hearing) to be provided within, say, a week after the end of the stretch of hearings, and file them with the each day's Transcript, without more.

A poor Transcript causes unnecessary expense. A Transcript based only on a tape recording is a disaster. Ask anybody who has actually seen one.

### 664.   Q: What should a Presiding Arbitrator say at the close of the hearing?

A: First, draw the attention of the Parties to the waiver provision in the Arbitration Rules or the *lex arbitri*:[190] "We are not fishing for compliments, just say, no objection."

Have the Transcript reflect exactly what the Parties answered. An objection, once made, need not be repeated, but a Party should make sure that it does not waive an objection even by implication. A Party should also make sure not to miss a deadline, for instance, to file separately for setting aside an (implied) decision on the proper constitution of the Arbitral Tribunal.

Do not forget to thank the interpreters and the Court Reporters: "We are all looking forward to receiving the Transcript."

Finally, thank the Parties and wish them a good trip home.

---

189. See question 621.
190. For example, Art. 39 ICC Rules.

## (d) Arguing the Law

### 665. Q: Should one argue the law only in Post-Hearing Briefs?

A: In most cases, yes. But the law on threshold questions should be argued before the main Evidentiary hearing, to make it possible to decide the threshold issues or to put them aside before the main Evidentiary hearing.

### 666. Q: Which law applies to the question whether the Arbitral Tribunal is properly constituted?

A: This is a question to be decided by the *lex arbitri*, and this should be discussed early in the arbitration.

### 667. Q: Does *lex arbitri* mean the law of the arbitrator?

A: Not exactly.

Watch out. Originally, one asked: "Which is the *lex fori* of an Arbitral Tribunal?" Then one coined "*lex arbitri*" as the counterpart of "*lex fori.*" There, "*arbitri*" is used as a *genitivus subjectivus* (in analogy to "*lex fori*") to mean the private law at the seat.

However, by now *arbitri* is often a *genitivus obiectivus*, so one should translate as, "the law concerning the arbitrator." This is a law at the seat dealing with the relationship between the Arbitral Tribunal and the State Courts at the seat. In German, this would be "*Schiedsverfassungsrecht.*"

### 668. Q: Why?

A: The *lex arbitri* deals mostly with three peripheral things, not the arbitration itself.

First, it deals with the way arbitrators are appointed, supervised, deposed and replaced. This is relevant mostly early in an arbitration.

Second, the *lex arbitri* also deals with the way State Courts at the seat may assist the Arbitral Tribunal during the arbitration. This depends on the assistance that one is seeking.

Finally, the *lex arbitri* deals with the way arbitral Awards may be reviewed and possibly set aside by the State Courts at the seat. This is relevant mostly towards the end of an arbitration.

### 669. Q: So the lex arbitri deals with State Court intervention concerning just these three subjects?

A: Normally, yes. However, in the United States the following additional matters may also be brought before a federal or state court:

- motion to compel arbitration;
- motion to stay litigation;
- motion seeking an anti-suit injunction;
- motion seeking an anti-arbitration injunction; and
- motion to confirm an arbitral Award.

**670.  Q: In England, one hears the expression "curial law." What does it mean?**

A: Presumably those who use the expression know, but nobody else. Avoid this term unless you wish to create confusion. The idea was probably to have a function similar to "*lex fori*," so it means all the things that "*lex arbitri*" means, but on top of that, the law (not statutory as the expression, "*lex*" may suggest) applied or created by the Arbitral Tribunal itself, including its Procedural Orders for the arbitration itself.

**671.  Q: Which law applies to the question whether the Arbitral Tribunal has jurisdiction?**

A: This is answered by the *lex arbitri*. This includes the question whether the subject matter of the dispute is arbitrable, the impact of parallel proceedings which may preempt the jurisdiction of the Arbitral Tribunal, questions of *res iudicata*. All this is governed by the *lex arbitri*, but possibly also by the New York Convention. You may have to distinguish formal validity of the arbitration agreement, intrinsic validity, interpretation, scope *ratione materiae*, and scope *ratione personae*.

**672.  Q: Which law applies to the questions of the construction of the arbitration clause or choice of law clause?**

A: These should be governed by the substantive law on Contract interpretation of the *lex arbitri*. However, some people believe that the law generally chosen (by implication? by hypothetical will?) as the law applicable to the merits should apply even here.

**673.  Q: Which law applies to the question whether *Provisional Measures* may be issued if requested?**

A: This should be governed by the *lex arbitri* and possibly the law applicable to the merits.

**674.  Q: Which law applies to the merits of the contractual issues?**

A: This choice-of-law question is governed by the private international law often included in the *lex arbitri*. By choosing Arbitration Rules, the Parties may indirectly choose the law applicable to the merits. The Parties often choose the law applicable to the merits in their applicable law clause. Watch out, however. This does not mean that the chosen law applies to *all* questions arising in the arbitration.[191]

### 675.   Q: When should the law applicable to the merits be discussed?

A: This is mostly for the Post-Hearing Briefs. The Arbitral Tribunal should not start worrying about the law applicable to the merits too early. The law must be applied to the facts, but until the facts are established there is little point in the Arbitral Tribunal worrying about what the law would be if the facts turned out one way or another.

This is, of course, not to say that in an *Award* an Arbitral Tribunal should not discuss the crossroads in the procedure, in its reasoning about the facts, and in its opinion on the law. Or how the case might have come out if, at these crossroads, a different route had been taken. If that other route would have ultimately led to the same outcome, this should be explained. If, on the contrary, there is an issue, factual or legal, that makes all the difference to the outcome of the case, the Arbitral Tribunal should make sure that its reasoning on that issue is sound.[192]

### 676.   Q: Should a Party Representative also wait until after the hearing before thinking about the law applicable to the merits?

A: Oh, no. Think about it all the time, but wait for the right time to write or talk about it.

### 677.   Q: When and where should a Party argue about the law applicable to the merits?

A: Mostly in its Post-Hearing Briefs, but perhaps even earlier, in the written submissions and in oral pleadings.

### 678.   Q: How should one argue the law applicable to the merits in an international arbitration?

A: There is not just one law, and one should distinguish, in each law, between various areas of the law.

### 679.   Q: Does the *lex contractus* also apply to the assessment of damages and the *Quantum*?

A: Yes, and in many systems of law. The same law also applies to a claim for interest.

---

191. See questions 121, 122, and 679.
192. See question 830.

163

**680. Q: Does it apply to the power of an individual to act for a company?**

A: This may be governed by a different substantive law for each company.

**681. Q: Which law applies to the question of *costs*, their assessment, and allocation?**

A: This has nothing to do with the law chosen to apply to the merits. This must be separately argued, possibly under the *lex arbitri* and the applicable Arbitration Rules. The fee schedule issued by a local legislator or bar association may have an impact.

**682. Q: That is many different laws. Should they all be argued by the same person?**

A: No. It is rather odd to hear a barrister argue some exotic law in beautiful English, while a real specialist of that law is sitting in the back and looks on.

One should also be aware of the sources of law in the various fields. In some fields there is generic or detailed statutory law, in some there is case law.

Unfortunately, the Arbitral Tribunal often receives a hodgepodge of sources of law from Party Representatives, dealing directly or remotely with a particular question, and cited without regard to conflicts of laws, the law on sources of law, and the way sources of law are used in various legal systems.

Further, sources of law are often used in an unpersuasive way.

**683. Q: What type of legal agreement is unpersuasive?**

A: If one is told that some professor somewhere is of a particular view, this may not be persuasive in itself. Even famous professors change their minds. Is the professor right or wrong in this particular instance? That is what should be discussed for the benefit of the Arbitral Tribunal.

One author's views may be discussed in detail and shown to be correct. This is more persuasive than citing many authors who are said to be of the same view, but without any argument in support.

Similarly, to say that a particular Arbitral Tribunal was of a particular view is not helpful. One would need to know which tribunal this was, who were the members, where it was sitting, who were the Parties, what were the issues. In short, all the things that, as one learns in law school, must be discussed when one reads a precedent.

It is better to use one case, but one on point, and discuss it in all its aspects, rather than to use many cases, none of which are properly relevant to the instant case.

**684.   Q: What are the provisions of the law that apply to the merits of the contractual issues?**

A: In short, first the Contract. But the Contract must be interpreted according to principles of the applicable law, with gaps filled by the method and the means provided by that law. Then the statutory law, or case law or doctrinal writing if that is also a source of law, are relevant.

**685.   Q: So you need to know the applicable law right from the start?**

A: Yes, even though somebody will say that the Contract speaks for itself.

**686.   Q: The *lex arbitri* and the chosen Arbitration Rules give the Parties the right to choose the law applicable to the merits. Should they exercise that choice?**

A: Yes. There are replacement mechanisms, but it is far more convenient if the Parties exercised their choice.

They should however choose carefully, after having done their homework.

**687.   Q: In negotiations, each Party usually starts insisting that the law applicable to the merits should be its own. Is this unreasonable?**

A: Not entirely. Usually a Party has easier access to lawyers in its own jurisdiction. Obtaining their opinion on a proposed agreement will be easier and cheaper than obtaining an opinion on the basis of another law. And if your local lawyer, applying your own law, has already told you that your position is strong, why stick your neck out for another law? However, your case may be equally strong under another law, and perhaps even stronger.

Unfortunately, there are local lawyers who are too close to their client and too weak to do what they *should* do: advise their client honestly and objectively, even if the case is weak.

Local lawyers may unfortunately also support the local law approach for less admirable reasons. All things being equal, they may be greedy and prefer the option that gives them more work.

Local lawyers are at the root of many problems in international arbitration. *A lawyer's foremost concern should be the interest of the client, not the lawyer's own.*

**688.   Q: Surely certainty should be valued? And there is more certainty about one's own law than about some faraway, exotic legal system.**

A: Sometimes this is true, but it all depends on the legal systems.

One reason for legal uncertainty may be that the applicable legal system is simply not designed to deal with complex commercial matters on a large scale. All domestic laws started out as laws dealing with small local disputes in agricultural societies. Some laws have not evolved beyond that stage, even though society has.

### 689.   Q: Why are laws often backwards?

A: Change is costly.[193]

Change may sometimes even be impossible, because the law has a religious foundation that cannot be shaken. It would be blasphemous to try and improve law that was given by God personally.

### 690.   Q: In modern societies ...?

A: Regardless of the development of society, even non-religious law may be mysterious. The outcome of any dispute before the State Courts is then too certain or too uncertain.

### 691.   Q: Too certain?

A: Because the local courts will in reality just follow the principle that the local or more influential Party must win, regardless of the legal situation.

### 692.   Q: Too uncertain?

A: In some State Courts, the outcome will not depend on the law but on bribery. Try to obtain a legal opinion about the law of a country low on the list of Transparency International. The legal opinion will be very long, learned, and convoluted. It will be, in one word, useless, because State Court decisions in such countries are not taken on the basis of the law at all.

### 693.   Q: Under these circumstances, is it not better to go for one's own law?

A: Not necessarily. Even if our own jurisdiction is one where the law is reasonably developed, and really and honestly applied, there may be a realistic possibility of another law being chosen that is *also* reasonably predictable in its outcome. So it would be foolish to prefer one's own law without having engaged in a comparative law analysis.

---

193. See questions 695 et seq.

### 694.   Q: An example?

A: There are countries where local distributors succeeded in obtaining protective legislation providing for substantial severance payments upon termination of an agency relationship. In other countries, there is no such protection for commercial agents.

In one case, an Italian distributor believed that its own law would favor it. However, on this point, it did not. Its German supplier readily agreed to the application of Italian law. This was, for the German supplier, an elegant way to get out of the substantial protection for commercial agents provided in German legislation. Had the German Party insisted on German law, this would have been an own goal.

### 695.   Q: We often hear that the applicable law does not really matter, because most laws lead to the same result. Is this not true?

A: In many cases, but not always. There are many different laws out there. Each law is the product of the interplay between various *interests*,[194] and the interests that are at play are not always the same.

### 696.   Q: Do you have examples?

A: We just had one on commercial agency.[195] Here are some more: Some countries were once emigration countries but are now immigration countries. Some economies import goods and export technology. Some produce raw materials for export. Some have important banks that provide credit worldwide. Some have important debtors. Comparative law reflects economic interests of the kind just mentioned, and these change. Some laws will favor manufacturers, some will favor bankers, some will favor debtors or farmers and so on. Religion and ideology also have an enormous impact. Change is costly, so even if you would do things differently if you could start from scratch, in the short run it is cheaper to just leave things as they are. *Inertia* explains why legal fossils are encountered in many jurisdictions.

### 697.   Q: Are there special areas where the applicable law *regularly* makes a difference?

A: Yes, for instance with respect to statute of limitations questions. For example, under Swiss law the statute of limitations on claims in construction Contracts for plant and equipment is just one year, but if the Contract is a building Contract, the statute of limitations is five years. Or take the whole area of *interest*.[196] This is often heavily influenced not just by debtors (as in the Midwestern states of the United States), but by religion and ideology. Depending on the rates and on the way interest is calculated, the

---

194. See above question 694.
195. See above question 694.
196. See questions 845 et seq.

interest in an international arbitration may easily exceed the principal sum. In other words, interest may more than double the money.

The applicable law is also influential on the question of *deadlines*. Depending on which statute of limitations applies, a claim may already be time-barred.

Other areas where the applicable law may make an important difference include: what constitutes *breach*, fundamental or not; calculation of *damages*; validity of *limitation of liability* clauses; of *penalty* clauses; and beyond the scope of substantive law, the way facts are *proven* and the content of the *law* is established.

Above all, one area where the applicable law – common law or civil law, and there are further subdivisions – may make an important difference, is the *interpretation of Contracts*. This is frequently overlooked.[197]

### 698. Q: Comparative law research is expensive. Is it really worth the trouble?

A: As the last examples show, in some cases the applicable law may make an economic difference that far outweighs the expense of obtaining even a thorough review of a draft Contract from a foreign lawyer. Ignorance may be bliss, but a waking up can be expensive.

Occasionally one sees entire arbitrations conducted in total ignorance of the applicable law, and lawyers from that jurisdiction are brought in only in the last minutes to answer questions from the Arbitral Tribunal. By that time, it is far too late to develop a factual basis to support one's desirable conclusions of law under the applicable law, and to prevent conclusions that one would like to avoid.

### 699. Q: Can one not just read what the Contract says?

A: No. It is all well and good to say that all depends on the language of the Contract, but much depends on *how* the Contract is *read*.

In some legal traditions, particularly the common law, one begins interpreting a Contract essentially on the basis of the words and the usual meaning that these words have in the language of the Contract, and nothing else.

Some believe that they must simply answer a linguistic question. They argue that, as a matter of the "English language," the Contract means a particular thing. However, there is no authoritative body that defines with any precision what words mean in English (and even for French, the Académie Française is still working on its dictionary).

The "dictionary" argument is often encountered but is a waste of time. People who negotiate Contracts do not consult the Oxford English Dictionary or Black's Law

---

197. See questions 699 et seq.

Dictionary. English is not the same throughout the world. Many Contracts are written by non-native speakers of English, with another language "shining through." They rarely distinguish properly "may" from "will," or from "shall" or "expect." Watch out for "false friends": "control"; "delay"; "depose"; "statement"; "shortly"; "joke."

### 700. Q: How does one work without the "plain meaning rule"?

A: Many laws have elaborate rules on the interpretation of Contracts. They say which meaning should be ascribed to a particular ambiguous word. Its ordinary, non-technical meaning? The meaning that the Parties ascribed to it, possibly wrongfully – *falsa demonstratio non nocet*? The meaning that an expression has in a particular context, possibly even as a legal term related to a particular law (perhaps even a law that is not the applicable law)? Which body of interpretation rules applies? This is a matter of the law applicable to the Contract.

### 701. Q: How do you interpret the Contract in the civil law tradition?

A: In the civil law, Contracts are interpreted according to their genesis, their structure, and their commercial purpose.

### 702. Q: Does this favor a broader reading of a Contract?

A: Sometimes, but it necessarily leads to the admission of broader evidence on the context.

### 703. Q: In the civil law tradition, at least before the State Courts, little evidence is admitted at all?

A: One indeed must wonder whether the truth can be found without evidence. However, in international arbitration this is different.

### 704. Q: Does English law favor a narrower reading of a Contract?

A: Many think so. There is a Latin maxim that leads to a narrow reading, *inclusio unius est exclusio alterius*, and the idea that every word used in a Contract must make a difference.

However, by now, English law is not so simplistic. The "factual matrix" (a fancy expression meaning the circumstances) comes in.

**705.  Q: In English law, the goal is to find out what the Parties – not just one of them – must have understood the Contract to mean at the time when it was made?**

A: Yes. For each side, what counts is how that *other* person must have understood what was said or written.

And, for the other side, one must look at reasonable and fair-minded business people under the circumstances, not at the proverbial "man on the Clapham omnibus."

**706.  Q: Is all this really different from civil law concepts?**

A: No.

**707.  Q: What was said, written, and above all, done, *after* the Contract was made, may throw light on the common understanding of the Contract?**

A: Yes, and this is also admissible in English law.

**708.  Q: Could what was said or written *earlier* also help in understanding the Contract?**

A: In English law this is treated as irrelevant. This exclusion has, however, only a practical basis, because it is thought that earlier utterances could *hardly ever* be helpful. How can you know whether they were followed?

**709.  Q: So here, there is a difference?**

A: In theory yes. Less so in practice in many cases.

**710.  Q: If the Contract is governed by, say, English law, do you then exclude evidence that is irrelevant under that law (such as pre contractual exchanges)?**

A: In practice, one lets in whatever a Party wishes to submit, without deciding from the start that it is irrelevant.

**711.  Q: You mentioned that the law applicable to the Contract is also there to fill possible gaps in the Contract language?**

A: Yes. In civil law type analysis, gap-filling is a further function of the applicable law. But this function comes into play only once the Contract language *has* already been interpreted, if, after following the interpretation rules of the applicable law, one sees that there is a gap.

**712. Q: How do you know if there is a gap in the Contract language that must be filled?**

A: This is in itself a legal question that should be answered by the applicable substantive law. Some gaps are "inside" the language, for instance, if a particular term is used, but not defined with any precision. What does it mean? This is an "internal" gap.

But there are other types of gaps: If a point that *should* be covered is simply not covered at all, that is an "external" gap. This may be unintentional, or the gap may have been left intentionally.

**713. Q: How do you fill such an "external" gap?**

A: This depends on the applicable law. In the civil law tradition, where systematic codes are used, it works as follows: The code covers various *types* of Contracts, such as employment Contracts, Contracts for work, partnerships. One takes the Parties' agreement and assimilates it to a particular *type* of Contract covered in the code. To the extent that the Parties left gaps in their contractual language, intentionally or not, the provisions of the code on the relevant Contract *type* are used to fill those gaps.

**714. Q: In civil law, are there also types of Contract that are not covered in the civil code?**

A: Yes. These types of Contract are called *innominate Contracts,* and they are mostly governed by case law (as opposed to the 'nominate' Contracts governed by the civil code). If the Contract between the Parties can be assimilated to one of these types of *innominate Contracts,* the (case) law on the innominate Contract will be used to fill any gaps in the contractual language.

**715. Q: This sounds easy, but is it?**

A: It is not quite that simple and easy, particularly in international arbitration. Many agreements between the Parties cannot be so easily assimilated to a particular Contract *type.* They are then called "mixed Contracts" or "Contracts *sui generis."* Then it is not so clear from where one can take the law to fill any gaps. We encounter this often in arbitration.

**716. Q: And in the common law, what do you do with gaps?**

A: Then there is no code to cover Contract types. Well, almost. There is the UCC, the SGA and other statutes.

### 717.   Q: So the Contract types are mostly innominate Contracts?

A: One could say that. However, the analysis is not the same. One does not talk about *gaps* in the Contract, and one rarely looks for an innominate Contract *type*. Rather, one talks about Contract terms that are *implied* by the particular Parties in their particular Contract.

### 718.   Q: This sounds more like a fiction. If the Parties did not think about the question at all, or intentionally did not provide an answer, how can one then say that they "implied" anything?

A: Indeed, this is a bit of a fiction. But one often sees that the law, or adjudicators such as arbitrators, like to say that they did not make up whatever they decided – they merely followed what the Parties had already provided, by implication, or by their hypothetical will. That is to say, it is what the Parties *would* have said if they had thought about it, or if they had thought about it some more. This, it is hoped, makes the (arbitral) decision more acceptable. It is more psychology than law.

### 719.   Q: Is it a good idea to provide for a non-national applicable law, such as general principles of international law or the UNIDROIT principles, under the common features of two or three laws? Is it a good idea to provide for a decision *ex aequo et bono*?

A: All this is very rarely done, and for a good reason. One loses too much predictability.

One should never forget that the primary point of an arbitration agreement and an applicable law clause is not to provide for the resolution of a dispute through arbitration, or for interesting questions for students and law professors. The main function of these clauses is to make the outcome as predictable as possible right from the start.

Incidentally, the substantive provisions of the Contract already pursue that same goal. The best arbitration is the one that one could avoid, and the best arbitration clause is the one that helps avoid arbitration. The best Contract is the one that has already solved all questions that arise.

### 720.   Q: Should one then fight for one's preferred applicable law of the Contract?

A: Yes, but not just for the applicable law.

### 721.   Q: Is the seat of the arbitration more important?

A: In a way. The *lex arbitri* will have a conflict of laws rule of its own, which usually lets the Parties choose the applicable law, but also deals with many other important matters.

**722. Q: So it is a good compromise for a Party to say "we pick the seat, you pick the law"?**

A: Yes. This is often a good compromise, if one knows which law will be picked by the other side. If a Party in a negotiation has done its homework, it will be able to counteract many of the pitfalls of the (potentially) applicable law by drafting against them.

Above all, a Party must fight not just for a suitable seat, but for an arbitration clause that will lead to a competent Arbitral Tribunal that will make a reasonable decision.[198] By contrast, if the Arbitral Tribunal is inept, as may often happen with the wrong Arbitral Institution and the wrong seat, a well-chosen and well-researched applicable law clause will not prevent the Arbitral Tribunal from getting it wrong.

**723. Q: How does an Arbitral Tribunal ascertain the law that it must apply to the facts that it has found?**

A: This is quite tricky. An Arbitral Tribunal is called to apply all kinds of law that are applicable to various questions, and within all these laws the sources of law are manifold. We can only give a few examples here to show the complexity of the comparative law analysis that is required.

**724. Q: Is this a matter of the distinction between civil law and common law?**

A: To some extent it is, but that distinction is far from uniform. In comparative law, the Rhine is sometimes wider than the English Channel.

**725. Q: Is it not true that in the common law, case law is predominant, and in the civil law statutory law prevails?**

A: Roughly, yes, but in the civil law there also are entire areas of the law that are essentially case law, and in the common law some areas are primarily statutory. Everywhere there is an interplay between statute and case law, or between the legislature and the judiciary. And doctrinal writing also plays a role, even where it is not formally recognized as a source of law.

**726. Q: Does *iura novit arbiter* apply in international arbitration?**

A: This depends on the internal procedural law applicable in an arbitration. In common law jurisdictions, particularly England, the idea is often that it is for the Parties to present the applicable law to the Arbitral Tribunal. The Arbitral Tribunal's primary job is to choose between the various propositions of law advanced by the Parties. An

---

198. See questions 293 et seq.

arbitrator has the role of an umpire between two Parties and should not apply legal propositions of his or her own.

The corollary of this is that a barrister is required to present not only the cases that are favorable to his or her client, but also to distinguish the other, less favorable cases.

Many in arbitration, especially in France, emphasize Party autonomy and the right to be heard. If an Arbitral Tribunal comes up with legal ideas of its own, ideas on which the Parties were not heard, their right to be heard may be infringed.

Under French and English influence, the ICC Court requires Arbitral Tribunals to state, for each proposition of law, whether this proposition was submitted to the Arbitral Tribunal by one Party or the other, when and how.

By contrast, in the civil law tradition following the German model, the idea is: *da mihi facta, dabo tibi ius*. The Arbitral Tribunal can come up with legal ideas that the Parties did not suggest, and it need not submit these to the Parties for comment. It must apply the law regardless of the quality of the legal representation by the Parties.

### 727.   Q: Does the applicable law have an influence on the way the various sources of law should interact with each other?

A: Yes, statutory interpretation and the role of case law and legal doctrine differ from jurisdiction to jurisdiction, and even within the same jurisdiction, from one area of law to the next.

The question is whether the *genesis* of the statute (travaux préparatoires), its systematic position within a statute, and its purpose (called *teleological* interpretation) shed light on the meaning of a particular statutory provision.

The weight of case law is also determined by the legal system itself. To put it simply: is there *stare decisis*? How does one distinguish *dictum* from holding? This sounds like a mechanic distinction that can be applied at once, but only with time can one be sure what is *dictum* and what is holding.

The way case law is recorded also differs widely from jurisdiction to jurisdiction. There are jurisdictions where judicial decisions are fully reasoned, and dissenting and concurrent opinions are fully set out as well. Other jurisdictions have succinct judicial decisions. These are, however, often accompanied by copious notes by legal scholars. Think of France.

### 728.   Q: In any legal system case law, like air, is richer at the bottom of the pyramid and gets thinner and thinner as one goes up. Where should an Arbitral Tribunal take its case law? From the bottom or from the top?

A: This is a frequently overlooked aspect. In a system where there are three tiers of judicial review above it, an Arbitral Tribunal may be concerned about the way the law is applied at the next level above. That level may have a high density of precedents to follow.

**729.   Q: Does this concern the procedural law or the law applicable to the merits?**

A: Here we are talking about the law applicable to the merits, on the assumption that the law that must be applied is the substantive law of the *lex arbitri*, which is frequently the chosen or otherwise applicable law.

But if the internally applicable procedural law is derived from the procedural law before a State Court at the seat of the arbitration, an Arbitral Tribunal may be worried that the lower State Courts at the seat will second-guess it on this as well.

**730.   Q: So an Arbitral Tribunal will like to sit where there is only one level of judicial review (as in Switzerland or Austria)?**

A: Yes, such an Arbitral Tribunal will breathe more freely. There will be fewer precedents that it must observe. The decisions by lower courts at the seat will not bind the Arbitral Tribunal any more than decisions by lower courts will bind the reviewing court.

The level at which the Arbitral Tribunal sits will be the same as the level of the reviewing court, or just below it. An Arbitral Tribunal in Switzerland will sit high in the Alps, so-to-speak, while one in London sits at the bottom near the River, with several State Courts sitting uphill or upstream.

## (e)   Closing Proceedings on the Merits and Costs Submissions

**731.   Q: Before an Award is issued, the proceedings on the issues decided in the Award are normally closed. When and how does this happen?**

A: Closing the proceedings is even a requirement in some systems, particularly the ICC, which requires the closure of proceedings on any question to be decided in an Award.

One should close the proceedings by a simple letter sent to the Parties *promptly* after receiving the last Post-Hearing Briefs. Otherwise, many Parties will keep arguing forever and try to have the last word, and the next after the last. Put an end to this.

**732.   Q: Should the Arbitral Tribunal also close the proceedings on costs?**

A: Yes, but separately. Costs should be exempted in the first close of proceedings letter, because the Parties usually take some time to establish their Party Representation costs, including those of the Post-Hearing Briefs. Often they have them available only at the end of the month when all the time-sheets at a law firm are in, and there may be some outside advisors or in-house people as well.

As soon as all the Party Representation costs are in, the Arbitral Tribunal should separately close the proceedings on costs as well.[199]

### 733. Q: Should the initial costs submissions be simultaneous or sequential?

A: Simultaneous is better. There is no good reason why a Party would need to know which costs were submitted by the other Party before submitting its own. Each Party must simply say what were *its own* costs.

### 734. Q: Why ask for a mere one-page statement of costs rather than for a fully-fledged submission?[200]

A: One page is normally good enough for the Arbitral Tribunal to see what the Parties are asking by way of costs. If one needs more, one can ask for more afterwards.

### 735. Q: What do you do to counteract the risk of Parties exercising their fancy to inflate Party Representation costs, especially the Party that expects to win?

A: You ask about costs already paid by the client, cost already billed, about to be billed, and expected.[201] Then you compare the statements with each other and with the effort observed during the arbitration. Often the costs claimed are quite similar.

It is not the Arbitral Tribunal's task to pick on Party Representation costs. The Arbitral Tribunal is in no good position to judge, except in a rough way, whether these costs possibly in a faraway jurisdiction are reasonable or not. Some clients and some Experts may have been difficult to work with. Developing one's strategy may have taken time. One may have been working with other law firms that handle parallel cases. These are all things that affect costs and that the Arbitral Tribunal may not know.

The Parties should receive an opportunity to ask to comment on the costs of the other Party, and the Arbitral Tribunal itself can always ask the Parties to comment.

In most cases, simple statements of costs prove perfectly sufficient to assess and allocate Party Representation costs.

---

199. See Annex (J), Procedural Timetable.
200. See Annex (L), Procedural Order No. 1, para. 30.
201. See Annex (L), Procedural Order No. 1, para. 30.

**736. Q: In England, traditionally a (Partial Interim) Award on the merits is first issued, and only then are separate proceedings conducted on costs, since, it is said, the costs must follow the event. Is this a good idea?**

A: Nothing wrong with the idea that costs must follow the event (but what exactly is the event?). However, it does not follow that an Arbitral Tribunal cannot decide both on the merits and the costs in the same Final or last Award. The English practice is influenced by English State Court procedure, where costs are assessed and allocated by special masters. Singapore has a similar system in arbitration.[202]

In international arbitration, the Arbitral Tribunal must do this by itself.

---

202. Art. 39 Singapore Arbitration Act Version 2012.

# CHAPTER 7

# Deliberation and Award

## (a) Deliberation

**737. Q: Now let us move to the deliberation phase of an arbitration, seen from the perspective of the Arbitral Tribunal. Do you need a formal *mise en délibéré* to start deliberation?**

A: As in a French State Court? No. It is not always clear when deliberation starts, but there is no real need to know this anyhow.

**738. Q: Should deliberations start at once, as some say?**

A: This depends on what you call deliberation, and also on the arbitrators. Some come from cultures where saying nothing is a virtue or a strategy for survival.

**739. Q: How do you further camaraderie in an Arbitral Tribunal?**

A: Foster a congenial attitude between the members of the Arbitral Tribunal right from the beginning.

"Eat before you meet" is an important rule. At the outset, before holding an initial Case Management Conference, the arbitrators should preferably share a meal together. Some recommend that the Presiding Arbitrator pick the same appetizers as one of the Co-arbitrators, and the same main dish as the other, but this is probably taking it a bit far.

In ICC arbitration, the Terms of Reference provide a welcome opportunity for a meeting. If you set the Terms of Reference meeting for an afternoon, a lunch together will be easy, and towards the end of the afternoon all participants will be eager to fly home, which will further their willingness to agree.

### 740.   Q: What should the Arbitral Tribunal discuss at its first meal?

A: Not the case, not the arbitration, but rather other, more human things. You will discover that this arbitrator loves opera, that the other studied at this particular school, that you have met the same people. Irrelevant? Certainly not. None of the Party Representatives' business, true, but they will sense the beneficial effect on stage.

In the middle phase, and throughout the arbitration, *think ahead and remain friendly.* Go to the opera together, share meals, swap stories …

Continue cultivating a pleasant atmosphere, especially towards the end of the arbitration when the chips may be down and masks may soon be falling.

### 741.   Q: Will the arbitrators deliberate on the substance during the *main part of the arbitration*?

A: During that period a constant stream of exchanges is normal, but not yet much on substance.

The full Arbitral Tribunal will deliberate and decide on all the procedural things that the Arbitral Tribunal must *do* (unless delegated to the Presiding Arbitrator), particularly threshold issues, and the question whether these should be decided by Preliminary Award. This will usually be done by email, or by telephone conference.

On these occasions the personality of the various arbitrators may surface.

### 742.   Q: In the lead up to the hearing, should a Co-arbitrator be quick to respond to the Presiding Arbitrator?

A: Yes. It is easy to do and helpful for an impatient Presiding Arbitrator. A Co-arbitrator should try to build up goodwill.[203]

### 743.   Q: And will the Arbitral Tribunal deliberate at the Evidentiary Hearing?

A: Yes, the arbitrators will talk at meals. Ideally, a first, more formal deliberation should be conducted immediately following the Evidentiary Hearings. This will mostly concern the structure of the Award, and the way forward in the deliberation.

---

203. See question 287.

**744.   Q: Occasionally one hears that the Arbitral Tribunal should not make up its mind before it has heard the entire evidence. True?**

A: True, of course, but nothing prevents the Arbitral Tribunal, if it works well, from discussing its impressions of a particular witness, or a particular issue, well ahead of the Final Award. Provisionally, of course.

By this time, at the latest, a skilful Presiding Arbitrator will have perceived whether an arbitrator is partisan.

**745.   Q: Sometimes it is worse: An arbitrator does not play by the rules. What do you do in that case?**

A: If the Presiding Arbitrator suspects that a member of the Arbitral Tribunal is passing on information to "his or her" Party, or is worried that leaks might happen in the future, there is unfortunately no good way to stop or prevent it at this stage. It used to be that you could go to the proverbial mountain hut, with no telephone connection, but we now enjoy being accessible and connected at all times. So then, remain tight-lipped even behind the scenes.

**746.   Q: Could the Presiding Arbitrator discuss things only with the arbitrator who appears to play by the rules?**

A: This should be avoided. Once discovered, it may be used against the Presiding Arbitrator and harm the arbitration.

**747.   Q: So, even if only one Co-arbitrator is leaking, the Presiding Arbitrator will feel lonely?**

A: Yes, but there is nothing one can do.

**748.   Q: Back to an Arbitral Tribunal that works well. Does this include a Co-arbitrator who is biased?**

A: Yes.

**749.   Q: What happens behind the scenes in the middle phase of the arbitration?**

A: In a well organized Arbitral Tribunal, it may be possible to distribute tasks even *before* a hearing. For instance, if one still works with paper, one can ask each of the arbitrators to bring along a particular part of the file that not everybody has studied and annotated yet, for instance legal materials or technical reports that, at best, only one arbitrator has read in detail.

181

**750. Q: So you divide up the work?**

A: Yes.

If there are many subclaims, one can assign these subclaims to individual arbitrators. I like to joke and say: "*You* take the even-numbered ones, *you* take the uneven-numbered ones, and I will take the rest."

Take care to distribute the work evenly, even if you expect that one Co-arbitrator will do a better job than the other. The Parties' claims, the amounts, the difficulty of the questions, all these must be taken into account. Your aim should be to treat the Co-arbitrators, and by extension the Parties, equally, in the interest of an even-handed decision.

**751. Q: Do you continue with this division of labor?**

A: Yes. For each subclaim, one arbitrator will prepare a one or two page summary of the position of one Party, and then the other, and make these summaries available to the other arbitrators. This makes it far easier for everyone to prepare for a hearing involving many subclaims.

The arbitrator who has done the homework on a particular subclaim will usually also be in a good position to question witnesses regarding that subclaim, or at least to ask additional questions when witnesses are being examined.

The next step is, of course, that the arbitrator will prepare a one or two page draft of the Arbitral Tribunal's proposed decision on this particular subclaim.

**752. Q: So, nothing will be left for the Presiding Arbitrator?**

A: In an ideal world, perhaps. But the arbitrators will not do an equally fair and thorough job preparing the draft decisions on each of the individual subclaims. If one of the Co-arbitrators is biased and provides one-sided drafts, or if both Co-arbitrators do, the Presiding Arbitrator will have some work to do. In any event, he or she may have to improve the drafting.

Or one of the arbitrators will have a different view on a particular subclaim. If somebody disagrees with a first draft, it will be up to that person to do a better job. It is not good enough to simply say "I do not like it. Please try again, and perhaps I will like it better."

**753.   Q: Can you assign work according to abilities?**

A: Yes, and one should, provided, of course, that the work is assigned evenly.[204] One arbitrator may be a professor of law and may be entrusted with the discussion of legal points. The other may be stronger on technical matters. Or one of them may be particularly good at writing in English.

Either way, by distributing the work it is more likely that you will soon have, on the whole, a good draft. By contrast, if everybody is expected to do everything at the same time, this may result in many doing nothing at all.

Through this method you also avoid something that fortunately one rarely sees, that within an Arbitral Tribunal a *bargaining process* sets in. "If you give in on this point, I will give in on the other." Or: "This Party clearly has the better case, but we must find something in favor of the other Party, so that we look more balanced even if the case is not." This type of bargaining happens with weak Presiding Arbitrators, and is arbitration at its worst.

So always be well *organized and efficient*, and keep every member of the Arbitral Tribunal busy and focused on a number of specific points.

**754.   Q: Now we come to the final phase. What happens behind the scene?**

A: At the end of the arbitration, a Presiding Arbitrator should simply proceed quickly.

**755.   Q: First-time arbitrators who wish to do an especially good job may want to find the truth. Is there anything wrong with this?**

A: Yes. Beware of the over-eager arbitrator who becomes inquisitorial. A Presiding Arbitrator must be quite forceful in fighting misplaced curiosity about "the truth" and well-meaning attempts to be thorough. One may explain to a scientifically minded Co-arbitrator that the role of an arbitrator is more like that of a historian than a scientist. An arbitrator's sources are limited. She or he must seek the truth, but on the basis of that which is made available to the Arbitral Tribunal, not by going out on her or his own, as an inquisitor or detective.

Make sure that the Co-arbitrators do not read more than they should. Warn them against surfing on the internet.

Also warn the Co-arbitrators of possible attempts by a Party to make extra submissions and submit further evidence, for instance on the main claim when the pleading should be limited to the counterclaim.[205] If a Party makes such an attempt, use an assistant[206] to identify the documents that should not be considered and ask your Co-arbitrators to

---

204. See question 753.
205. See question 404.
206. See questions 107 and 108.

*seal* them. Yes, physically seal them, right away, and date the seal. People are forgetful and when, sometime later, the Award must be prepared, they may no longer recall which documents were excluded, and their file may not be sufficiently organized to find the Presiding Arbitrator's letter about this.

**756.   Q: Has it ever happened that a Co-arbitrator deliberately went ahead anyway, and read what he or she should not have read?**

A: Unfortunately, yes, and it was not easy to correct.[207]

**757.   Q: If reading the prohibited material does not influence the decision anyway, then surely nothing bad has happened?**

A: Some jurisdictions may permit this type of analysis. Other jurisdictions, however, have a *per se* rule: *Any* prohibited information that a Party was not given an opportunity to answer leads *per se* to unequal treatment and violates that Party's right to be heard, which is a *per se* basis for setting aside an Award.

**758.   Q: Where?**

A: Switzerland, for example.

**759.   Q: This may throw out the baby with the bathwater?**

A: Yes, but imagine the dispute over whether a particular piece of information did or did not influence an Award.

**760.   Q: Can an arbitrator ask friends for technical or legal advice?**

A: Absolutely not. Co-arbitrators should also be warned against this. The Parties chose *them* to do the job, a job that they knew full well to be demanding, and the Parties must now live with their choice.

**761.   Q: How does an Arbitral Tribunal remedy the situation if one of the Co-arbitrators, ineptly or otherwise, behaves improperly?**

A: It is not easy to correct the inappropriate behavior of Co-arbitrators *after* it has happened.

---

207. See question 761.

In its draft Award, the Arbitral Tribunal may go out of its way to reach its decision and state the precise basis for it in detail, thereby pointedly omitting the information improperly received by one of the arbitrators.

One may reopen the proceedings to restore the balance, by setting out for both Parties the information unilaterally discovered and asking them to comment. This should be reflected in the procedural history of any Award.

In the Award, one can then write (if it is true) that the additional information did not lead the Arbitral Tribunal to change its mind.

**762. Q: This may easily lengthen the arbitration by a month or two?**

A: Yes, which is why one should be forceful and proactive to avoid these problems in the first place.

**763. Q: In the ICC system, closing the proceedings triggers an informal deadline of three months for the submission of the Final Award. Is this a realistic deadline?**

A: In most cases, it is.[208] By the time the proceedings are closed, the Arbitral Tribunal may easily have an advanced draft of the introduction and the procedural history, and a rough draft of the structure of the substantive part of the Award. A date should already have been set for a deliberation meeting of the Arbitral Tribunal, at which the operative part of the Award should be agreed, leaving at least a month for the finalization of the entire text.

**764. Q: Are there ways to defer the closure of the proceedings and so, indirectly, the three months deadline to render a Final Award?**

A: Now we are into some tricks. A second round of Post-Hearing Briefs, perhaps designed to deal with specific questions of the Arbitral Tribunal, or further submissions just on costs, will not substantially impede the Arbitral Tribunal's deliberation and drafting work on the substance. That way the draft Award can be already further advanced when the proceedings are formally closed.

**765. Q: Are three months realistic if there is a dissenting opinion?**

A: Even then it is reasonably feasible. The important thing is to know early on whether there is likely to be a dissenting opinion. Once the word "dissent" has been uttered, the

---

208. See questions 764 and 765.

majority can move forward and meet the deadline. It may be that the dissenter will have to scramble, but this is not the majority's problem.[209]

It may be that the three months' deadline leads to more dissents generally, but this is not necessarily unhealthy, if it is a result of there being less time for bargaining within the Arbitral Tribunal.[210]

### 766.   Q: In an ICC arbitration though, a dissent may lengthen the scrutiny process?

A: True, by perhaps a month. Moreover, after the draft Final Award has been scrutinized, the majority may be requested by the ICC Court to "clarify" various points in the Award, which may add another week or two to the process.

### 767.   Q: Nevertheless, worst case scenario the Final Award should be issued within half a year of the Evidentiary Hearing?

A: In the worst case. And in the best, within perhaps two months.

### 768.   Q: Do you keep a record of deliberations?

A: Not normally. One can keep drafts (which should always have an automatic bottom line date on each page). The draft Award as it is prepared, or at least furthered during the deliberation, should be a sufficient record of what was discussed.

### 769.   Q: Should only the arbitrators take part in deliberations?

A: Yes, one should generally avoid having others present at deliberations. There should be a record of any attendance by persons *other* than the members of the Arbitral Tribunal, and of their function.

In one case, the Presiding Arbitrator made a point of inviting the Co-arbitrators to his hotel room rather than to a conference room. This way, the "minder" of one of the Co-arbitrators could not easily join the meeting. This did not prevent her from making a room-to-room phone call to make sure that the arbitrator in question really was in the Presiding Arbitrator's room, not on his way to defect.

The Award should set out when and how the arbitrators deliberated.

---

209. See question 903.
210. See question 885.

## (b)   Award Writing[211]

### 770.   Q: When there are parallel proceedings, do the parallel Arbitral Tribunals or State Courts talk to each other?

A: If they know about each other, then yes, they normally do. The purpose of these communications is not, however, to discuss the decision on the merits.[212] Rather, the parallel *fora* have an interest in minimizing the interference between their proceedings.

### 771.   Q: An example?

A: If decisions on the merits are rendered in two parallel proceedings around the same time, one can expect that the decision rendered first may be used in the still pending proceedings, as a basis for a request to stay those proceedings, or as at least persuasive evidence on the facts or the law. The parallel *fora* may wish to avoid this effect by agreeing to render their decisions on the same day. This is just reasonable case management.

### 772.   Q: Why should the two *fora* not talk to each other about the merits of their cases?

A: This would violate the Parties' right to be heard. Unless the information is notoriously well known, a *forum* should not consider any material, from whatever source, that the Parties have not seen and have not had an opportunity to comment on.

Even once a parallel *forum* has issued a decision, it is still up to the *Parties* to decide, subject to confidentiality, whether one of them wishes to make this decision known to the other *forum*. Neither *forum* should preempt that right from the Parties and try to obtain the information directly from the other *forum*, which may be contrary to confidentiality.

### 773.   Q: So, the Arbitral Tribunal should not send its Award to the other *forum*?

A: No. This may violate confidentiality.

---

211. An earlier version of this subchapter was published by the author under the title "How to write Awards – ICC Awards anyway", The Danubia Files: Award Writing Lessons from the VIS Moot – Ed. Louise Barrington et al., Cisgmoot 2013, pp. 19–36. The author thanks the copyright owner for the permission to use the earlier publication.
212. See question 772.

**774.  Q: What if a decision is made available online?**

A: Then it is in the public domain and may be used.

**775.  Q: Now to Award writing. When is the Award due?**

A: We just discussed the informal three months ICC deadline after the proceedings are formally closed.[213]

**776.  Q: But what about a statutory overall deadline in the *lex arbitri*?**

A: Sometimes the *lex arbitri* allows the Parties to delegate the power to extend the overall deadline to the Arbitral Tribunal, but often only once or twice. Beyond this, normally a State Court at the seat has jurisdiction to extend a statutory deadline, but again, unfortunately often only once or twice, and by an unrealistically limited time.

**777.  Q: However, the arbitration agreement or the Arbitration Rules sometimes provide for short overall deadlines say, six months starting at the beginning of the arbitration or when the Terms of Reference come into force within which an Arbitral Tribunal must render its Award. Are these to be taken seriously?**

A: Those in the contract, unfortunately, yes. These deadlines are usually far too short or do not depend on the Arbitral Tribunal but on the good will of a Party which may not be cooperating. The question, therefore, is how such an overall deadline can be extended.

**778.  Q: If the overall deadline is contractual, presumably the Parties may extend it?**

A: Yes, but both must agree. If they do not agree, it may not be clear which State Court at the seat, if any, may extend a contractual deadline. This is a question on which an arbitration lawyer from the *lex arbitri* should be consulted.

In institutional arbitration, the Arbitral Institution may extend a deadline provided in the Arbitration Rules, which is of course contractual in nature. The ICC does this routinely for its overall six months deadline, even if the Arbitral Tribunal does not request an extension. This means that the ICC overall six months deadline after the Terms of Reference is little more than a marketing gimmick.

---

213. See questions 773 et seq.

**779. Q: But then the overall deadline has little function?**

A: Yes, it just causes trouble. The deadline is at best a way to tell users of a particular arbitration system that the Arbitral Institution will monitor the time taken by an Arbitral Tribunal.

**780. Q: Does this have a beneficial effect?**

A: Not really. Good arbitrators will have a sense of urgency regardless of deadlines, and do not need be told to work quickly.

Unfortunately, a deadline may in fact have a pernicious effect. Some arbitrators, used to court-set deadlines in domestic litigation, tend to believe that in arbitration also it is good enough, and even wise, to sit on their hands until just before a deadline expires. An Arbitral Institution such as the ICC is therefore faced with an unpleasant dilemma: either it sets unrealistically short deadlines, but then must extend them all the time, which is inefficient, or it sets generous deadlines, but then some Arbitral Tribunals will act only when the deadline is about to expire.

**781. Q: In which language should an Arbitral Tribunal write its Award?**

A: The language of the arbitration. If the Arbitral Tribunal has a choice, it should use English.[214]

**782. Q: When should an Arbitral Tribunal start writing its Award?**

A: Some wait until they are sure that they indeed need to write an Award, because if the case settles, no Award may be necessary. However, as one drafts the Award, one becomes familiar with the case. Therefore, it is preferable to start writing the Award very early. In ICC arbitration the Arbitral Tribunal should start as soon as it has the Terms of Reference, the Procedural Timetable and Procedural Order No. 1 (the "three documents").[215]

**783. Q: What if the case settles?**

A: Much of the draft may still be useful for a Closing Order or Consent Award.

**784. Q: Are ICC Terms of Reference useful for the Award?**

A: Yes. Substantial portions of the Terms of Reference can already be written in such a way that they can be inserted unchanged (with their automatic numbering of

---

214. See question 145.
215. See questions 345 et seq.

paragraphs) into a first draft of an Award. The overall structure should be adapted to the case. The draft should be structured from the start to provide slots for further inserts.[216]

As the arbitration goes forward, the Arbitral Tribunal should add as much information as possible into its draft, or at least into the Procedural Timetable from where the information can easily be retrieved.

One can write in the past tense even about what has not yet happened. Just do not forget to strike that which did not eventuate after all.

The ICC Checklist for Awards should be used from the start. It is easier to comply with this Checklist if, during the arbitration, one gathers the information in the draft Award or in the Procedural Timetable.[217]

For instance, the ICC requires that the Award specify the date when the Request for Arbitration was *received* by the ICC (because the statute of limitations may have been interrupted on that date). In France, the days on which the ICC deadline to present the Final Award was extended must be specified, and the ICC also requires this for non-French arbitrations. If such details are recorded in the Procedural Timetable as they occur, the information will be easy to retrieve when one writes the Award.

**785.   Q: In non-ICC arbitration, do you also start drafting early?**

A: Yes.

## (c)   Cover Page and Introduction

**786.   Q: Let us then go through the ICC Terms of Reference. Will you reuse the title page as your Award cover page?**

A: Yes. That page should be drafted as a *Dramatis Personae*, in such a way that it can be reused and updated throughout the arbitration. The title page of the Terms of Reference[218] should contain the names and addresses of all participants, including the ICC Secretariat. This may require smaller print, but having everybody on one page, grouped according to their functions, is helpful for your clerical staff, for interpreters and Court Reporters, for everybody.

Make sure you have the Parties' names correct – as they appear in the Register of Commerce if there is one – yes, in the original language, in the script used in the register, Cyrillic or whatever it may be. Upper or lower case? Any dots or diacritical signs? Are there several individuals bearing the same name? This seems irrelevant at

---

216. See Annex (R), A Few Tables of Contents of Awards.
217. See Annex (J), Procedural Timetable.
218. See Annex (H), ICC Terms of Reference or Constitution Order.

the outset (what is in a name?), but once an Award must be enforced this needs this to be correct on the cover page. Add "also known as" ("a.k.a.") names in Latin script.

You should put one Party, Claimant, on the left, and one, Respondent, on the right. Later, when hearings are conducted, in fact already at the initial Case Management Conference, you can ask the Parties to sit accordingly, to the left and the right of the Arbitral Tribunal.[219]

**787. Q: Even if the State Courts at the seat do it otherwise?**

A: Yes. You can always say that you are following the World Court. There, the Claimant sits on the Court's left.

**788. Q: Will you use the *Dramatis personae* throughout the arbitration?**

A: Yes.

In ICC arbitration, the *Dramatis Personae* title page of the Terms of Reference[220] can be used, with handwritten arrows and numbers, as a *Routing Sheet* for the signature merry-go-round of the Terms of Reference.

The same *Dramatis Personae* page can be used for Procedural Order No. 1,[221] and later orders and Interim Awards, and, of course, for the Final Award.

Update the *Dramatis Personae* constantly and informally.[222]

Be aware that your Award may have to be enforced one day, perhaps into a bank account inscribed to a slightly different name. There was a Russian Party that had the Russian word for silver in its name, "platina." This had been mistranslated as "platinum" when a bank account was set up in Austria. "But that is somebody else," the Russian Award debtor said. This was an expensive translation mistake! It took a year to sort out.

**789. Q: Do you include the ICC Secretariat?**

A: Yes, but some people are afraid that the Award might be taken to have been *made* by the Secretariat, so they ask that their names be removed from the *Dramatis Personae*. You may avoid the problem by writing: "Under the auspicies of ..." or put the Secretariat into a footnote.

---

219. See Annex (L), Procedural Order No. 1, para. 50.
220. See Annex (H), ICC Terms of Reference or Constitution Order.
221. See Annex (L), Procedural Order No. 1.
222. See question 786.

**790.   Q: For the introduction in the Award, do you start with Claimant, then Respondent?**

A: Not necessarily. Avoid boring the reader early on with all the tedious details concerning the Parties. You can put this into the *Dramatis Personae*.

**791.   Q: Part C of ICC Terms of Reference usually contains some sort of introduction. Can you carry this one over to begin your Award reasoning?**

A: Yes, but only as a first draft. The beginning of an Award will need substantial redrafting.

In a dispute between a main contractor and a subcontractor, for example, the reader will first want to know about the project and the employer. Then one can go on to the main contractor, and then the subcontractor, even if the subcontractor is the Claimant and the main contractor is the Respondent, as can happen.

To introduce the project, one may need to start with something about its geographical setting and its purpose. Example: "Aluminum smelters are often close to sources of aluminum ore (Bauxite) and have easy access to hydro-electric power. In the present arbitration ...."

Another way to start is to explain the technology involved, especially if it is highly sophisticated.

**792.   Q: So one should tell a story?**

A: Definitely. Start from the top.

Example: There is a dispute about a tube made by a Party out of special steel. The tube is part of the engine of a stage two rocket used to propel a satellite into orbit. If one commences the reasoning of the Award with the company that made the tube, the reader will find it hard to understand the relevance of the company. Instead, start with the stationary telecommunication satellite, then go to the multi-stage rocket used to put it in place, then to stage two of the rocket, then to the engine for that stage, and then to that particular tube made of special steel. The reader will be able to relate to the satellite and probably the rocket, and so be led gently down to the subject-matter of the dispute.

If a Party belongs to a group of companies, introduce the group and its top company first, which may be a household name, then the Party appearing in the arbitration (perhaps a special purpose vehicle set up for the performance of the Contract in dispute).

If there is a licensing agreement, start out by explaining what the licensor does, that it has this patent or know-how, and only then move to the licensing agreement with the licensee. Then perhaps say that various disputes arose, and the licensing agreement was terminated, effective a particular date.

Feel free to shape the story. Some details may be so well known to the Parties that they may not have set them out for the benefit of those who are new to the case (often unfortunately including the arbitrators). Provide these details even if they just "flesh out" the story. For instance, the subject-matter of the license dispute may be a drug. The reader will be curious to know what this particular drug is supposed to do (say, fight intestinal cancer). Tell him or her even if it does not matter for the law.

### 793. Q: Should one summarize the story at the end?

A: No, the other way around. It is better to start with a shorthand description of the dispute.

One can start in a catchy way, such as: "This arbitration is about a treasure found and a friendship lost." The first page should hook the readers, not lose them.

Or one can give a summary as follows: "Claimant A sold a particular factory to Respondent B and now claims the remainder of the purchase price, but B objects that the factory was deficient and brings counterclaims against A."

Only then can one say, "The details are as follows," and go into who is who, the agreement, its arbitration clause, who started the arbitration, and how.

### 794. Q: Any suggestions on mundane technical points, abbreviations, names, and the like?

A: Abbreviations should be used sparingly. Why do we have abbreviations? Because there was a time when one wrote on parchment, which was expensive. Nowadays, with computers, using full names costs nothing. Experience shows that abbreviations waste more time than they save.

Once an abbreviation is introduced, the ICC insists on it being used all the time. If the same word or name is abbreviated differently in contemporaneous documents quoted in the Award, then several abbreviations should be given in the *Dramatis Personae*, because the text in a quotation cannot be changed.

A list of abbreviations is often provided and can be easily generated electronically. This may be facilitated by putting newly introduced abbreviations in boldface in the text.

Put quotations in italics, but the ICC wants to see quotation marks anyway.

Sometimes a Party, or both Parties, use certain expressions improperly, or spell them incorrectly. It is not particularly elegant to highlight this with the expression "sic." A typing error may simply be corrected, adding "[recte]," or even silently, if irrelevant. Let somebody else be pedantic over nothing.

Fortunately, only very rarely does a Party write almost unintelligible gibberish, or argue outrageously. This is best ignored, but if one needs to make the point, one should simply reproduce such text as is, introducing it by saying: "X wrote the following, reproduced here in its entirety: ..." The quoted text will speak for (or rather against) itself.

When reproducing a Party's point of view, start every paragraph with, "According to Claimant," or the like. Some readers tend to ascribe everything said in an Award to the Arbitral Tribunal unless it is flagged otherwise.

### 795. Q: When referring to individuals, should one call them Mr., Ms., etc.?

A: Definitely, it is only polite. The Award is likely to be read by some of the individuals participating in the arbitration. One should show them respect. Remember that in some countries, being a Dr. is more prestigious than being a professor.

### 796. Q: And what should one call the Parties?

A: In the body of the Award, the Parties should preferably be called by their short names as they normally appear in the file, for instance in the agreement – not "Claimant" and "Respondent." It avoids confusion.

For clarity, use these names liberally in your titles, such as "Y Corporation's Counter-claim 2."

Parties often provide materials about themselves that are of a promotional nature. They may think that it is rude if the Arbitral Tribunal simply discards their glossy advertising. In such cases, it is best to say: "Company X describes itself as a leading manufacturer of ..." This way, the Party in question has its text, but the text is not endorsed by the Arbitral Tribunal.

### 797. Q: More technical details?

A: Capitalize defined terms.

All text in languages other than that of the arbitration must be translated, and the source of the translation must be indicated.[223]

Internal cross-references are helpful to the reader and should be used liberally. They are easy to create if the paragraphs are numbered automatically. One may also cross-reference issues for arbitration, as listed in the Terms of Reference, or particular requests in the Prayers for Relief, or the text of a particular contractual clause.

---

223. See Annex (L), Procedural Order No. 1, para. 26, 32.

**798.   Q: Should one also cross-reference to the record?**

A: No. Most readers will not have access to the record, and they should be able to understand the Award as it stands alone. When in doubt, quote.

**799.   Q: What do you do about important documents?**

A: Quote them. In the Award, and even during the arbitration, nick-name particular important letters or versions of the same thing (e.g., talk about the "hundred factories letter" or "tests number 3, 4, etc."). One should try to make it easy for the reader to follow the story as it developed.

Patents or bank accounts have long unwieldy numbers which may be abbreviated to the last three digits.

**800.   Q: Can an Award include pictures, diagrams and the like?**

A: There is no reason why not, but the author and origin of each picture should always be stated.

Before you use color, ask yourself how a black-and-white copy will look.

If a full page is to be inserted into an Award, say a particular spreadsheet or a complicated diagram, insert it as a full page and fill any blank in the previous page with, "left intentionally blank," or words to that effect.

**801.   Q: How do you end the introductory story?**

A: End by stating in simple terms who wants what from whom. It will then be easier to understand the often cumbersome Prayers for Relief that will have to be reproduced *verbatim* in due course.

## (d)   Procedural History and Prayers for Relief

**802.   Q: What comes after the introduction?**

A: Normally a summary of Claimant's position, leading up to its Prayers for Relief (from Part C of ICC Terms of Reference). Then follows a summary of Respondent's position, leading up to its Prayers for Relief (again, from Part C). Somewhere, the Prayers for Relief must be reproduced *verbatim*, even if verbose, often in a separate chapter.[224]

---

224. See questions 818 et seq.

**803.   Q: The Prayers for Relief are often hard to locate, poorly written, and change all the time. What do you do?**

A: Unfortunately true. As Prayers for Relief change, the new Prayers for Relief should always be reproduced chronologically and *verbatim*. This is something that should be done as one goes.[225]

**804.   Q: ICC Terms of Reference contain summaries of the Parties' respective positions. Is this useful for this part of the Award?**

A: These summaries were prepared at a very early stage, but they were drafted or accepted by the Parties and are there to be used at little if any cost. One can always justify leaving an *initial* summary as it is, on the basis that it explains what led to the *original* Prayers for Relief and to the Terms of Reference, including the issues for arbitration.

The facts that emerged later may then be set out in a separate chapter *after* a description of the proceedings before the Arbitral Tribunal. After all, they are the *result* of these proceedings, and the first product of the Arbitral Tribunal's work beyond the ICC Terms of Reference.[226] One may certainly discuss facts in conjunction with claims based on them.

**805.   Q: Any general suggestions about style?**

A: You are often writing for non-native speakers of English. Short sentences please. Avoid casual language. No elisions (don't, hasn't, etc.), please.

The reasoning in an Award can be easily improved by inserting words such as: "therefore"; "hence"; "accordingly"; "thus"; "by contrast"; "however"; "yet"; "for instance"; "it follows that"; "under these circumstances"; "precisely"; "in particular"; "in the Arbitral Tribunal's view"; "Claimant says"; "as he put it"; "sometimes also called"; "also"; "likewise"; "similarly"; "in short"; "in other words"; "to sum up"; "in sum"; "this is not to say that"; "true"; "it must be conceded that"; "to be sure"; "rather"; "this being said"; "there are exceptions; however"; and, "so far so good."

**806.   Q: As you edit the text of an Award, are there also words that you should just delete?**

A: Yes: "clearly"; "unanimously"; "without hesitation"; "with some hesitation"; "forcefully"; and, "Claimant overlooks ..."

---

225. See questions 820 et seq.
226. See Annex (H), ICC Terms of Reference or Constitution Order.

**807. Q: Should the Arbitral Tribunal call a spade a spade?**

A: Not necessarily. Be a little subtle. It is often sufficient to say: "The Arbitral Tribunal is not persuaded." "This argument strikes the Arbitral Tribunal as far-fetched." "A more natural interpretation ....." "This is a sophisticated argument, but ....." "This testimony was contradicted by ....." Or use terms such as: "unusual"; "surprising"; "complex"; "a countervailing consideration"; and, "one should not overlook ....."

**808. Q: Will an ICC Award also include a section on the Terms of Reference?**

A: Yes, but it needs to appear at the right point in the chronology, after one has set out how the Arbitral Tribunal was formed, when one finally reaches the history of the proceedings.

**809. Q: Part E of the ICC Terms of Reference contain material on the initial stages. Is this useful?**

A: Definitely, and you do not even need to change much there. Simply reproduce that part early in your Award *before* you reach the Terms of Reference.[227]

In non-ICC abitrations without the benefit of Terms of Reference, this part should be drafted early, as things develop. It is difficult to reconstruct things that are long forgotten.

**810. Q: Is *res iudicata* also a consideration?**

A: It is. This is a difficult area of the law, because the concept of what is *res iudicata* or collateral estoppel differs from jurisdiction to jurisdiction. If the *lex arbitri* is that of a common-law country, it is particularly important for Claimant to know what the ambit of *res iudicata* is going to be. Say, a particular money claim is made on the basis of a particular theory, but in the course of the arbitration Claimant abandons this theory and bases its claim on another. Has the claim based on the first theory been waived? What about a third theory? Can this still be brought in another arbitration? A Party must say exactly what it means, or it may be misunderstood.

**811. Q: Can the Arbitral Tribunal help here?**

A: Yes. Since it has a general duty to ensure that it understands the Parties' positions, it should ask when uncertain.

The Arbitral Tribunal, however, cannot and should not decide the ambit of *res iudicata* of its own Award. This is for others to decide.

---

227. See Annex (H), ICC Terms of Reference or Constitution Order.

What an Arbitral Tribunal can do, however, is to say that it understands that a particular claim was waived, or that a Party expressly asked that the Arbitral Tribunal not deal with a particular potential claim, but that the Party "reserved" its right to bring that claim before another *forum*. However, it is not for the first *forum* to decide whether a subsequent *forum* will have jurisdiction on this "reserved" claim.

Never forget that one can *say* that one reserves something, but one can only *reserve* something that one *has*. "Reserving" sounds good, but it adds nothing to the position.

### 812. Q: Next in the Award comes the general procedural history?

A: Yes. Call it "Proceedings" (please note that "procedure" should be distinguished from "proceedings" in English; do not get confused by the false friend "procédure" in French, which often means "proceedings"). Present what has happened in a chronological way. This makes it easier to update your draft as the arbitration develops. It is tedious to write it all in one go.

### 813. Q: Do you set out the entire proceedings before the Arbitral Tribunal?

A: Yes, within reason.

Extensions of deadlines are normally irrelevant for the outcome. Dealing with them by formal numbered Procedural Orders is not required, and an Award that sets out every numbered Procedural Order (dozens of them) will be boring to read.

Frequently you have threshold issues that were bifurcated in the proceedings. If so, these special proceedings should be set out separately up front, in a separate chapter, leading to the resulting decision or Preliminary or Partial Award.

If the details of the bifurcated proceedings were set out in those separate decisions, there is no need to repeat those tedious details in the Final Award.

One should, however, set out the *operative part* of any earlier Partial Award or other resolution or special proceedings.

### 814. Q: Why?

A: The Final Award should contain everything that is necessary to understand the proceedings and the decisions on costs (in any event, those on the arbitration costs, which in ICC arbitration are made only with the Final Award, partly by the ICC Court, partly by the Arbitral Tribunal).

Some Awards even provide that the earlier Awards are all made an integral part of the last Award, which, the Arbitral Tribunal hopes, will make them enforceable all in one go on the basis of just one document. The Partial Award may have reserved some decisions, such as those on arbitration costs, or particular merits, which the Final Award will have to address.

### 815.   Q: The procedural history cannot be taken from ICC Terms of Reference, can it?

A: No, the procedural history is mostly about what happened *afterwards*. The updated Procedural Timetable is useful here though. If the Procedural Timetable is structured in a way similar to the first page of the Terms of Reference, as a "ping pong table,"[228] and kept current, it will be easy to describe the proceedings chronologically.

### 816.   Q: How detailed should the description of the proceedings be?

A: Essentially, you should describe what you see as you stand before the file on your bookshelves: the various submissions and their dates, but not every extension of a deadline, every letter, or every Procedural Order.

Of course, a procedural dispute may still remain open. This dispute should be set out in the Award at the chronological point at which it arose, and its resolution by the Arbitral Tribunal may have to be explained and defended. But normally the reader will be glad to be spared mere old kitchen quibbles, and will be interested only in what in fact came to the table.

### 817.   Q: Some present the procedural history in the form of a table, perhaps taken from the Procedural Timetable. Is this a good idea?

A: At first glance this appears convenient, but one may need more flexibility to discuss special procedural problems as they have arisen.

### 818.   Q: Should Prayers for Relief be provided in detail?

A: Yes. They should preferably be gathered in a separate chapter, and one may highlight the new elements ("emphàsis supplied") for better understanding.

### 819.   Q: Why are many Prayers for Relief so poorly worded?

A: Because in domestic litigation, Prayers for Relief do not have the same function and importance, particularly in the common law world. In the French-speaking areas of the world, Parties often ask for declarations ("donner acte," "constater"), and on the basis of these declarations, for money.

---

228. See Annex (J), Procedural Timetable.

Sometimes it is useful to ask the Parties to simply tell the Arbitral Tribunal what kind of an Award they wish to receive, specifically the operative part of the Award. Once the Party has drafted the operative part that it wishes to obtain, it has already done the job of drafting its Prayers for Relief.

There was a case where this method brought a Party's Prayers for Relief down from ten pages to five. The Arbitral Tribunal then brought the five pages down to one, and asked the Party whether *this* was the Award that it was requesting. The answer was, yes, precisely.

### 820.   Q: How can you tell which Prayers for Relief apply? Can the Parties change their Prayers for Relief at will?

A: In theory, they cannot. But the Arbitral Tribunal normally has *discretion* to accept new Prayers for Relief. They will normally bend over backwards to do so provided the right of the other Party to be heard is safeguarded (perhaps with some cost consequences), and the arbitration will not be too much delayed.

### 821.   Q: How do you know that the issues that have been raised really are *new*?

A: This is often difficult. Hence, in ICC arbitration, an Arbitral Tribunal may write in its Award: "Applying Article 23 subs. 4 of the ICC Rules, the Arbitral Tribunal notes that *arguably* new issues were presented by a Party's amended Prayers for Relief, but whether the issues are *really* new need not be decided, because if they *are* new, the Arbitral Tribunal accepts to deal with them in the present arbitration."

New Prayers for Relief should not be accepted in Post-Hearing Briefs, even if they are claimed to be (and perhaps *are*) mere updates or improved wording.[229]

### 822.   Q: Would it not be better if the Prayers for Relief that one had at the start - in the Terms of Reference in an ICC arbitration - did not change?

A: Ideally, yes. But as the examples just mentioned show, drafting Prayers for Relief is not easy for some, and cases evolve.

### 823.   Q: Do Prayers for Relief ever legitimately change in the course of an arbitration?

A: Quite often. For instance, at the commencement of the arbitration the basis for liability for damages can be argued by Claimant, but perhaps not yet the precise amount, or the amount may increase with time. It is then wise for a Party to announce

---

229. See Annex (L), Procedural Order No. 1, para. 9.

in its Prayers for Relief that the final amounts will be specified at a later date, and the Prayers for Relief will be amended at that time. The Germans call this "Stufen-klagen."[230] This must be done clearly, so that the later stages do not hold up commencing the arbitration. The statute of limitations may even force a Party to initiate the arbitration earlier.

### 824. Q: How do you interpret Prayers for Relief?

A: Procedural Order No. 1 may deal with this.[231] If needed, ask.

### 825. Q: What do you do if the Prayers for Relief change?

A: In your draft, you set out every new Prayer for Relief that supersedes a previous Prayer for Relief (highlighting the changes for better readability), but leave the old Prayer for Relief in, all the way back to the original Prayers for Relief that appeared in the Terms of Reference (though not *still* earlier versions).

Give them nicknames. In one case, it so happened that the Prayers for Relief changed once in every calendar year, so they could easily be identified by their vintage.

One must also specify which new Prayers for Relief are accepted.[232]

### 826. Q: A change of Prayers for Relief may lead to a change of value in dispute. How do you handle this?

A: In non-ICC arbitration, keep track of this, and it must be set out in the Award.

In an ICC arbitration, this is for the ICC Court, and all you can do is help it to reach the right decision and to increase the advances adequately. However, the various advances and how they were paid should not be part of the procedural history. This was handled by the ICC, not the Arbitral Tribunal.

In the part of the Award on costs, one may need to set out the end result of the advances made, but that part should only be drafted at the end of the arbitration.[233]

### 827. Q: Why?

A: Because, for costs, substantial elements are not available before the end of the arbitration.[234] If submissions on costs are made at various stages of the arbitration, one cannot foresee whether this will have an impact in a particular arbitration. Depending

---

230. See Annex (L), Procedural Order No. 1, para. 11.
231. See Annex (L), Procedural Order No. 1, paras 9 to 14.
232. Art. 23 subsec. 4 ICC Rules, and questions 820 et seq.
233. See question 856.
234. See question 732.

on the outcome, the chapter on costs may or may not require a more elaborate presentation.

**828.  Q: Why is this? An example please.**

A: Suppose one Party's procedural behavior leads to rescheduling, or to an extra hearing that could have been avoided had that Party acted more diligently. Regardless of the outcome, the extra costs of rescheduling, or of the unnecessary hearing, will have to be borne by the Party that caused them.

However, if that Party fully loses on the merits anyway, it will, for that reason alone, be burdened with all the arbitration costs and reasonable Party Representation costs, probably already automatically increased, The Arbitral Tribunal therefore will not need to elaborate the point.

## (e)  Substance

**829.  Q: How should one structure the main part on substance?**

A: As one can see from these first very rough explanations, the entire Award (but not its operative part) should consist of automatically numbered *paragraphs* (as with ICC Terms of Reference), with cross-references to other paragraphs automatically adjusted. Use automatic Arabic numbering of paragraphs for this.

Moreover, the overall structure should be divided into about two dozen *chapters*, of which not more than half should be devoted to setting up the arbitration and the arbitral proceedings, and at least half to the discussion of the various issues by the Arbitral Tribunal.

Arabic numbering of titles is likely to interfere with the automatic numbering of the paragraphs. Split-Arabic numbers are inconvenient because it is hard to spot a dot, and it is even harder to work with further subdivided numbers. Roman figures are inconvenient because they are hard to read from about Roman *vii* onwards. It therefore follows that the chapters should be labeled with upper-case (capital) letters.

Chapters should be further subdivided by *subparts* labeled with lower-case letters.

**830.  Q: Should you provide a decision tree or rail map?**

A: For the deliberation one could develop an outline that may go into the middle part of the draft Award. A rail map, however, is substantial work if one outlines in all details where the rails go each time there is a switch.

However, this method may be good if one has Co-arbitrators who will necessarily dissent from any decision that does not favor the Party that appointed them, and one does not wish to show them too early where one is going. They may even both agree on the entire rail map, but each simply wants to make sure that they arrive at the train station preferred by the Party that appointed them.

### 831. Q: Is there an easier way to organize the main part of your reasoning in your Award?

A: Often a few major issues emerge during the arbitration. It will be expedient to deal with these in separate chapters upfront, in a systematic way.

One may ask oneself whether a particular issue is a *threshold issue*, that is, depending on the outcome, dispositive of all or most of the claims. Obviously the threshold issue must be discussed first.

### 832. Q: Some examples of threshold issues?

A: Proper *constitution* of this Arbitral Tribunal and *jurisdiction*, but also arbitrability, whether a Party is properly represented, and waiver.

If there is a dispute as to whether the merits of the case should be decided according to particular rules of law, the substantive law of one particular country or of another, this *conflict of laws* issue will often also be a threshold issue.

Or there may be a threshold *statute of limitations* issue. If the statute of limitations has run, there is little point in discussing the merits of claims that are time-barred anyway.

If it is argued that a particular issue was decided elsewhere already, and is therefore *res iudicata* for the Arbitral Tribunal, this should be discussed upfront.

### 833. Q: How should an Arbitral Tribunal deal with *res iudicata*?

A: Whether a particular decision by a first Arbitral Tribunal is *res iudicata* for a second, must be decided according to the *lex arbitri* of the second Arbitral Tribunal. This is likely to be the same *lex arbitri* as that of the first, since it is likely that both arbitrations arose from the same arbitration agreement, which is likely to have provided for the seat. If the decision is *res iudicata*, the second Arbitral Tribunal cannot decide on the same matter again. The matter is dead, and there is nothing left for the second Arbitral Tribunal to decide. It cannot revive the issue and decide it a second time, let alone decide it differently than the first. It is not possible to kill a dead body again. The contrary view would lead to the absurd result that a third Arbitral Tribunal, on the basis of the same arbitration clause, might have jurisdiction to decide a third time on the same issue, which would be *res iudicata* not just once, but twice.

**834.   Q: Surely issues that were hotly debated between the Parties make a real difference to the outcome of the case?**

A: You would be surprised. Sometimes young lawyers get excited at an early stage of the arbitration about an interesting legal question, such as whether the Contract is a work Contract, a Contract *sui generis*, or has elements of a partnership agreement and is accordingly *uberrimae fidei*. In the end, this may have no relevance for the outcome, but for internal reasons the work product of associates must be "sold" to the client. So the Arbitral Tribunal is treated to it, for whatever it is worth (not much).

**835.   Q: As you then go into the details, should you simply take the first request in the applicable Prayers for Relief, then the second, and so on?**

A: No. It is better to zero in on those that are for "monetary relief." Only after all the monetary aspects have been decided should the Arbitral Tribunal then turn to requests for declarations and the like.[235] In some legal systems, declarations will be issued only if there is a special separate interest in a declaration. In other systems, declarations are issued freely. Regardless of one's attitude to this, it is wiser to deal with the money first, and only then with the words, which are often requested only in a preparatory way or merely for good measure. In an Award, one may often say that in view of the monetary Award, there is no need to discuss a request for a declaration.

**836.   Q: How do you structure the discussion of every subissue or subclaim?**

A: The easiest and recommended way is to first state what one Party says, then what the other Party answers, and then what the Arbitral Tribunal has decided.

**837.   Q: So you start with Claimant?**

A: Normally, but for a separate plea or defense, or a counterclaim, you will obviously start with Respondent.

**838.   Q: You recommend writing the Award as you go. Do you then let the earlier sections of your draft just sit there?**

A: Not completely untouched. Each time you add to the draft, you can easily review once more what is already written, and improve on it. Moreover, one sometimes welcomes a bit of easy work. Before a hearing or a deliberation, rereading the current draft of an Award and, as always, editing that draft as one goes, is a good way to remind oneself of the case.

---

235. See Annex (R), A Few Tables of Contents of Awards.

**839.  Q: How do you deal with the law in the Award?**

A: For each legal question that arises, one should never forget that a preliminary question is which law, and which area of that law, should answer that particular question.

In determining the law applicable to a particular question in any arbitration, the starting point must always be the *lex arbitri*, which in many cases contains, at least by implication, a conflict of laws rule. This rule, incidentally, will be different from the conflict of laws rule applicable before the State Courts of the country of the *lex arbitri* (in the courthouse across the street from the hearing room, so-to-speak).

If the Arbitral Tribunal knows that the State Courts that will decide any setting aside or enforcement proceedings are not sophisticated and knowledgeable about international commercial arbitration, the arbitral Award should be written in a particularly didactic way. Include all the elements that will help the State Court uphold the Award.

**840.  Q: Should an Award include comparative law remarks?**

A: In some jurisdictions, e.g. former colonies, recent case law and doctrinal writing from certain other jurisdictions, such as the former colonial masters, continue to be discussed as if they applied directly.

Sometimes comparative law remarks may help the losing Party accept the outcome. In one arbitration the Parties had agreed that French law should apply, and the Japanese Party lost after having argued, against all odds, for Japanese law to apply, perhaps to keep face. The Arbitral Tribunal explained that Japanese law would have led to the same (mixed) outcome as French law. Accordingly, the Japanese Party did not lose the case (and not too much face) on the applicable law point.

**841.  Q: There was a famous arbitrator who said: "I do not know, nor do I care about the law at the seat. I am an Englishman, so I will presume that it is the same as in England, unless somebody proves something else to me."**

A: Outrageous arrogance. Never use this person again.

**842.  Q: Some Awards then take up the Prayers for Relief in their final version and reproduce them, giving a reference to the place where these Prayers for Relief are decided in the reasoning of the Award. Is this good practice?**

A: Yes. This way, one makes sure that one has not overlooked any of the claims, thus one does not remain *infra petita*. In ICC arbitration, this is work that the ICC Secretariat will have to do, but if you do it for them, they will be grateful.

**843. Q: What comes after the reasoning on the monetary claims?**

A: That last part will for a long time just be an outline.[236]

**844. Q: What is the outline?**

A: Something like this, or just the last parts:

- Interest
- Non-monetary claims
- The Arbitral Tribunal's decisions on the various Prayers for Relief
- Costs
- Operative part of the Award.

Some of this can already be drafted if there is no expected disagreement between the arbitrators. It is likely that disagreement, if any, will focus on the monetary claims.

## (f) Interest

**845. Q: If you deal with the money claims in your Award, what do you do about interest?**

A: Nothing at first. Principal and interest should be kept apart. Deal with the claims for principal first; without principal, no interest.

**846. Q: After the principal money claims, one provides a summary?**

A: Yes, and the total amount is the amount that will probably be included in the operative part of the Award.

**847. Q: Only then do you discuss interest?**

A: Interest issues should be argued separately by the Parties, sometimes only in the Post-Hearing Briefs, and the Parties may need some prompting for this.[237] The Arbitral Tribunal should cover interest in a separate chapter of the Award, or in the second part of a summary section concerning the money claims.[238]

---

236. See Annex (R), A Few Tables of Contents of Awards.
237. See Annex (L), Procedural Order No. 1, para. 13.
238. See Annex (R), A Few Tables of Contents of Awards.

**848. Q: Interest is quite a thorny subject, and the Parties often deal with it in a sloppy fashion. True?**

A: Unfortunately. That is why an Arbitral Tribunal should give itself some flexibility in Procedural Order No. 1.[239]

**849. Q: Is interest a matter of procedure, or of substance?**

A: By now there is consensus that interest is a matter of substance. However, the various legal systems deal with interest in completely different ways. For historical and religious reasons, even in secular societies, interest is downright prohibited or treated with distrust in many legal systems. Interest on interest[240] is prohibited in many systems.

Moreover, statutory interest depends on how stable the currency is. On soft currencies, interest rates tend to reflect expected inflation. Interest rates on hard currencies tend to be lower.

Some legislatures believe that by setting high statutory default interest rates, they encourage compliance by Award debtors. This introduces a punitive element into the default interest.

Some help is provided by the Unidroit Principles Article 7.4.9, which may be applied, depending on the applicable conflict of laws' rules, to reach a commercially sensible result.

## (g) Costs

**850. Q: One should distinguish arbitration costs and Party Representation costs, correct?**

A: Yes. Party Representation costs may incidentally include the client's in-house costs.

**851. Q: Do the various Arbitral Institutions deal with costs differently?**

A: Yes. Here, we will set out the position in ICC arbitration.

**852. Q: How are the advances for arbitration costs set by the ICC?**

A: Advances are usually set on the basis of the average arbitration costs, based on the amount in dispute.

---

239. See Annex (L), Procedural Order No. 1, para. 13.
240. Called by some, anatocism.

**853.  Q: And what is the amount in dispute?**

A: The principal claimed plus the principal counterclaimed, disregarding interest.

**854.  Q: And that is then split 50:50?**

A: Correct. However, the Parties may request that separate advances be set. The Claimant must then advance the entire arbitration costs for the main claim, based on the amount of the main claim only, and the Respondent must advance the arbitration costs of the counterclaim, based on the amount of the counterclaim. An average is used to determine each of these amounts, as explained earlier.[241] However, the entire amount advanced will be higher in this case.

**855.  Q: Why is that?**

A: The cost schedule of the ICC is degressive. In other words, the higher the amount in dispute, the lower the percentage rate paid on any additional amount claimed. By having separate advances, the Parties must thus each pay an advance based on a lower amount, which will be subject to a higher percentage rate. So the two separate advances, taken together, lead to a higher sum than if the advance is calculated on the single amalgamated amount.

The Arbitral Tribunal should realize, however, that in the end the ICC Court will set the arbitration costs independently from the way in which the advances were calculated. In the end, the amounts in dispute on the main claim and the counterclaim *will* be added together, and the arbitration costs will be assessed on that basis. They will then be allocated according to the decision of the Arbitral Tribunal, which often will apply the principle of costs follow the event. This means that the advances will often be more than sufficient to cover the arbitration costs, and any excess amount will then be refunded to the Party from which it came.

**856.  Q: In your Award then, what do you do about these advance payments to the ICC to cover the arbitration costs?**

A: The Parties like to say and repeat what advances they made lest one forgets. When you deal with Party Representation costs, always take the advances out. They are not Party Representation costs. In fact, they are not even costs yet, until the ICC assesses its own costs and sets them off against the advances.

---

241. See question 852.

**857.  Q: Can you already allocate Party Representation costs pending arbitration?**

A: Yes. If the principle of costs following the event is applied, it may be possible at various milestones even within an ICC arbitration to decide on the Party Representation costs concerning that particular event.

**858.  Q: So the question is what qualifies as an event for the purposes of applying the principle?**

A: Precisely. If the outcome is in a Final Award, this is normally the event. Same result for a Partial Final Award. For instance, if the Arbitral Tribunal declines jurisdiction in a Partial Final Award concerning only the jurisdiction *rationae personae* over one particular Party, that is the event.

**859.  Q: If jurisdiction is *accepted* in an Award, this is not yet the Final Award, correct?**

A: Correct. It is only in a Preliminary Award. Under the same circumstances, this should also be treated as a separate event.

If an ICC Arbitral Tribunal decides in a separate Award on principle that certain damage claims should be granted, and certain others rejected, the Arbitral Tribunal could decide at this point on the allocation of Party Representation costs concerning these claims. The difficulty, however, is that one does not yet know what the *Quantum* is going to be.

**860.  Q: Could some other decisions on preliminary questions also be seen as separate events, even if they do not become the object of a separate Award ?**

A: Yes, but then the answer is less clear.

**861.  Q: This would also apply to particular procedural questions, such as questions concerning the production of documents?**

A: Yes.

**862.  Q: Should a Calderbank or Sealed Offer be considered when deciding on the allocation of costs?**

A: Yes.

**863.   Q: Does all this concern only Party Representation costs, or also the arbitration costs?**

A: In non-ICC arbitration, both.

In ICC arbitration, only the Party Representation costs, since the arbitration costs are set by the ICC Court at the end of the arbitration in an USD figure.

**864.   Q: What is so special about the assessment and allocation of the arbitration costs?**

A: It appears tricky that an Arbitral Tribunal decides in its own favor about its own costs.

This explains why in Sweden an Award must tell the Parties how they can challenge the decision on costs before Swedish courts. Nothing need be said about the possibility of setting aside the Award on the merits.

In the Swiss Chambers' Institution system, the cost decision must be submitted to and approved by the Arbitral Institution.

In other systems, just as in the ICC, the cost decision is made in part at least by the Institution itself. In the ICC system, the cost decision with respect to the assessment of the arbitration cost is made by the Arbitral Institution, but the allocation is made, first percentage-wise, by the Arbitral Tribunal.

**865.   Q: But the final percentage-wise allocation of the arbitration costs may still be based on various "events"?**

A: Yes.

**866.   Q: What about tax on arbitrators' fees?**

A: Depending on where an arbitrator has a tax residence, value added tax on that arbitrator's fees may become payable to the country of residence. In countries that are members of the European Union, this amounts to roughly 20%.

**867.   Q: Can that be recouped by the Party that advanced the VAT on the arbitrator's fees?**

A: Yes, if that Party is a VAT taxpayer. As a result, the arbitrator's country of residence in the end receives nothing, and the participants have simply endured tedious administrative work.

However, if the Party in question comes from a country which does not have VAT, the VAT cannot be recouped, and that cost remains with that Party.

**868.   Q: Are there countries that charge no VAT on arbitrators' fees at all?**

A: Yes, Switzerland.

**869.   Q: This gives arbitrators with their tax residence in Switzerland a competitive advantage, regardless of the seat of the arbitration or of the Party that would otherwise have to make the advance, and also regardless of the applicable law?**

A: Correct.

## (h)   Operative Part

**870.   Q: How long should the operative part of the Award be?**

A: In most arbitrations one page should be sufficient.

**871.   Q: Are the Prayers for Relief the *petita*?**

A: Yes. The operative part of the Award should deal with all the *petita*, and only these. But the wording of the operative part should not necessarily follow the Prayers for Relief word-for-word, especially claims for money. For instance, in their Prayers for Relief, Parties often specify the legal basis on which they are claiming certain amounts of money. As Procedural Order No. 1 specifies,[242] Parties must be understood to claim for money on the basis of *all* possible legal theories, such as *restitutio in integrum*, contractual penalties, damages for breach of Contract, *culpa in contrahendo*, or tort. If a Party claims money on the basis of a particular legal theory with which the Arbitral Tribunal does not agree, the Arbitral Tribunal may grant the same amount, or less, on the basis of another theory.

**872.   Q: Must the operative part track the Prayers for Relief?**

A: The decision on interest may depart from a Party's Prayers for Relief, as provided in Procedural Order No. 1.[243]

Prayers for relief are often, of necessity, generic on costs. Later costs submissions may be more detailed. They must be understood to amend the Prayers for Relief *pro tanto*. The Arbitral Tribunal's decision on costs will be based on these latest costs submissions.

---

242. See Annex (L), Procedural Order No. 1, paras 10 et seq.
243. See Annex (L), Procedural Order No. 1, para. 13.

It will often also include details on the advances made to the Arbitral Institution, so that the amounts that must be paid are fully explained in the operative part of the Award. [244]

### 873.   Q: Why this special way of dealing with costs in an Award?

A: The reason for these departures from strict adherence to the formal Prayers for Relief is practical. The people who deal with enforcement of money claims should be able to work with just the operative part of the Award, without having to go into the reasoning of the Arbitral Tribunal. This is relevant even in-house, where costs are often allocated to particular profit centers. Further, you should help the enforcement authorities in the various countries understand what it is that you ask them to do.

### 874.   Q: To make sure that you do not remain *infra petita*, the operative part should dismiss "all other or furthergoing claims." Correct?

A: Yes.

### 875.   Q: When one writes an Award, should one keep in mind the possibility of setting aside proceedings at the seat?

A: Yes. However, distinguish between issues concerning the proper constitution of an Arbitral Tribunal and its jurisdiction on the one hand, and main decisions on the merits on the other. Distinguish also between due process and other procedural aspects, and the merits. For all these issues, distinguish between factual and legal questions (and in which law?). The applicable criteria for setting aside are not the same for each of these questions.

### 876.   Q: An example?

A: In Switzerland, the findings of fact by an Arbitral Tribunal can be challenged only indirectly, if they were reached in violation of due process. This applies to *all* findings of fact, whether they are facts relevant to jurisdiction or facts relevant to the decision on the merits. If due process was violated, the Award will be set aside regardless of the effect that the violation may or may not have had on the Award.

On the *proper constitution* of an Arbitral Tribunal and *jurisdiction*, the review on the law, on the basis of the facts found without violation of due process, is unfettered.

On *merits*, by contrast, the review on the law is extremely limited. Only a violation of *truly international public policy* could lead to setting aside.

---

244. See question 856.

**877.   Q: Is the law similar elsewhere?**

A: Roughly, yes.

**878.   Q: What is so magical about jurisdiction?**

A: Good question. But everywhere, not just in Switzerland, people seem to believe that Arbitral Tribunals are too easily inclined to accept jurisdiction, out of self-interest in having more cases. They think that State Courts know better about arbitral jurisdiction and deserve the Parties' trust.

One should certainly prevent abusive jurisdiction decisions, but many jurisdiction decisions involve difficult legal issues.

It is doubtful whether it actually serves the Parties' interest to err generally on the side of the State Courts, rather than to simply fight abuse.

An incorrect negative jurisdiction decision will take an important international case out of the hands of an Arbitral Tribunal, and place it into those of some potentially distant State Court. This may be even more of a disaster than if arbitral jurisdiction had been accepted when it should have been declined.

About half of the Awards that were set aside by the Swiss Federal Supreme Court over the last twenty years were set aside for reasons of lack of jurisdiction.

**879.   Q: Does this mean that, in Swiss arbitration practice, one has to be particularly careful as far as jurisdiction is concerned?**

A: Yes, but not just in Switzerland.

**880.   Q: And what is the next worry?**

A: Due process. The other half of the Awards set aside in Switzerland since 1989 were set aside on procedural due process grounds.

**881.   Q: What about public policy?**

A: In practice, this should not cause worry in Switzerland. Swiss Awards are hardly ever set aside on international (transnational) public policy grounds. Elsewhere this may be a concern.

## (i) Non-unanimous Tribunal[245]

**882. Q: Should one say that the Arbitral Tribunal is unanimous?**

A: This would require that all arbitrators did genuinely and spontaneously agree on a truly *unanimous* Award.

However, even then it is better *not* to say so. Avoid the word "unanimous."

**883. Q: Why?**

A: Next time, you may not be able to say, "unanimous," and somebody will then ask: "Ah, this time you did not say, 'unanimous.' What happened?"

**884. Q: What is the best answer to this question?**

A: You could then answer: "You may draw your own conclusions, if you can, because we may have been sloppy in our drafting." Or, "No comment." But it is better simply not to provoke the question in the first place.

**885. Q: Will a good Arbitral Tribunal always be unanimous?**

A: No. The positions that an arbitrator may take in the deliberation of any question in an arbitration are quite diverse, even with a good Presiding Arbitrator. The goal should be a *correct* Award, not an *unanimous* Award which may be the result of a bargaining process.[246]

**886. Q: Are there different types of minority opinions?**

A: About a dozen.

The Award may be made by *majority*, against the express views of a minority arbitrator. In that case, the Award may not disclose this fact at all, and there may be no dissenting opinion either, but the decision may still not be graced with the term "unanimous."

A minority arbitrator may not take *any* position on a particular point (but *quaere* whether this is allowed), in which case the Award on that point is made without adverse vote, but again may not be termed "unanimous."

It may also be possible that a certain decision is expressly characterized as having been taken "by majority." The minority arbitrator may then remain unidentified.

---

245. An earlier version of this subchapter was published by the author under the title "How to write Awards – ICC Awards anyway", The Danubia Files: Award Writing Lessons from the VIS Moot – Ed. Louise Barrington et al., Cisgmoot 2013, pp. 19–36. The author thanks the copyright owner for the permission to use the earlier publication.
246. See question 765.

Alternatively, the minority arbitrator may wish to be named.

It is possible, but not required, for the minority arbitrator's views (attributed or not) to be disclosed in the reasoning in an "embedded dissent," or simply as a footnote.

Finally, it is possible for the dissenter to issue a full, separate, signed dissenting opinion.

These are all possibilities for concurring views as well.

**887.   Q: Now, in practice, *which* of these possible methods should be used to express a different view?**

A: Whether it is in an Award, or a separate opinion sent to the Parties, an arbitrator should only ever express a different view when that arbitrator believes that it is absolutely necessary for him or her to do so.

This is a matter of distinguishing the good, the bad, and the ugly. Alan Redfern describes a good dissent as "one that is short, polite and above all restrained." Redfern classes bad or ugly dissents as those in which "the dissenting arbitrator does not merely disagree with his or her colleagues on issues of fact or law, or on their reasoning, but instead takes the opportunity of issuing a dissenting opinion to attack the way in which the arbitration itself was conducted."

**888.   Q: How can you avoid such an ugly attack by a dissenting arbitrator on the majority?**

A: A Presiding Arbitrator may anticipate that a Co-arbitrator may have a minority view. He or she should then take extra precautions to ensure that the deliberations will be conducted congenially. The other arbitrators may even travel to the town of that particular Co-arbitrator. This will make it more difficult for the discussions to become acrimonious. It could be awkward for the host minority arbitrator to leave a deliberation meeting slamming the door of his or her own office.

**889.   Q: Should exchanges between the arbitrators become more formal when a dissent is looming?**

A: Yes. The Presiding Arbitrator should invite the Co-arbitrators to a formal "final" deliberation, fixing the time and place, and announce that at the close of this deliberation a vote will be taken on the operative part of the draft Award, after which it will be promptly submitted to the ICC Court for scrutiny.

If one of the arbitrators (normally the one about to dissent) does not show up, possibly with an honest-sounding excuse, be cautious. Document every subsequent attempt to contact that particular arbitrator and to deliberate.

**890.  Q: And once the arbitrator in question has uttered the word "dissent"?**

A: Breath a sigh of relief.

The majority should immediately make it clear that it will now feel free to draft the majority Award as it thinks fit, and that it will send only the near-*final* version of the draft majority Award to the dissenting arbitrator. The dissenting arbitrator should even then be invited to suggest improvements to the draft, or to send his or her draft dissent to the majority arbitrators.

Dissenting opinions are often predictable.

The majority arbitrators should, however, insist that *they* will have the last word on the majority Award, and will submit to the ICC Court *their* even more final version of the draft Award whenever they are ready, copying the minority arbitrator. Along with the draft majority Award, they should send the ICC Court the latest version of the draft dissenting opinion known to them.

**891.  Q: The minority arbitrator cannot be prevented from drafting yet another version of his or her minority opinion?**

A: No, they cannot. The newest version, however, is often not very different from the previous draft. When asked about this by the ICC, the majority will then normally say that it stands by its opinion.

**892.  Q: Is *secrecy of deliberation* important?**

A: It fulfills valuable functions, particularly *pendente lite*.

*Pendente lite*, free discussion and dialogue further quality. If the ability to discuss freely within the Arbitral Tribunal is curtailed, including the possibility to change one's mind, the quality of the discussion suffers.

**893.  Q: Are there limits?**

A: The secrecy of deliberation has its limit where the deliberation process *as such* was faulty. Thus, an arbitrator may claim that he or she was mobbed by his or her Co-arbitrators in the deliberation process. This was famously claimed, but proved untrue, in the CME investment protection arbitration against the Czech Republic.

**894.  Q: What about leaks *pendente lite*?**

A: If one of the arbitrators *leaks* information about the deliberation *pendente lite*, equal treatment of the Parties is in danger.

Moreover, if a Party privately knows towards the end of an arbitration that it is going to lose, it may be tempted to start challenging the arbitrators personally. It may also take measures against enforcement, for instance hiding assets. It could have taken these measures earlier, but may have been reluctant to do so that early for other reasons.

Conversely, if a Party knows that it is likely to win, it may take measures towards enforcement that, possibly for cost reasons, it would otherwise not yet have taken, such as retaining lawyers in the country of enforcement, or seizing assets there.

The Parties' positions on costs may also be tainted if they know what the outcome on the merits is going to be. Losers pay, but try to pay as little possible.[247] Winners may beef up their cost claims.

**895. Q: Once the final deliberations stage has been reached, sometimes marked by a declaration that the proceedings are closed, is secrecy of deliberation still important?**

A: Less so, because the worst threat, unequal treatment as a result of leaking, is now less of a concern. Leaking cannot affect proceedings that are already closed. Still, the freedom of arbitrators to speak their mind may be affected even *ex post facto*.

**896. Q: And once the Final Award is rendered, and the Arbitral Tribunal is *functus officio*?**

A: At that stage, knowing the various positions taken by the arbitrators has an even less pernicious effect. That is why those who put the secrecy of deliberation as an absolute, and claim that *any* violation of that secrecy should lead to the Award being set aside, take a good point too far.

## (j)   Final Deliberation Meeting

**897.   Q: Back to the deliberation. Should the subjects for discussion be listed in advance to structure the deliberation?**

A: Not necessarily. However, it is important to say *at which time* the final *vote* on the entire operative part will be held, and to provide a paper trail of this.

**898.   Q: In many State Courts, the most junior member of a panel usually talks first. Is this a good rule?**

A: Yes, also in arbitration.

---

247. See question 735.

Ugo Draetta says that the Presiding Arbitrator should talk last, because by changing one's mind one loses authority. There, I disagree. This may be a cultural thing.

### 899. Q: Should the Presiding Arbitrator come to the deliberation with a *draft* of the Final Award?

A: Some say absolutely not. But one should distinguish. There is nothing wrong with a draft of the procedural history, of the Prayers for Relief, perhaps also the part on the applicable law if that it is undisputed. Cover as much undisputed ground as possible before you reach the thorny part.

What really counts is the tricky decision on the *merits*. There, one should definitely not bring a draft to show the Co-arbitrators. The Presiding Arbitrator should not even suggest orally how the decision on the merits should be. A Presiding Arbitrator who does so may deprive him or herself of valuable input from the Co-arbitrators. The Co-arbitrator nominated by the Party that wins on the particular point may then limit his or her comments to minor drafting points, while the arbitrator nominated by the losing Party may be prompted to prepare a dissenting opinion.

As long as the Co-arbitrators do not know where the Presiding Arbitrator is going, and particularly if one or both are biased Co-arbitrators, they will make more substantial efforts to develop their own views, or what they will *say* are their own views. They will try to persuade the Presiding Arbitrator to accept that view rather than the other.

### 900. Q: And the Co-arbitrators? Should they arrive with their own drafts?

A: A Presiding Arbitrator should not encourage this. These *notes en délibéré* are too easily transformed into dissenting opinions.

This is of course different from the drafts of decisions on individual claims, which we talked about earlier.[248]

### 901. Q: What do you do about partisan dissenters?

A: They are not necessarily bad people. Often they merit our sympathy. Some arbitrators *must* be *partisan*.

One such arbitrator indicated by a gesture that, if he did not issue a dissenting opinion, he might have his head cut off. He came from a country where free speech is guaranteed in the Constitution, but not in reality. Capital punishment is frequently applied. That he made the gesture silently confirmed my suspicion that he might even have been wired by his minder, who traveled with him but was not present at that deliberation. A case that was much more sad than it was bad.

---

248. See question 752.

Such arbitrators are easily spotted early on in an arbitration. Their contribution is sometimes still useful, even beyond choosing the wine at meals.

*Be kind to the captive minority arbitrator.*

### 902.   Q: Should dissenting opinions simply be prohibited because they might make an Award null and void?

A: This was a view frequently voiced in French, but it is heard less and less. That a dissenting opinion makes an Award null and void is just not true.

As long as there are Party-appointed arbitrators, nothing will prevent some of them from issuing dissenting opinions, and from sending them directly to the Parties if the Arbitral Institution does not send them itself.

### 903.   Q: How does the minority draft the dissenting opinion?

A: An arbitrator who is likely to be in the minority may be inept, slow and even lazy.

Initially, a partisan arbitrator hopes to be in the majority with the Presiding Arbitrator and will not contribute much. If the Presiding Arbitrator voices an opinion favorable to the appointing Party, the partisan arbitrator will simply say that he or she entirely agrees with the Presiding Arbitrator's views, and form, if needed, a majority with him or her. It is only if the Presiding Arbitrator, unfortunately for the partisan arbitrator, turns the other way, that the partisan arbitrator will start working in an effort to sway him or her. At a late stage, this may be quite a scramble. At least the Presiding Arbitrator will have done his or her homework, but the partisan Co-arbitrator will have to catch up and take on a difficult uphill task.

Sometimes the dissenting opinion is even drafted by one of the Party Representatives! Far more admirably, occasionally the Presiding Arbitrator helps the dissenter with the dissenting opinion!

### 904.   Q: Does the Presiding Arbitrator draft the majority opinion?

A: Yes together with the other majority arbitrator.[249]

Unfortunately, a partial Co-arbitrator nominated by the winning Party is not likely to contradict the Presiding Arbitrator in any substantial matter. It is sometimes said that a Co-arbitrator's task is to make sure that the Party that appointed him or her is granted a procedurally equal right to be heard. If that Party's viewpoint is accepted by the Presiding Arbitrator, that Party has obviously been *heard*.

---

249. See question 890.

So a Presiding Arbitrator should hold back his or her views and scare that lazy arbitrator into contributing.[250]

### 905. Q: Are there ways to speed up the issuing of a Final Award?

A: If the Presiding Arbitrator anticipates that there will be a dissenting opinion, he or she might as well draft the entire (majority) Award and keep it ready. As soon as it is *clear* that there will be a dissenting opinion, that fully drafted majority Award can come out of the bag overnight as a draft, to the minority arbitrator's surprise, and the majority Co-arbitrator's surprise and delight.

### 906. Q: What is particularly dangerous is the partisan arbitrator who is also leaking information. How can these problems be managed? Should one try to trap the leaking partisan arbitrator, for instance by "salting" a draft? Should one report partisanship to the Parties? To the Arbitral Institution?

A: Generally not. Removing a leaking partisan arbitrator would take a long time, and would result in a successor being appointed who is equally bad.

It is better to *beat* the leaking arbitrator *to the finishing line*.

One technique that has worked is the following: The Presiding Arbitrator announces that on a certain issue only two views are possible, and invites each Co-arbitrator to put his or her view on paper, though not more than, say, three pages. The Presiding Arbitrator also announces that both three-page statements will find their way into the Award *verbatim*, be it as a summary of the majority's view, or as a succinct embedded statement of a minority arbitrator's point of view.

This has the advantage that there will not be an extensive and perhaps acrimonious dissenting opinion, which will take a long time to be ready and may hold up the Award. The dissenting arbitrator will also be shielded from accusations that the arbitration might have gone the other way, if only he or she had argued more forcefully and at greater length in the appointing Party's favor. The minority arbitrator can point out that all he or she *could* do was to write the three pages, and that these pages are now embedded and integrated in the Award itself.

### 907. Q: How do you handle the signatures?

A: The signature page of an Award should be just that – a signature page, identifying the Award in a running title, but initially unnumbered and completely undated. This way, the Co-arbitrators may be invited to provide their signature well in advance without much risk. When the text has been finalized with everybody's approval, the

---

250. See question 899.

signature pages may be added to it. Only at that time will the signature pages be dated (perhaps by a legible stamp) and numbered.

On the signature page, the "place" of arbitration must be given. Even though many Arbitration Statutes use the word "seat," you may not use this word in ICC arbitration.

## (k) Scrutiny of Awards[251]

**908. Q: The ICC scrutinizes draft Awards and must approve them before they are issued. Is this unique in the ICC system?**

A: The formal scrutiny is indeed unique in the ICC system, but other systems have some sort of informal scrutiny. In these other systems one is advised to submit a first draft of an Award to the Arbitral Institution, and it will then informally have a look at it and may give helpful suggestions.

**909. Q: Once it receives a draft Award, what does the ICC Secretariat do?**

A: First, the Secretariat reads the Award and may have various suggestions and corrections, mostly of a formal nature.

Ideally, the Presiding Arbitrator should hear such suggestions promptly and informally (preferably even by telephone), and may then promptly send in "replacement pages" or a full "replacement version."

The Secretariat then sends the draft Award with its suggestions in a written report (called "Agenda") to the ICC Court.

**910. Q: How does the ICC Court scrutinize Awards?**

A: There are two methods by which the ICC Court then scrutinizes a draft Award. Most draft Awards and the Secretariat's Agenda go before a *committee* of the court consisting of three people, usually the Chairperson or a Vice Chairperson of the Court presiding, and two members of the Court. The two members are usually one senior member with substantial experience in international arbitration, and one of the newer members.

In special cases, those involving a state or those where there is a Dissenting Opinion, or cases raising important policy issues, draft Awards go before the *plenary session*. There, a member of the Court, usually a senior and experienced person, prepares a short written report in addition to the Secretariat's Agenda, and these two written

---

251. Earlier versions of this subchapter were published by the author under the title "How to Write Awards – ICC Awards anyway", The Danubia Files: Award Writing Lessons from the VIS Moot – Ed. Louise Barrington et al., Cisgmoot 2013, pp. 19–36; "Awards and Orders – Labels Matter After All", Tijdschrift voor Arbitrage, 2004, pp. 57–62, ©Kluwer Law International. The author thanks the copyright owners for the permission to use these earlier publications.

reports go the plenary session. There are then short presentations by the Secretariat and the Rapporteur, discussion, and a decision by the plenary session.

**911.  Q: What happens to a Dissenting Opinion in the ICC Scrutiny process?**

A: In an arbitration system where arbitral Awards are scrutinized, formally as at the ICC or informally elsewhere, a draft Dissenting Opinion is also submitted for consideration, but is not subjected to scrutiny as such. At the ICC, if a draft Award is accompanied by a draft Dissenting Opinion, both frequently go before the Plenary Session of the ICC Court rather than a Committee of the Court.

Before the ICC Court, in my view, the secrecy of deliberation does not hold. The draft Dissenting Opinion at that time may be quite sharp in argument, not in tone – *suaviter in modo fortiter in re*. It is only a draft that, if and when it becomes final, may be amended to delete those passages that were meant only for the ICC Court and should not go to the Parties, as a Dissenting Opinion ultimately will. So the Dissenting Opinion will in the end comply with Alan Redfern's admonitions to be short, polite and above all, restrained.

**912.  Q: What does the ICC Court finally do?**

A: The ICC Court then decides whether (a) to approve the Award as is, (b) approve it subject to certain conditions, or (c) to reject it, in which case it goes back to the Arbitral Tribunal for a new decision.

**913.  Q: What is the most frequent outcome?**

A: Most frequently, (b) is used: The Award is approved subject to certain conditions, and the Secretariat must then monitor compliance with these conditions. The draft Award does not go back before the ICC Court.

**914.  Q: Has it ever happened that a draft Award was rejected and the case went back to the same Arbitral Tribunal several times?**

A: *Several* outright rejections of type (c) by the ICC Court in the same case? Very rarely.

**915.  Q: Once the text is finalized …?**

A: Only once the text of the Award is finalized may it be dated and signed by the Arbitral Tribunal.

**916.   Q: If the signature page then still must be sent all around the world, this is tedious and means delay?**

A: Yes. If one fears that one of the Co-arbitrators will neither sign nor even send on a set of signature pages, one can set the signature merry-go-round in motion in both directions, and monitor the signing process closely. One set can then be retrieved early before it falls into the same trap as the other.

**917.   Q: Is there a way around this?**

A: Yes, The signature pages can be pre-signed,[252] *inter praesentes* at the close of the deliberation, ideally in far more than the required number of copies (say, nine copies). It is only fair that the pages should be identified (by a head title) to the arbitration in question, but yet undated and unnumbered, and really just the signature pages, nothing of the operative part of the Award which then comes in on its own page before the signature page. This is done in such a manner that the pre-signed and newly dated signature page can be added to each final version of the Award once the final version is produced.

If the minority arbitrator is already refusing to sign at this time, that can be handled then and there as well. And once the Award is finally approved, there will be no need to set the signature merry-go-round in motion.

This makes it possible for the Award to be issued sooner than would otherwise have happened, and even if the operative part is leaked, the harm is limited.

**918.   Q: Has it ever happened that tricks were played with a pre-signed signature page?**

A: No, never in my experience.

**919.   Q: How do you send out an Award?**

A: In ICC Arbitrations this is done by the ICC. In other systems you have to do it yourself. Here are some practical suggestions:

In the course of the arbitration you may have been able to prompt the Parties to designate an easily accessible recipient for all notifications by the Arbitral Tribunal. If not, consider the diplomatic service, or ask for the advice of (even in non-ICC cases) the ICC National Committee for the recipient's country.

Be aware that a deadline to file a request to have the Award set aside will depend on the day on which the Award is *notified* to the Party. Do not notify Awards by email, not even as a courtesy copy.

---

252. See question 907.

223

To treat the Parties equally, if a document will trigger a deadline, consider sending it briefly before the weekend. That way the deadline will start running for both Parties the first day after the weekend, usually a Monday, and will also end simultaneously for both Parties.

# CHAPTER 8

## Judicial Remedies at the Seat

**920.   Q: Suppose a Party wants to have the Award set aside at the seat. Should it use a local lawyer?**

A: Yes. Use a specialist at the seat, not a lawyer from another jurisdiction, and certainly not the lawyer who lost your case in the arbitration.

**921.   Q: Even if the Party is allowed to represent itself in the setting aside proceedings? Even if it may use non-local lawyers?**

A: Yes. It is just too risky. One must keep a deadline, sometimes very short – in Switzerland, 30 days from the receipt of the Award in the language in which it was issued – and with special rules about holidays. There will also be special rules about how specific the setting aside request must be, and which grounds are available – fewer than one may think. It is not good enough to simply complain that the Award is wrong. You also need to consider language; normally the request cannot be presented in the language of the arbitration, but rather must be expressed in an official language of the seat.

**922.   Q: How long do setting aside procedures take in Switzerland?**

A: More often than not, less than five months, and hardly ever more than seven.

**923.   Q: Will setting aside proceedings hold up enforcement at the seat?**

A: Not in Switzerland, unless a "stay of enforcement" was specifically ordered by the Swiss Federal Supreme Court (or rather the presiding judge of the Second Civil Chamber), which rarely happens.

225

It is surprising that many successful Parties do not initiate enforcement proceedings in other jurisdictions at once, even though, there, enforcement may take a long time.

### 924.   Q: When an Arbitral Tribunal writes an Award, it should make sure that it writes an enforceable Award, correct?

A: Many say that it is required by the ICC Rules, but this is not what the ICC Rules say.[253]

### 925.   Q: Should an Arbitral Tribunal try to write an Award that will not be set aside under the *lex arbitri* at the seat?

A: Yes. From the very beginning, the Arbitral Tribunal should know exactly what is required by the *lex arbitri*.[254] There are sometimes surprising requirements, such as that all witnesses must be sworn in a particular way before they testify, that the Arbitral Tribunal may not apply *lex mercatoria*, or that the Award must be issued in the name of the Ruler.[255]

### 926.   Q: Are these requirements not a little old-fashioned?

A: They are, but the Parties choose the seat of the arbitration, directly or indirectly. They must live with the perhaps antiquated or peculiar requirements that come with that choice. They should do their homework beforehand.

### 927.   Q: Are there other things that an Arbitral Tribunal should observe depending on where it is sitting?

A: The Arbitral Tribunal should generally understand the procedural context in the *lex arbitri*, and act accordingly. It is helpful if a member of the Arbitral Tribunal is familiar with it.

### 928.   Q: Once an Award has been rendered, do the Parties ever negotiate as to its enforcement or partial enforcement?

A: Yes, mostly the latter. Once the arbitration is over, some Parties may be able to settle and go on with their common business. Claimant may think that it has now taught Respondent a lesson. Respondent may think that a prompt partial payment and the prospect of future business are more attractive than a possibly protracted enforcement dispute that will kill any hope of further business between the Parties.

---

253. Art. 41 ICC Rules. One should read the entire text of this Article.
254. See question 443.
255. For other unusual features in some *leges arbitri*, see above questions 63 et seq.

**929.   Q: If the Arbitral Tribunal is asked to send the entire file to a State Court, should it comply without delay?**

A: Before sending in the entire file, the Arbitral Tribunal should contact the State Court that ordered it (perhaps purely out of routine, using its standard form). The State Court may have no idea what is in the file, or how big it is, and may not be eager to receive a truckload of entire shelves of documents in English. Nobody will pay you for this anyway.

**930.   Q: If asked to take a substantive position on a challenge of an Award, what should the Arbitral Tribunal do?**

A: If the challenge concerns the Award itself, the Arbitral Tribunal should refrain from taking a position. The Award should speak for itself, and the winning Party should be capable of defending the Award that it obtained. In that case, simply answer: "The Arbitral Tribunal has nothing to add to its Award."

Whatever you do or write, remain cool. Do not attack the challenge, let alone the challenger. Let the Party that won do this; do not do its work for it.

The case may ultimately be remanded to the same Arbitral Tribunal, and you do not then wish to be challenged personally for having tried to help one Party against the other.

**931.   Q: Suppose, in a request to set aside, the internal workings of the Arbitral Tribunal are attacked, perhaps on the strength of what the attacking Party heard from the arbitrator that it appointed?**

A: Then the situation is different. The Arbitral Tribunal must answer this particular point about internal matters that are not dealt with in the Award. But remain factual, cool and dry in your response.

**932.   Q: Must the full Arbitral Tribunal answer, including the leaking arbitrator?**

A: Yes, probably by majority. If the minority arbitrator wishes to submit a (scathing) dissent, then so be it.

# CHAPTER 9

# Enforcement of Awards in the Country of Enforcement

**933.  Q: When people say that the Arbitral Tribunal should make every effort to ensure that the Award will be enforceable at law, they often mean enforceable in the *country of enforcement*. Is this so?**

A: This is an entirely different matter. There, one cannot be so sure. In the first place, one does not know *where* the country of enforcement is likely to be. There are more than 200 jurisdictions out there.

**934.  Q: Is it then the Party Representatives' job to think about enforcement, rather than the Arbitral Tribunal's?**

A: Yes. The Party Representatives should know what their client's goal is: Does the client really wish to obtain enforcement? Where? How will this be done? One will need legal advice about the law of the country of enforcement as well as practical considerations.

**935.  Q: But there is the New York Convention almost everywhere?**

A: Let us not kid ourselves. The New York Convention is honestly applied in about 30 countries. Forget about the rest.

**936.  Q: But one then can go into investment protection arbitration about this?**

A: Good luck.

**937.   Q: Some things may be tricky to enforce in particular countries, for instance claims for interest?**

A: Yes, and an Arbitral Tribunal should put such tricky matters into a separate paragraph of the operative part of the Award, so that, if worse comes to worst, the other paragraphs may still be enforced. *Utile per inutile non vitiatur.*

Interest is in any event a particularly difficult area. There are jurisdictions where, if an arbitration clause even talks about interest, this may make the entire arbitration clause null and void.

In some jurisdictions there is a distinction between pre-arbitration interest, interest *pendente lite*, and post-Award interest. These jurisdictions believe that there *must* be such a difference. They may believe that interest that ran pre-arbitration is covered by substantive law. Interest *pendente lite* is, they say, procedural because this pertains to the procedure before the Arbitral Tribunal. Post-Award interest, they think, cannot be awarded by the Arbitral Tribunal *in futurum*, when it will no longer be around, but can only be a granted in the country of enforcement, because it is of a procedural nature in that particular country.

**938.   Q: If an Award has been set aside at the seat, can it be enforced in other countries under the New York Convention as if it had not been set aside?**

A: Generally only in France, for ideological reasons.[256]

**939.   Q: Also in the United States?**

A: Yes, but only in individual cases, and for a different reason. The analysis is as follows: Whenever an Award is annulled at the seat, there is not just the Award but also the annulment decision, and that is a decision by a State Court. Thus, the question arises as to whether that State Court decision should be recognized in the enforcement country. Sensibly, the law on recognition and enforcement of foreign State Court decisions should apply to that question. Within that law, there is reference to the public policy of the country of recognition and enforcement. In two cases,[257] the particular setting aside decisions of foreign courts in Egypt and Mexico where held to be contrary to United States' public policy. As a result, the arbitral Awards were resurrected, or rather were deemed to never have been struck down, and thus could be enforced in the United States under the New York Convention.

---

256. See question 977.
257. Chromalloy, 939 F. Supp. 907 (D.D.C. 1996) and COMMISA, Corporacion Mexicana de Mantenimiento Integral, S. de R.L. de C.V. v. PEMEX-Exploracion y Produccion, Case 1:10-cv-00206-AKH, August 27, 2013.

**940.   Q: If an arbitrator is asked to testify before a State Court in the country of enforcement, should he or she comply?**

A: It is probably part of an arbitrator's "after sales service," though not so much to the enforcing Party as to arbitration itself, which is not always well understood in some countries. If a State Court judge sees that the Arbitral Tribunal conducted serious proceedings with professionalism, this may help enforcement.

**941.   Q: If the State Court judge wishes to revisit all the issues in the arbitration, should the arbitrator assist?**

A: No. For instance, the Presiding Arbitrator may limit his or her testimony to what he or she *remembers* of the case, not having studied the record again, and only regarding the Award. It is surprising how little one remembers about a past case.

**942.   Q: If requested by the Parties, should an Arbitral Tribunal conduct a *post mortem* of an arbitration?**

A: Obviously this would presuppose that the case is completely finished. However, the possibility of a revision does not depend on a deadline, and thus can *never* be excluded. A *post mortem* should therefore be avoided.

The point of an arbitration is not to assess the performance of the Party Representatives. An Arbitral Tribunal is not in the worst position to do that, of course, but it is not in the best position either. It does not know, for example, about the relationship between the Party Representatives and the clients. It does not know things that the Party Representatives may, for good reason, not have disclosed.

**943.   Q: So it is not a good idea for the Arbitral Tribunal to teach the Party Representatives how to do their job?**

A: They should learn by themselves from their own experience, and perhaps that of others.

# CHAPTER 10

# History of Arbitration

**944. Q: Now let us move to a more historical and philosophical view of the entire process. Is it true that the history of international commercial arbitration reaches back thousands of years?**

A: It is true, of course, that whenever people interact there may be disputes, and these may be resolved either peacefully or by force.

**945. Q: And by peaceful resolution of disputes we mean arbitration?**

A: Not necessarily. Peaceful resolution is the goal not just of international commercial arbitration, but of the Rule of Law generally.

**946. Q: Disputes may be resolved peacefully by the state or by states, or by some means of private dispute resolution?**

A: This is the way we think today, but the state as we now know it is a relatively recent phenomenon. Emmanuel Gaillard dates the current system of sovereign States back to the treaty of Westphalia of 1648, which put an end to the 30 Years War, a disastrous conflict between European warlords.

Before that time, even during much of the Roman Period in Western Europe, the state had only a small role to play in the resolution of business disputes. There was law, but for most of the Roman Period disputes were resolved in a way that was substantially different from today's court litigation, and had quite a bit in common with modern-day arbitration.

**947.  Q: The Roman praetor *was* a state official, was he not?**

A: He was, but if you went to a praetor (there were different types), he would not give you a decision. He would appoint a judge, as we would call him, however then sometimes called an *arbiter*. The praetor would give the judge what we would call ICC type Terms of Reference, then known as *litis contestatio*, and the judge would hear the Parties and render a decision.

**948.  Q: This sounds like arbitration today, but was the judge not a full-time state official?**

A: No. In the classical period, the judge was a private person entrusted with the task of rendering a decision that would be binding upon the Parties.

Only in the late Roman Empire did the Emperor's Court become more like our current State Courts.

**949.  Q: Today public functions are not exercised by private entities?**

A: Hardly at all. Although, in Hong Kong the setting aside of arbitration Awards, even *ad hoc* and those administered by other Arbitral Institutions, is entrusted to HKIAC, which then exercises a public function.

**950.  Q: Back to the Romans. Was there also arbitration as we know it, as a separate phenomenon?**

A: Yes, but not exactly the same. For instance, one used *sole* arbitrators only, called "*arbiter*," hence today "*lex arbitri*." The *arbiter* probably had to swear an oath of office. If an *arbiter* died, there was no replacement mechanism. An arbitration agreement could be used only once.

The *arbiter* issued a "*sententia*," it seems *orally*, as the word indicates. "*Arbitrium*" means, of course, "will" (remember *De libero/servo arbitrio* by Erasmus and Luther), not "arbitration" or "award."

**951.  Q: An arbitral Award is called "sentence" in our modern languages?**

A: Yes, "sentence" in French, but in other languages "award," "vonnis," "lodo," "Schiedsspruch," and so on. These other expressions do not derive from Latin legal parlance.

**952.  Q: In Roman law, why would the Parties have an incentive to honor an arbitration agreement?**

A: They mostly used *stipulatio*, an abstract formal oral promise. A stipulated sum of money was payable under certain conditions, for instance, if a Party went to a State Court instead of arbitration, or did not honor an arbitral Award.

**953.  Q: So this operated as an abstract contractual penalty?**

A: Yes.

**954.  Q: Another area of the law that the Romans hardly knew was the conflict of laws (as we know it). True?**

A: Yes, and accordingly we have different words in different languages for this also. In Roman times the entire known civilized world, or almost, so it was believed, was under Roman rule. Even though cultural diversity was enormous within the Roman Empire, local laws in Greece, Egypt or elsewhere were not on an equal footing with the laws of Rome.

**955.  Q: One used a different technique then? The *jus gentium*?**

A: Yes, this was an area of Roman law developed by the Romans to deal with relationships between people from different corners of their Empire.

**956.  Q: So actually something similar to the CISG? A special substantive law to deal with international sales that leaves local national sales laws applicable to local national disputes?**

A: Yes.

It is only in the Renaissance that a *conflict of laws* approach was developed, to deal with the fact that there were local enactments called "*statuta*" in various parts of Italy, and one had to determine which of these *statuta* would apply in which case. Which law should apply "*si Bononensis conveniatur Mutinae ...*" ("if a person from Bologna should make a Contract in Modena ..."), as Bartolous discussed in his seminal commentary to the beginning of the *Codex Justinianus*. Roman law, at the time, was theoretically the law of the whole Roman German Empire. This was the basis of the universalist approach to conflict laws, which was abandoned only later with the advent of the nation state. Yes, first in France.

**957.   Q: All this means that the conflict of laws and international commercial arbitration that we know today must have developed more recently. Sometime later than the French Revolution?**

A: Yes, as is the case with most of our modern law, even Anglo-American law.

Our modern approach to the conflict of laws goes back to Savigny and Story.

Modern Arbitral Institutions were created only in the late nineteenth century, by Chambers of Commerce, beginning with the London Court of Arbitration in the 1880s (forerunner of the LCIA), followed by local Arbitral Institutions in Switzerland, Sweden and Finland all still before World War I, the ICC in 1921, and countless others since then. Arbitration Law everywhere became comprehensively codified, and later, in many civil law countries, Private International Law as well.

**958.   Q: 100 years ago, was there really arbitration as we know it?**

A: Pretty much as we know it. If you read arbitral *awards* that are about 100 years old, they read very much the same as today's Awards.

Nowadays we have different types of arbitration. We still have public international law arbitration.[258] We have investment protection arbitration and sport arbitration, and in the commercial field there is maritime, construction and classical commercial arbitration.

**959.   Q: Was international commercial arbitration different from today?**

A: International commercial arbitration was still a rare occurrence in the early 1900's. Moreover, at the outset what was called "arbitration," even within the ICC system, was often what we would today call conciliation. In any event, many decisions were made *ex aequo et bono*, not on the basis of a particular law.

**960.   Q: Have the players changed?**

A: Yes. Originally the arbitrators were *important business leaders*. They drew their prestige from their position. As Gerold Hermann puts it, an arbitrator was not thinking that he (still *he* at that time) was rendering a judicial decision. He would see himself as presiding over a power lunch, hearing what the Parties had to say and then giving his suggestions that would invariably be followed. The Award would be rendered informally at the time when the cigars would come out and the peace pipe was smoked (they still did this).

It is only after World War II that a new, second phase began. A typical international commercial arbitrator would then be a prominent legal scholar, or professor of private

---

258. As the Alabama and Taba cases.

international law. As Barth and Dézaley described it in their sociological book, this was the period of the *"grand old men."*

The third phase, the time of the *arbitration specialists* who would engage in international commercial arbitration all through their professional lives, would come even later, some forty years ago, and continues to this day. Now international commercial arbitration has become far more intricate and complicated, some might say legalistic. Some romantically deplore these developments that favor large law firms over brilliant sole practitioners as Party Representatives. But this nostalgia, though popular, is misplaced. Many experienced arbitration specialists set up their own "boutique" law firms, from which they practice mostly as arbitrators. Some are specialists of investment protection, or sport, transportation, pharmaceutical, or construction arbitration.

Today, a fourth phase has been reached. International arbitration is now a mass phenomenon. Just to take the ICC: in the last 10 years alone it administered more arbitrations than in its first 80 years, and they were larger as well. In all systems taken together, well in excess of a thousand international commercial arbitral Awards are now issued every year. Future arbitration specialists are already getting involved in arbitration during their studies, when they participate in the VisMoot in Vienna or Hong Kong. They then work at Arbitral Institutions before joining large law firms and working in Party Representation teams.

# CHAPTER 11

# Philosophy of Arbitration

**961. Q: Is it true that philosophical underpinnings have far-reaching consequences in the practice of international commercial arbitration?**

A: There is an impact, but the consequences are not as far-reaching as sometimes argued.

**962. Q: Let us start with the fundamental philosophical differences.**

A: This concerns the *foundation* of international commercial arbitration law. Many, not just in France, say that international arbitration is the creation of the Parties, of the will of the Parties, of *Party autonomy*. Without an arbitration agreement between the Parties, there can be no arbitration.

**963. Q: And that is true, is it not?**

A: Yes, without an arbitration agreement, there can be no international commercial arbitration.

**964. Q: But the question is, *why* is the agreement of the Parties valid and binding?**

A: When Parties make a Contract domestically, as happens all the time, nobody says that they must keep that promise because of some philosophical reason, or the general principle of *pacta sunt servanda*. No, rather one says that the substantive law applicable to the Contract *says* that when Parties make a Contract, they are bound by it. Normally, at least, because the substantive law also provides that, under certain circumstances, the agreement of the Parties is *not* valid. So the foundation of the validity of the Contract is in the *applicable law*.

**965.  Q: Is this not also the case for international arbitration law?**

A: Many in France think not.

**966.  Q: Because it is international?**

A: Yes. Many in France think that there is a body of *international* arbitration law out there, created by the will of the Parties, or more precisely, by the will of the *international business community*. They believe that it is quite apart from the law of this or that country and is rather some sort of *law merchant*, akin to public international law.

**967.  Q: As customary law?**

A: Perhaps as customary law that is part of public international law. But it is not clear how this particular customary law could exist. Where would one find *longa consuetudo* and *opinio necessitatis?*

**968.  Q: But now the content of the law of international commercial arbitration. Is that also, according to French theory, public international customary law?**

A: Not so fast. Remember, the will of the Parties, or Party autonomy, reigns supreme. So if the Parties devise their own international arbitration system, or refer to a *lex arbitri* by choosing a "place" of arbitration, or international Arbitration Rules, or both (as happens all the time), that choice is valid, French theory has it, because it was made *by the Parties in exercise of their Party autonomy.*

**969.  Q: But this then still means that, according to them, the Award is binding upon the Parties again because of Party autonomy?**

A: Exactly. Even then it is ultimately the will of the Parties.

**970. Q: Those who say that Party autonomy reigns supreme in international matters, do they also believe that private international law is based on Party autonomy?**

A: Yes, they do. The Parties may, of course, refer to a particular private international law (and many civil law countries by now have comprehensive statutes on this), or some special arbitration-specific private international law that may be contained in the *lex arbitri.*[259] But what makes it valid or applicable, they say, is the will of the Parties.

**971. Q: But then the Parties could also, even by implication, refer to a body of substantive law to apply *directly,* instead of the law designated by the conflict of laws rules. This would be a body of *substantive* law developed by the community of international merchants?**

A: Yes, and that is what is often called *"lex mercatoria."*

**972. Q: If the Parties have, directly or indirectly, designated the applicable law to the substance of the dispute, can an arbitrator nevertheless decide to simply apply *"lex mercatoria"*?**

A: Some think so. Even in such a case, they think, the Arbitral Tribunal should try to apply the *true* will of the Parties, which may differ from the idiosyncrasies of the applicable law that they designated.

**973. Q: The proponents of this theory would prefer something else to the *actual* will of the Parties, namely their *hypothetical* will, or what the Arbitral Tribunal thinks that they *should* have wanted?**

A: Yes, and this sounds adventurous.

**974. Q: Do you not see the beauty of seeing arbitration law as an emanation of the transnational community of business people and business lawyers, dissociated from citizenships, countries, local laws, and truly international?**

A: Yes, the idea is indeed beautiful and attractive.

However, what business people seek is not romantic, beautiful and attractive ideas. They need practical and foreseeable decisions, and reasonably fast. One should give them what they want.

---

259. Think of section 34 English Arbitration Act 1996, or Art. 187 Swiss PIL Statute.

**975.   Q: But *should* they not want something else? Truly international justice?**

A: Who are we to say what they *should* want? We should pay respect to the *actual* will of the Parties, even if we find it less attractive than our own ideas. It is their business, not ours, their money, not ours.

**976.   Q: Did the Parties not choose *where* they would conduct the arbitration?**

A: They did, but the question is, what was the scope of this choice? Outside of France, most say that by choosing the *seat* of arbitration, the Parties chose the *lex arbitri*, and one should make a distinction between the seat and the place where the Parties and the Arbitral Tribunal meet, which may be somewhere else. The seat is a legal concept.

In French theory, by contrast, and few outside France and the ICC agree, there is no such thing as the seat. All the Parties chose was the *place* of arbitration, and this was just a place where they would actually meet. That place, they say, has only a tenuous connection with the arbitration, far more tenuous than the country of enforcement. The Parties want an Award, perhaps rendered somewhere, yes, but above all they want to enforce it. By choosing a particular place to arbitrate, they say, the Parties just chose hotels and meeting rooms, not law.

**977.   Q: An Award rendered outside France, and set aside where it was rendered, can still be enforced in France because it is an Award. Is this a consequence of the French "internationalist" view of international arbitration law?**

A: In France, it is.

**978.   Q: Is there not value in making it possible for an arbitral Award to be set aside where rendered?**

A: Indeed, the advantage is that there is *one forum* that will primarily deal with setting aside proceedings, under the *lex arbitri*, and a *forum* that knows well the *lex arbitri*, as well as the local Arbitration Rules and local substantive law, if they are applicable. An Arbitral Tribunal will know within which framework it is operating.

This does not preclude the possibility of a Party invoking the New York Convention in the country of enforcement, but setting aside at the seat of the arbitration may weed out the worst Awards. If setting aside is handled properly at the seat, one can be fairly certain that Awards that passed the test at the seat will be enforceable in other countries, particularly in countries that try to apply the law fairly. That is why the suggestion by the late Professor Fouchard that there should be no setting aside proceedings at all in the country of the place of arbitration, that all one needs is the New York Convention, fell flat, even in France.

**979.  Q: Whether an Award that was set aside at the seat can be enforced elsewhere, is this necessarily a question of philosophy?**

A: No.

**980.  Q: This all concerns the theoretical underpinnings of international arbitration law. So you say this philosophy has no influence on the substance of the law?**

A: None. While Swiss and French international arbitration law are based on funda-mentally different philosophical ideas, *in substance* they are very similar. Whereas, many systems that are based on the idea that *lex facit arbitrum*, not *voluntas partium*, may in substance be worlds apart.

**981.  Q: Why is this?**

A: Quite apart from the philosophical basis that gives international arbitration law its quality as law, one may view Party autonomy as a good thing. This is a liberal principle. One may also think that interference by State Courts should be kept to a strict minimum. Another liberal principle. One may seek to institute an arbitration-friendly regime. Still a liberal idea. Many people in international commercial arbitration are weary of local specialties, even their own. Many people are internationally-minded. All this has a philosophical basis of its own, going back to the eighteenth century.

**982.  Q: In other words, if all depends on how liberal and internationally-minded a country's arbitration law is?**

A: Yes. The philosophy that applies is liberal, and it is not necessarily based on Party autonomy.

**983.  Q: Locke rather than Rousseau?**

A: Yes.

**984.  Q: Is an international and liberal attitude furthered by drawing a distinction between international arbitration and domestic arbitration?**

A: In practice, yes. In domestic arbitration, domestic customs will be influential. If the same law applies for domestic and international arbitration, the Arbitration Law will take on an unwelcome and unwelcoming local accent.

By contrast, if one makes a distinction between international and domestic arbitration, local influences may play their role in domestic arbitration, but international arbitration will be freed from them. This is the most important practical reason for distinguishing international from domestic arbitration, even if the distinction has a relatively weak theoretical or philosophical basis.

### 985.   Q: So you may have a dual system even if you do not accept French philosophy?

A: Yes. Switzerland is an example.

### 986.   Q: Does the distinction have an effect when the law changes?

A: Then especially. This is another practical advantage of a dual system. International arbitration law charges ahead, and domestic arbitration law limps behind.

One can modernize international arbitration law, leaving domestic arbitration law as it is. Once that has been achieved, one can later try and pull domestic arbitration law forward to come close to the position of international arbitration law, and then repeat the process. Over the years, this Laurel-and-Hardy effect could be observed not just in Switzerland, but in all jurisdictions where the distinction is made between international and domestic arbitration.

By contrast, if domestic and international arbitration laws are governed by a unitary Arbitration Law, domestic arbitration will (in part) hold back the development of arbitration law, to the detriment of international arbitration. This could be observed in England and Sweden.

It is easier to walk ahead step by step than to stumble forward with feet bound together.

### 987.   Q: Is international arbitration law an extension of private international law?

A: Yes. In fact, it uses the method initiated by Savigny, of identifying a particular area of law or set of questions and then selecting a *connecting factor* to determine the applicable law (or rules of law). This is the classical puzzle or mosaic technique well-known in private international law.

A particularly important connecting factor is found in any choice-of-law provision agreed by the Parties.

By contrast, domestic arbitration is closer to civil procedure and is often taught by professors of civil procedure.

**988.   Q: Is international arbitration law not close to the law applicable in State Courts?**

A: To some extent, but the analogy is not close. If Parties choose international arbitration, it is precisely because they want to get away from the local court practices followed across the street. In an international arbitration, you do not want to hear any references to the "White Book." And you do not want your case to be discussed by people wearing wigs.

The private international law in international Arbitral Tribunals is not the same as in the courthouse across the street from the hearing room.

The *lex arbitri* actually does not deal with the civil procedure to be followed before the Arbitral Tribunal. That is something that the Parties may determine *as they please*, failing which it will be determined by the Arbitral Tribunal. The only thing the procedure must guarantee is equal treatment of the Parties and their right to be heard, or, to put it even more succinctly, due process. As long as the Arbitral Tribunal safeguards *due process*, it can do whatever it wishes.[260]

**989.   Q: What does the *lex arbitri* do then?**

A: It deals with the question of the relationship between the Arbitral Tribunal and the court system at the seat. It is not civil procedure, it is more like a judiciary act or "Schiedsverfassungsrecht." The State Courts at the seat do three entirely different things, and the *lex arbitri* describes these three things.[261]

**990.   Q: If Party autonomy is not the philosophical legal foundation for the validity of the entire international arbitration process, what is?**

A: Many say that the foundation of the binding effect of any law, not just domestic, but also in international cases, is to be found in the law of a *sovereign state*. A Contract is valid because the substantive law of a sovereign state applicable to the Contract *says* that it is valid. It is invalid, or invalid in part because that law says so.

**991.   Q: But the Parties can still say what they want in their Contract?**

A: Yes, but only because the applicable law *lets* them, and grants them, *pro tanto*, the right to make law.

---

260. See questions 77 et seq.
261. See question 667.

**992. Q: And in international commercial arbitration?**

A: The same thing. The law gives the Parties the right to enter into an international arbitration agreement, and it will enforce that international arbitration agreement, but the international arbitration agreement still takes its validity from the law. *Lex facit arbitrum.*

**993. Q: But which law?**

A: In an international case, this is indeed a slightly more difficult question. Those who say *lex facit arbitrum* answer that the law applicable to international commercial arbitration is necessarily the *lex arbitri.*

**994. Q: The *lex arbitri* chosen by the Parties?**

A: Yes. If that international Arbitration Law does not allow the Parties to provide for arbitration, because, for example, it does not consider the subject-matter of the dispute to be arbitrable, then the choice of Arbitration Law is not valid, and the arbitration cannot proceed.

**995. Q: All this sounds like Kelsen. By chance?**

A: No, for good reason. Ultimately, something is law because a state says so, and the norm that institutes the state and confers to it law-making power is Kelsen's *"Grund-norm."*

**996. Q: With that approach, all states are put on an equal footing, even the most abhorrent?**

A: Yes. To mitigate this, one can reach back into public international law and borrow its notion of state. According to public international doctrine, a state must have a territory, people, and some consistent authority, or else it is just the territory of a warlord, of a criminal gang, etc.

**997. Q: Some states pass the test, but they are still no better than criminal gangs. If statehood is the criterion, then ultimately it is might, not right?**

A: True, and this idea of statehood is the idea that has prevailed in continental Europe since the treaty of Westphalia, and which our friend Emmanuel Gaillard therefore calls "Westphalian."

He wishes to get away from such a public international law concept. His idea is to found the validity of arbitration law *entirely* on the will of the Parties and a mythical community of merchants.

**998. Q: Do all differences of opinion in international arbitration ultimately stem from this difference in the underlying philosophy?**

A: No. Philosophy is at best one factor that shapes the law. There is also history, and most of that is tradition, inertia, and fear of change.

**999. Q: An example?**

A: Suppose an Arbitral Tribunal issues Provisional Measures. For some reason, a Party wishes to have these "reinforced" by a State Court. The question is whether the State Court should simply "recognize and enforce" the Provisional Measures, or whether it should "issue" similar measures of its own in parallel. The answer to this question has nothing to do with philosophy, but may be shaped by tradition or practicality.

**1000. Q: Other influences?**

A: The competing analogies of private international law and civil procedure law. In some traditions, and especially in domestic arbitration, arbitration law is (wrongly) considered an extension of civil procedure law.[262] This leads Parties to choose judges or retired judges as arbitrators, and then arbitration all too easily takes on a flavor of domestic litigation.

There was one case where the first hearing was conducted in the Presiding Arbitrator's courtroom. The Presiding Arbitrator-judge started the hearing by saying "Welcome to the commercial court, sorry, ... this arbitration."

**1001. Q: So history has more influence on arbitration than philosophy?**

A: Yes. Arbitration theory is shaped by many historical influences. A philosophical view of the foundation of arbitration is but one of them.

However, one should never underestimate the everyday impact of the rule of law (which has a philosophical basis) or its absence in the country of the seat and the countries of enforcement, not so much on arbitration theory, but on arbitration practice.

---

262. See question 987.

# ANNEXES

# Our Arbitration Team, and Theirs, Internal Party Worksheet[263]

*Party Representatives and witnesses may find an overview of the team helpful.*

**Our Team**

| Overall Team Leader: | | |
|---|---|---|
| | **Appearing team** | **Back-up team** |
| | Outside law firm/client | Outside law firm/client |
| Team leader: | | |
| Arbitration law specialist: | | |
| Applicable law specialist: | | |
| Other laws specialists: | | |
| Arbitral Institution specialist: | | |
| Technical aspects of case: | | |
| Basic technical questions: | | |
| Specialized technical questions: | | |
| Experts: | | |
| | | |
| | | |
| Liaise with management: | | |
| Manager in charge: | | |
| Fact witnesses: | | |
| | | |
| | | |
| | | |
| | | |
| Logistics, IT: | | |
| Travel arrangements: | | |
| Manager in charge: | | |

---

263. See questions 176, 194, 198, 336, 337, 625.

## Their Team (as far as we know)

| Overall Team Leader: | | |
|---|---|---|
| | **Appearing team** | **Back-up team** |
| | Outside law firm/client | Outside law firm/client |
| Team leader: | | |
| Arbitration law specialist: | | |
| Applicable law specialist: | | |
| Other laws specialists: | | |
| Arbitral Institution specialist: | | |
| Technical aspects of case: | | |
| Basic technical questions: | | |
| Specialized technical questions: | | |
| Experts: | | |
| | | |
| | | |
| Liaise with management: | | |
| Manager in charge: | | |
| Fact witnesses: | | |
| | | |
| | | |
| | | |
| | | |
| Logistics, IT: | | |
| Travel arrangements: | | |
| Manager in charge: | | |

# First Letter from Co-arbitrators to Parties on Appointment of Presiding Arbitrator

*After having contacted each other by telephone, the Co-arbitrators could write this kind of common letter to the Party Representatives, or, if none are yet appointed, to the Parties themselves.*[264]

**E - MAIL**

Dear Party Representatives:

I am writing this letter also on behalf of my Co-arbitrator ….

We both would first like to thank you for the trust put in us. We are looking forward to working with you and the Parties towards a just, fair, and speedy resolution of this dispute.

As you undoubtedly know, in view of the arbitration clause, if we do not do anything, then the ICC Court will appoint the Presiding Arbitrator. This would then rule out the appointment of any member of the ICC Court itself, some of whom would otherwise be suitable.

The ICC normally asks one of its national committees to make a proposal, and that proposal is normally accepted. Often this works satisfactorily, but we can only keep our fingers crossed that the "ICC Roulette" will not put an inept or dangerous person in the driver's seat.

Our suggestion is not that, instead, the Co-arbitrators alone should appoint the Presiding Arbitrator, as this would also leave the Parties with no say in the matter. Rather, we believe that *all* participants should have a role in this process, and that this can be achieved as follows:

---

264. See questions 290, 292 and 298.

We have jointly established a shortlist of suitable Presiding Arbitrators from which the Parties might indicate their preference.

Here it is, in alphabetical order:

.............................

.............................

.............................

.............................

We have not contacted these candidates, and we suggest that neither should you. We suggest that by ...................., each Party simply writes us to give us its ranking of these possible Presiding Arbitrators. On this occasion, please write without copy to anybody. Just a ranking please, no comments, no "up to you," or *ex aequo* ranking.

The two of us will then combine the ranking (breaking any tied ranking according to criteria already agreed between us). We will then go down the list to find a suitable candidate who is willing to serve, and trusted by all.

Very sincerely yours,

cc: ICC Secretariat

# Letter from Co-arbitrators to Parties after Having Found a Presiding Arbitrator Candidate[265]

Dear Party Representatives:

Many thanks for having complied so carefully with the procedure mapped out in our letter to you, dated ...[266]

On the basis of your rankings, we have proceeded as planned and are happy to report that

...................................

has agreed to chair our arbitration, if confirmed by the ICC Court.

Our Presiding Arbitrator candidate will no doubt contact you shortly.

Very sincerely yours,

cc: Presiding arbitrator candidate

    ICC Secretariat

---

265. See question 299.
266. See Annex (B), First Letter from Co-arbitratiors to Parties on Appointment of Presiding Arbitrator.

# First Letter of the Presiding Arbitrator Candidate to the Co-arbitrators

My dear Co-arbitrators,

If I may call you that already, but I am really grateful to you, and hope that the ICC will confirm me.

From the ICC's letter of ........................, and in view of the arbitration clause, it appears that we will soon be in business. I am very pleased about this.

As you know, our first task will be to establish our Terms of Reference together with the Parties, and to have them signed. We will do our best to do this in writing, but experience shows that it is often unavoidable, and in any event useful for all of us to meet for a half-day Case Management Conference. I do not know about you, but for me, in the next two months or so, the following days look best: ...................... On which of these dates would it be *impossible* for you to be in ................. (or, if that makes a difference for you, in .................... ...) for an afternoon? Please advise promptly.

You will no doubt notice that I am asking for the *impossible* dates, not those that may be the most convenient. We will have to continue this little auction with the Parties. If people only pick their favorite dates, we will never find one that even halfway suits all of us.

Very sincerely yours,

# Letter of the Presiding Arbitrator to Co-arbitrators Re the Draft "Three Documents"

My dear Co-arbitrators:

Please find enclosed a first rough draft of our Terms of Reference,[267] of a Procedural Timetable, and of our Procedural Order No. 1.[268]

My suggestion is to deal with the three documents one by one.

First, our draft *Terms of Reference*[269] for which we have a deadline. This is largely a cut-and-paste job. Your prompt corrections and suggestions are welcome, always with a copy to your Co-arbitrator. When you have several players working on the same document, it is often more convenient to use the very old-fashioned method of making corrections and suggestions by hand on the document itself, which can then be sent back by PDF or fax. This way, even if the document evolves, everybody knows exactly who would like to change what, where, and in which way. If you wish to conduct a call-in telephone conference on the draft Terms of Reference, please let me know, and I will organize it.

The draft *Procedural Timetable*[270] is of course mostly blank, and we will definitely need input from the Parties, most conveniently at a call-in telephone conference.

The *Procedural Order No. 1*[271] can be done in many different ways. Some people like to have as much flexibility in an arbitration as possible, because they want to "play it by ear." I, for one, think that it is better to have a very detailed document covering many

---

267. See Annex (H), ICC Terms of Reference or Constitution Order.
268. See Annex (L), Procedural Order No. 1.
269. See Annex (H), ICC Terms of Reference or Constitution Order.
270. See Annex (J), Procedural Timetable.
271. See Annex (L), Procedural Order No. 1.

points that would otherwise lead to difficult discussions, and to suspicion by each Party that the other is seeking a procedural advantage. Anyway, this draft is for the Parties to discuss. The Parties are more likely to agree on such matters at the outset of an arbitration. Besides, if the rules of the game are known well in advance, the Parties may even play by them!

If you would like to discuss any aspect of this draft Procedural Order No. 1, the three of us could first conduct a call-in telephone conference.

Indeed, my idea is not to do to the Parties what I am doing to you, namely to bombard you with a lot of paper all at one time. Rather, I would like to go easy and, as soon as possible, send the Parties just our first draft of the Terms of Reference and see how they react. Only once we know that the Terms of Reference are well on their way will I send them the other documents, emphasizing that they are just drafts.

I hope that you agree with this approach.

Very sincerely yours,

(No copy to anybody!)

# First Letter of the Arbitral Tribunal to the Parties

*The Co-arbitrators write the ICC and identify the person whom they jointly propose to chair the arbitration, with copy to the Party Representatives and the candidate.*

*Once confirmed, the Presiding Arbitrator writes the Party Representatives along these lines.*

Dear Party Representatives:

Now that I have been confirmed, I feel honored to serve as the Presiding Arbitrator in the above arbitration. My Co-arbitrators and I are very much looking forward to working with you and the Parties towards a just, fair and speedy resolution of the dispute.

As you know, our first task will be to draw up, finalize and sign our Terms of Reference. This must be done within two months of our receiving the file, which was on ................ This is a very short deadline.

We are aware that Claimant, ................, has filed a request for a time extension to respond to Respondents' counterclaim. In any event, the Terms of Reference is only a snapshot of the dispute at this point in time. They are simply established in the light of the Parties' latest submissions. The Terms of Reference deadline must be kept.

We are planning to draw up a first draft of our Terms of Reference shortly. With your help, and a bit of luck, it may well be possible to finalize the text of the Terms of Reference through email exchanges and possibly a telephone conference or two. Still, it often turns out necessary to have a hearing in the end.

Apart from the Terms of Reference, we will also need to map out the arbitration in a Procedural Order No. 1 and a Provisional Procedural Timetable.

In the course of the coming two months, my Co-arbitrators and I are available on the following dates for an afternoon Case Management Conference in ………….. or …………:

…………………………

…………………………

…………………………

Would any of these dates and times be completely impossible for you? Please note that we are not looking for your preferred date, just those that are halfway possible for all participants. Otherwise, we could never meet.

In this arbitration, there will be general liberty to apply. Upon a Party raising an issue, the other should respond promptly without awaiting the Arbitral Tribunal's invitation to do so.

Very sincerely yours,

cc: ICC Secretariat
    Co-arbitrators

# Cover Letter to Parties for the Arbitral Tribunal's First Draft Terms of Reference

Dear Party Representatives:

Many thanks for your responses regarding possible dates for an initial Case Management Conference in person in ........................... May we kindly ask you to reserve ....................... for a possible afternoon meeting starting at 2 pm and ending no later than 5 pm?

Our first task will be to finalize and sign our Terms of Reference on the spot. It is important that from each side a person attends who has the power to sign the Terms of Reference for that Party.

Here is our first, still very rough, draft, based essentially on your written submissions.[272] As you know, the final version must be established on the basis of the Parties' latest submissions. Any corrections and suggestions are now welcome.

If you so wish, we can also conduct a call-in telephone conference to discuss your suggestions and further develop our draft. Just let us know, and we will organize it.

If we could receive your first corrections and suggestions (which do not preclude any further corrections and suggestions from you) by, say, ........ Please always copy your opponent, my Co-arbitrators, and the ICC Secretariat. When you have several players working on the same document, it is often more convenient to use the very old-fashioned method of making corrections and suggestions by hand on the document itself, which can then be sent back by PDF or fax. This way, even if the document evolves, everybody knows exactly who would like to change what, where, and in which way. We can then promptly produce a new draft of our Terms of Reference. With a bit of luck, we may even then be able to finalize our text.

---

272. See Annex (H), ICC Terms of Reference or Constitution Order.

Whether we will actually have to meet depends on how we progress on the Terms of Reference and the other documents that we might afterwards discuss with you, our Procedural Timetable and our Procedural Order No. 1.

Very sincerely yours,

cc: ICC Secretariat
    Co-arbitrators

# ICC Terms of Reference or Constitution Order[273]

*This sample includes many features that one will not necessarily need in every case.*

*Some special features[274] may already be found in the Arbitration Rules (which are the will of the Parties, just like signed Terms of Reference) or the lex arbitri chosen directly or indirectly by the Parties. Otherwise, signed Terms of Reference are the best, most realistic, and practical opportunity to the Parties to agree on certain points.*

*If not all Parties sign the Terms of Reference, they must be submitted to the ICC Court for approval. The text must then be pared down so that it does not contain matters that appear as though they been agreed, which is not true if a Party has not signed the document. Specifically, the matters marked with * should then be pared down.*

*Some provisions must be harmonized with Procedural Order No. 1.*

---

273. See questions 347, 375, 378, 784 786, 787, 804, 809.
274. See Annex (H), ICC Terms of Reference or Constitution Order, paras 1, 30, 35, 36, 38.

| Under the auspices of<br>**International Chamber of Commerce**\* | Date |
|---|---|

### Terms of Reference

Pursuant to Article 24 of the ICC Rules of Arbitration (ICC Rules) as in force from
January 1, 2012
of the Arbitral Tribunal

| **Name**<br>Address<br>Tel.+<br>Fax+<br>e-mail<br><br>*Co-arbitrator nominated by Claimant and confirmed by the Secretary General in accordance with Article 13(1) of the ICC Rules* | **Name**<br>Address<br>Tel.+<br>Fax+<br>e-mail<br><br>*Presiding Arbitrator upon joint nomination by the Co-arbitrators and confirmed by the Secretary General in accordance with Article 13(2) of the ICC Rules* | **Name**<br>Address<br>Tel.+<br>Fax+<br>e-mail<br><br>*Co-arbitrator nominated by Respondents and confirmed by the Secretary General in accordance with Article 13(1) of the ICC Rules* |
|---|---|---|
| | in the matter of<br>**ICC No** ..........<br>in ............... | |
| **C**<br><br>*herein referred to as C or Claimant or counter-Respondent* | **R1**<br><br>*herein referred to as R1* | **R2**<br>**a.k.a.** [275]<br><br>*herein referred to as R2* |
| | *herein collectively referred to as RR, Respondents, or Counterclaimants* | |
| represented by:<br>**Name**<br>**Name**<br>Address<br>TF:+<br>FX:+<br>Email<br>Email | | both represented by:<br>**Name**<br>**Name**<br>Address<br>TF:+<br>FX:+<br>Email<br>Email |
| concerning | | |
| *1. Contract 1*<br>*2. Contract 2* | | |

\* Ms. GZ, 33-43 avenue du Président Wilson, FR-75116 Paris, TF: +33 1 49 53 28 91, FX: +33 1 49 5330 30.

---

275. See question 786.

## Table of Contents

## A.   Names and Description of the Parties

1.

\*

See the first page. Should any of the details change, the Parties shall promptly notify the Arbitral Tribunal.

For the following, a Party must promptly request the Arbitral Tribunal's agreement, which shall not be unreasonably withheld:

- keeping a particular lawyer on its Party Representation team after the lawyer has moved to a different firm;
- adding a lawyer to its team after that lawyer newly joined the firm;
- adding a further law firm to its team;
- changing law firm;

– and any other circumstance or new development that may give rise to a conflict of interests with any member of the Arbitral Tribunal.

## B. Notifications

2.

\*

Other than skeleton submissions, if any (which shall be limited to six pages, shall not be accompanied by any exhibits, and shall be sent to the Presiding Arbitrator only, who will monitor compliance with these limitations), all written submissions, Witness Statements, and exhibits shall be sent to the Presiding Arbitrator in one hard copy, together with enclosures. To make it easy to quote or summarize, written submissions shall also be sent to the Presiding Arbitrator as downloadable and alterable Word documents (not PDF files, and cleaned of earlier versions). At the same time, one single hard copy with enclosures should be sent directly to the two Co-arbitrators, together with a USB Stick or CD-Rom containing the full digital record of documents submitted. However, a rejoinder on the counterclaim and skeleton submissions, if any, should not be sent to the Co-arbitrators until approved by the Presiding Arbitrator. The Parties shall keep a further full set of their submissions and all their exhibits, including Witness Statements and Expert Reports, in hard copy ready to be consulted by the Arbitral Tribunal, to be shipped according to its instructions, for instance to a Tribunal-appointed Expert or to a hearing room. All other communications shall be sent to the Presiding Arbitrator and the two Co-arbitrators in one copy each, by letter, fax, or email.

3.

\*

Written submissions, Witness Statements, and exhibits shall be sent to the Party Representatives in hard copy, together with enclosures, at the same time as they are sent to the Arbitral Tribunal and by equally fast means. Additional hard copies of the briefs, Witness Statements, and exhibits shall be sent directly to the further persons having an asterisk or two (two asterisks: two copies) on the first page. All other communications shall be addressed to the Party-Representatives only, at the same time and by equally fast means (letter, fax, or email). All communications sent by fax or email shall also be sent in hard copy to the Party-Representatives and the Arbitral Tribunal, at the same time and by equally fast means.

4.

The International Court of Arbitration of the International Chamber of Commerce ("ICC Court") shall receive all written submissions (with enclosures) and all communications in one hard copy and/or e-mail.

5.

*

Please provide a distribution list on the document itself or on the covering letter (the covering letter should then specify what it is covering, not just say: "please see attached").

6.

*

Normally, the local time at the respective business address of the Party applies, but where submissions are due from both sides simultaneously, the local time at the seat of the arbitration applies (the Relevant Time). A time limit is observed if the written submission or communication:

- *reaches* the Arbitral Tribunal in hard copy (by hand or by mail) before expiry, local time at the seat of the arbitration, or
- *is sent* to the Arbitral Tribunal by email or fax before expiry, local time at the seat of the arbitration. Any fax or e-mail must be followed by a full hard copy, with all exhibits, sent the next day at the latest.

If a private courier is used, a time limit is observed if the submission or communication addressed to the Arbitral Tribunal, with all its exhibits, *is handed over* to the courier service before expiry, local time at the place of dispatch, provided the courier's receipt is emailed or faxed to the Arbitral Tribunal the same day.

7.

*

In case a time limit is not respected by a Party, the Arbitral Tribunal shall, without further notice, be entitled to disregard any submission made by the Party after the expiry of the deadline.

## C.   Summary of the Parties' Claims

### (a)     *Undisputed Introduction*

*

8.

By signing these Terms of Reference, neither Party subscribes nor agrees to the summary of any other Party's position set forth below.

9.

Claimant C describes itself as a company incorporated ...........................

269

10.

C is a company producing and selling ..............................

11.

Respondent R1 describes itself as ..............................

12.

R1 was established in ...........

13.

R2 describes itself as one of the top ..........................

14.

Both Respondents are members of the .... Group. The ... Group is a multinational group of building material companies oriented towards sustainability.

## *(b)* *Jurisdiction of the Arbitral Tribunal*

15.

*

Any jurisdiction that the Arbitral Tribunal may have is based on Article ... of Contract 1 and Article ... of Contract 2.

16.

Article ... of Contract 1 and Article ... of Contract 2 read as follows:

> ... *Disputes*
>
> *If any conflict or dispute arises among any of the Parties with regards to the interpretation, execution, non-compliance, existence, validity or termination of this Agreement (such conflicts or disputes, hereinafter referred collectively as "Disputes" and individually, as a "Dispute"), any Party shall be entitled to serve a written notice to the other Parties of the existence of a Dispute ("Dispute Notice") and the Parties shall then use their reasonable commercial endeavors to negotiate in good faith to settle such Dispute.*
>
> *Any Dispute between the Parties shall, if not amicably settled within a period of 30 days, be referred to arbitration as set forth below.*
>
> ... *ICC Arbitration*
>
> *If the Parties have not resolved a Dispute within thirty (30) days, a Party can have the Dispute referred to and finally resolved exclusively by arbitration in Vienna, Austria and in accordance with the arbitration rules (the "Rules") of the International Chamber of Commerce ("ICC") for the time being in force which rules are deemed to be incorporated by reference into this clause. If the Dispute is submitted to arbitration, the tribunal shall consist of three arbitrators, one to be appointed by the purchaser, one to be appointed by the Seller and the third to be appointed by the said two arbitrators. If the two arbitrators fail to appoint the third, such third*

*arbitrator shall be appointed in accordance with the Rules. The arbitration proceedings shall be conducted in the English language. The Parties may agree that a single arbitrator be appointed to settle a Dispute under this Clause, in which case such arbitrators shall be appointed in accordance with the Rules. The costs and expenses incurred by the prevailing Party in connection with any Dispute referred to arbitration under this Agreement shall be borne by the Party or Parties against whom the award is made to such arbitration proceedings.*

### (c)     C's main claim

*The following is a summary based on C's Request for Arbitration dated ......... received by the ICC on ............. This is C's position:*

17.

On ..., the Parties met concerning a transaction or possible cooperation on the ...........
business that C was involved with at the time, through a brokerage company acting as R1's consultant.

18.

Following these initial meetings and negotiations, the Parties agreed to consider a sale of C's production plants and a transfer of its ... business to R2.

....

....

### (d)     R1 and R2's Defense and Counterclaim

*The following is a summary based on R1 and R2's Answer to the Request for Arbitration, dated ... received by the ICC on .... This is R1 and R2's position:*

19.

In early ..., the ............ Group, of which R2 is a member, showed initial interest in the
... market after ... conducted a market and competition analysis. ............ Group contacted ..., a member of the ... Group, engaged in investment advisory and brokerage activities ("..."). As a result of this interest, R2 first initiated negotiations with ..., another large ... manufacturer in ....

....

....

....

### (v)

### RR's Counterclaim

....

....

....

### (e)     C's Answer to R1 and R2's Counterclaim

*The following is a summary based on C's Reply to Respondents' Answer and Counter-claims of .... This is C's position:*

20.

C has performed all of its obligations set out in Contract 1 and thus has not breached any of its obligations, representations or warranties set out therein. As a result, the Respondents have not incurred any damage or loss and have not become entitled to any compensation.

....

....

### (f)     C's Prayers for Relief

21.

C's Prayers for Relief on its main claim in its brief of ..... were as follows:

1. *Respondents be ordered to pay to Claimant ... plus the interest to be accrued as of ... until the full payment of the Retention Amount is made and the cancellation of the objection to the execution proceedings already initiated,*
2. *R1 be ordered to pay the compensation for unjust execution objection for the Retention Amount of ... with a minimum percentage of 40%,*
3. *Respondents be ordered to pay to Claimant the accrued interest of ... in relation with the Retention Amount, calculated on the basis of the three month EURIBOR rate applicable to each quarter as of the Closing Date until ...,*
4. *Respondents be ordered to pay to Claimant ... plus VAT, and interest to be accrued as of ... until full payment is made,*
5. *R1 be ordered to pay to Claimant ... due to its actions against business ethics,*
6. *Respondents be ordered to bear the full costs of arbitration and to pay to Claimant compensation for all of its costs of the arbitration, legal fees and other expenses.*

22.

C, in its Reply to Respondents' Answer and Counterclaims dated ..., addressed both the main claim and counterclaim. C's Prayers for Relief in its Reply were as follows:

1. *All relief sought by C in the Request be granted.*
2. *All relief sought by the Respondents in the Answer be dismissed and denied.*
3. *The Respondents be ordered to pay the full costs of arbitration and to pay to C all of its costs, legal fees inclusive of fees of the attorneys and other expenses for claims and counterclaims.*

23.

C reserves the right to amend its Prayers for Relief as may be required throughout the proceedings.

### (g) R1 and R2's Prayers for Relief

24.

R1 and R2 seek the following from the Arbitral Tribunal:

1. *The statement of claim submitted by the Claimant [C] be disregarded and the Claimant's claims be dismissed,*
2. *The Claimant be ordered to pay compensation in an amount of ... plus interest for the losses and damages suffered by R1 as a result of the Claimant's breaches of Contract 1 and to effect payment of the stamp taxes arising out of or in connection with the transactions contemplated under Contract 1 and provide evidence of the same to the Respondents,*
3. *Declare that the Retention Amount of ...00 shall remain with the Respondent,*
4. *The Claimant be ordered to pay the taxes arising out of Contract 1 as per Article ... of Contract 1 and to provide R1 with satisfactory evidence of the same,*
5. *The Claimant be ordered to pay the full costs of arbitration and to pay the Respondents compensation for all their costs of arbitration, legal fees and other expenses,*
6. *The Claimant be ordered to pay compensation in an amount not less than 40% of the amount claimed under the execution proceedings for initiating execution proceedings in bad faith.*

25.

R1 and R2 reserve their right to amend their Prayers for Relief as may be required throughout the proceedings.

### D. Issues for Arbitration

26.

Without prejudice to any rights under any agreement and Article 23(4) of the ICC Rules, the Parties refer for final determination by the Arbitral Tribunal all disputes or differences, including claims, counterclaims, defenses and setoffs and future submissions between them arising out of or related to the Agreement, including the arbitration costs and the Party Representation costs.[276]

## E.  Arbitral Tribunal

27.

On ... the Secretary General of the ICC Court, in accordance with Article 13(1) of the ICC Rules, confirmed ... as a Co-arbitrator upon nomination of C.

28.

On ... the Secretary General of the ICC Court, in accordance with Article 13(1) of the ICC Rules, confirmed ... as a Co-arbitrator upon nomination of R2 and R1.

29.

On ... the Secretary General of the ICC Court, in accordance with Article 13(2) of the ICC Rules, confirmed ... as the Presiding Arbitrator of the Arbitral Tribunal upon joint nomination of the Co-arbitrators.

30.

\*

The proper constitution of the Arbitral Tribunal is not in question. The Parties confirm at the time of signing these Terms of Reference that neither Party is aware of any grounds for objecting to the constitution of the Arbitral Tribunal.

## F.  Place of Arbitration, Lex Arbitri and Applicable Law

### (a)     Jurisdiction

31.

\*

There is no dispute over the jurisdiction of the Arbitral Tribunal (see above, paragraph)

32.

\*

The Arbitral Tribunal shall have the power to issue Preliminary and Partial Awards.[277]

---

276. This is based on the Goldman Formula.
277. See question 55.

### (b)   *Lex Arbitri*

33.

*

The place of arbitration is ....... After having consulted the Parties the Arbitral Tribunal may call hearings in any convenient city. It may meet internally wherever convenient. ........... Arbitration law is the *lex arbitri* of these proceedings.

### (c)   *Applicable law*

34.

*

Articles 18.5.1 of Contract 1 and 12.7.1 of the Contract 2 read as follows:

*This Agreement shall be governed by, and construed in accordance with the laws of ... and without regard to its rules of procedure.*

35.

*

... substantive law is to be applied to any Contract law questions.

### G.   Language, Applicable Procedural Rules and Disposal of Documents

36.

*

Two months after the Secretariat of the ICC Court has notified the Final Award to the Parties, the Arbitral Tribunal shall be at liberty to destroy the documents submitted throughout the course of the proceeding, unless the Parties have specifically asked within one month after notification of the Award for the documents to be returned to the counsel who initially sent them. This will be done at the cost of the requesting Party.

### H.

*

## Confidentiality

37.

Unless the Parties expressly agree in writing to the contrary, the Parties undertake to keep confidential all Awards and orders in the present arbitration, together with all materials in the proceedings created for the purpose of the arbitration, and all other documents produced by any Party in the proceedings, save to the sole extent that disclosure may be required of a Party by a legal duty, to protect or pursue a legal right, or to enforce or challenge an Award in bonafide legal proceedings before a court or other judicial authority. The Parties also undertake to use their best efforts to ensure that the terms of the present paragraph are respected by witnesses, Experts, counsel, and any other individuals who may be granted access to the materials referred to above in the context of these proceedings.

*

38.

*

Signed in five copies. Each signed original of these Terms of Reference shall be an original arbitration agreement in writing for the purposes of Articles II and IV(I) of the Convention on the Recognition and Enforcement of Foreign Arbitral Awards (New York Convention) of 1958.[278]

Place of Arbitration: ...

Dated:

The Arbitrators:

_____
Name

_____                    _____
Name                                                             Name

For the Parties:

C                                                                R1

_____                    _____

                                                                  R2

                                                _____

*

---

278. See question 371.

# Cover Letter to Parties for First Draft Procedural Timetable

Dear Party Representatives:

Now that our Terms of Reference are well on their way, we should start working on our Provisional Procedural Timetable.

Please find enclosed a first draft by the Arbitral Tribunal.[279] It is in the form of a "ping-pong table," still mostly blank.

May we suggest that we discuss this at the beginning of next week, say, on Monday ............... at ............... in a short call-in telephone conference? The number to call will be .......... Your access number will be ....... If there is any difficulty, please call this (mobile) phone: ........

Obviously, you will need your engagement calendars handy.

Looking forward to our conference.

Very sincerely yours,

cc: ICC Secretariat

---

279. See Annex (J), Procedural Timetable.

# Procedural Timetable[280]

*This may be nicknamed "Ping pong table."*

*The first example is a neutral standard draft. The second is taken from an actual, rather complicated, case.*

| | | | |
|---|---|---|---|
| **ICC**<br>**Name of ICC Counsel** | | | **CODE**<br>Date |
| | **Provisional Procedural**<br>**Timetable** | | |
| **Name of Co-Arb Claimants** | **Name of President** | **Name of Co-Arb**<br>**Respondents** | |
| | ICC No. 16453/GZ | | |
| **1. Claimant**<br>**2. Claimant** | Appl. Law:<br>.... | **1. Respondent**<br>**2. Respondent** | |
| **Represented by**<br>**Represented by**<br>**Represented by**<br>**Represented by** | | **Represented by** | |

| | | |
|---|---|---|
| Request/Complaint | | |
| | | Answer, Counterclaim |
| | File Received | |
| | | |

---

280. See also questions 379, 386, 388, 394, 402, 403, 404, 431, 471, 607, 626, 731, 732, and 815.

| | | |
|---|---|---|
| | **Case Management Conference:**<br>ICC Terms of Reference deadline:<br>..................................<br>......................... | |
| | | Full Answer, Facts, Documents, Witness statements, Party-appointed Expert's Report, Experts' questions, and profile for Tribunal-appointed Expert, Law.<br>Last opportunity for a Counterclaim |
| Reply, Answer to Counterclaim<br>Facts, Documents, Witness statements, Party-appointed Expert's Report, Experts' questions, and profile for Tribunal-appointed Expert, Law. | | |
| | | |
| | | Rejoinder, Reply on Counterclaim<br>Facts, Documents, Witness statements, Party-appointed Expert's Report, Experts' questions, and profile for Tribunal-appointed Expert, Law. |
| Rejoinder to Counterclaim only<br>Facts, Documents, Witness statements, Party-appointed Expert's Report, Experts' questions, and profile for Tribunal-appointed Expert, Law. | | |
| | Telephone Conference | |
| | | |

| | | |
|---|---|---|
| | | |
| | **Main Evidentiary Hearing** | |
| Post-Hearing Brief | | Post-Hearing Brief |
| | **Deliberation Meeting** | |
| | Closure of Proceedings Except Costs | |
| Statement of Costs | | Statement of Costs |
| | Closure of Proceedings on Costs | |
| | Final Award Overall ICC Deadline: | |
| Claimed: | Amount in dispute: | Counterclaimed: |
| Advance: | | Advance: |

| | |
|---|---|
| *Actual*/planned | scheduled/postponed after motion by * claimant, ** defendant, *** Parties |

*ICC*                                                                          **CODE**
Mr. ....                                                                        Date

Provisional Procedural
Timetable
Dr. Pierre A. Karrer
(appointed, 2 July 2009)
ICC No. ........
in Paris, France

1.                                                   Appl. Law: German
2.


Ms. ..... (Court Reporter)


| | | |
|---|---|---|
| Request/Complaint<br>24 October 2008 (received 24 October 2008)<br>Amendments: 25 February 2009<br>*29 May 2009* | | |
| | | Answer<br>*19 January 2009* |
| | File Received<br>*3 July 2009* | |
| | T/Ref signed<br>*16 August 2009*<br>ICC Deadline for T/Ref:<br>ca. 1 September 2009 | |
| | Order on language<br>*17 August 2009* | |
| | Tel Conference<br>~~24 August 2009*, 18:30 CEST~~<br>fall back date ~~26 August 2009** 18:30 CEST~~<br>*31 August 2009, 18:30 CEST* | |
| Subm. on stay, jurisd. etc., witn. stat. ♥<br>~~*25 September 2009*~~** *16 October 2009* ☺ | | Subm. on stay, jurisd. etc., witn. stat. ♥<br>~~*25 September 2009*~~**<br>*16 October 2009* ☺ |
| Subm. on stay, jurisd. etc., witn. stat. ♥<br>*30 October 2009* ☺ | | Subm. on stay, jurisd. etc., witn. stat. ♥<br>*30 October 2009* ☺ |

| | | |
|---|---|---|
| Witn. stat., 2nd round ♥, ~~submission~~** 16 *November 2009* ☺ | | Witn. stat., 2nd round ♥ *16 November 2009* ☺ |
| | Proceedings on stay, jurisd., etc. closed♥ *18 November 2009* | |
| Full Statement of Claim *30 November 2009* | | |
| | Tel. Conf. ~~*11 December 2009,*~~ ~~*18:30 CET*~~ ♥ | |
| | *Hearing* ~~or Telephone~~ ~~Conference,~~ ~~Paris,~~ Zurich ~~*7, 9, 20, 22, 23, 24, 27,*~~ ~~*28 July or 24 August or*~~ ~~*30 September 2009,*~~ ~~*14:00*~~ ~~15 December 2009 ?~~ ♥ ~~Radisson Blu, Zurich~~ ~~Airport~~ | |
| | | Full Answer *15 January 2010* |
| | (1st) ~~Fall-back~~ ♥ one-day ***hearing***, Zurich *2 February 2010,* Radisson Blu, Airport | |
| Req./Prod./Docs *18 February 2010* ♣ | | |
| | | Answer/Req./Prod. ♣ *1 March 2010* |
| Req./Prod./docs ♦ *9 March 2010* | | |
| | | Answer/Req./Prod./Docs ♦ *12 March 2010* |
| | Order and (First Phase) Award on stay, jurisd. etc. ♥ *26 March 2010* | |
| Statement of Reply, ~~*15 February 2010*~~* *1 April 2010* | | |

283

| | | |
|---|---|---|
| Witness Statements, Exp. op.<br>*~~15 February 2010~~* * 1 April 2010* | | |
| | Order Prod./Docs ♣ ♦<br>*April 2010* | |
| | | Statement of Rejoinder,<br>Witness statements<br>*~~15 March 2010~~* * 28 May 2010* |
| | Telephone Conference<br>*~~7 May 2010~~*, *2 June 2010*, ~~18:30 CEST*~~ ~~17:30 CEST~~** ***18:30 CEST ~~8, 9, 15, 16, 17, 18 June, 17:30 or 18:30 CEST~~* | |
| | | Subm.of Cl.Constr.Order, motion to stay *4 July 2010* |
| | (2nd) ***Evidentiary Hearing***<br>~~3-7 May 2010, Paris~~<br>~~Fall-back:~~<br>***30 August 2010, 10:00, -***<br>***4 September 2010,*** Zurich<br>~~Further fall-back:~~<br>~~21-26 March 2011, Paris, Zurich~~ | |
| Post-Hearing Brief<br>~~16 June 2010, 13 October 2010***~~<br>~~10 November 2010***~~<br>*10 December 2010* ☺ | | Post-Hearing Brief<br>~~16 June 2010, 13 October 2010***~~ ~~10 November 2010***~~<br>*10 December 2010* ☺ |
| | Closure of Proceedings Except Costs<br>~~21 June 2010, 18 October 2010***~~<br>~~15 November 2010***~~<br>*15 December 2010* | |

| | | |
|---|---|---|
| Statement of Costs<br>~~5 July 2010 ⊖5 November 2010~~\*\*\*<br>~~6 December 2010~~<br>*7 January 2011*\*\*\* | | Statement of Costs<br>~~5 July 2010 ⊖5~~<br>~~November 2010~~\*\*\*<br>~~6 December 2010~~<br>*7 January 2011*\*\*\* |
| | Closure of Proceedings<br>on Costs<br>~~5 July 2010, 5~~<br>~~November 2010~~\*\*\*<br>~~7 December 2010~~<br>*7 January 2011* | |
| | Second Partial Award<br>*7 June 2011* | |
| Request/2d Phase ■•;<br>Req./Prod./Docs ♠<br>*3 August 2011* | | |
| | | Answer/2d Phase<br>proceedings ■• ♠<br>*12 August 2011* |
| Reply/2d Phase Proceedings ■•<br>19 August 2011 | | |
| | | Rejoinder/2d Phase<br>Proceedings ■•<br>*26 August 2011* |
| | Letter: no stay, draft<br>Procedural Timetable<br>*31 August 2011* | |
| Time proposal<br>*9 September 2011* | | Time proposal<br>*9 September 2011* |
| | Procedural Timetable<br>13 September 2011 | |
| | Fine-tuned Procedural<br>Timetable<br>*3 October 2011* | |
| | | Answer on production<br>of docs. on Quantum<br>(if any) for ....<br>produced in the United<br>States from 1 to 27<br>October 2008, for<br>worldwide sales of ....<br>produced in the United<br>States on or before 27<br>October 2008, and for<br>worldwide sales of .... |

| | | |
|---|---|---|
| | | out of ... produced in the United States on or before 27 October 2008 (hereinafter .... after 1 October 2008) ♠<br>*14 October 2011* ☺ |
| Reply on production of docs. on Quantum (if any) for .... after 1 October 2008 ♠<br>*14 November 2011* ☺ | | Full 2d Phase Answer on principle of, and Quantum (if any) for, .... from 15 December 1998 to 30 September 2008 in the United States (hereinafter .... to 30 September 2008) •■<br>*14 November 2011* ☺ |
| | | Rejoinder on production of docs. on Quantum (if any) of .... after 1 October 2008 ♠<br>*14 December 2011* |
| Full 2d Phase Reply on principle of, and Quantum (if any) for, .... to 30 September 2008 □ ■<br>*16 January 2012* | | |
| | | Full 2d Phase Rejoinder on principle of, and Quantum (if any) for, .... to 30 September 2008 □ ■<br>*16 March 2012* |
| Reply to Respondent's Submissions of 16 March 2012 with Dr. ... ...'s Expert Report on Principle of ......□<br>*20 April 2012* | | |
| | 2d Phase (3rd) **Hearing** on Principle of .....in Frankfurt, Hotel ...........□<br>*27-28 June 2012* | |
| | 3rd Partial Award on principle of ..... ■<br>*05 September 2012* | |

| | | |
|---|---|---|
| 3d Phase Request Quantum for, ..... after 1 October 2008 • ~~5 October 2012 *~~ <br> *10 October 2012* | | |
| | | 3d Phase Answer on principle of, and Quantum for, ...... after 1 October 2008 • ~~2 November 2012 *~~ ~~12 November 2012~~ <br> *15 November 2012* |
| | Telephone Conference ~~16 November~~, *21 November 2012, 18:30 CET* | |
| | (4th) ***Hearing on Quantum*** (if any) for, ..... ■, in Frankfurt Hotel ........... *29 November 2012, 10:00* | |
| Post-Hearing Brief ~~17 December 2012, 20 November 2012~~ *4 January 2013* ☺ | | Post-Hearing Brief ~~17 December 2012, 20 November 2012~~ *4 January 2013* ☺ |
| Statement of Costs *22 December 2012* ☺ | | Statement of Costs *22 December 2012* ☺ |
| | Closure of Proceedings ~~24 December 2012~~ *4 January 2013* | |
| Statement of Costs *31 January 2013* ☺ | | Statement of Costs *31 January 2013* ☺ |
| | Closure of Proceedings on Costs ...... February 2013 | |
| | 4th Partial/Final Award 3d Phase on Quantum for ..... •, costs ~~Early~~ February 2013 Final Award ICC Deadline: *Originally* ca. 16 February 2010 (16 February 2010:) 31 May 2010 | |

| | | |
|---|---|---|
| | (6 May 2010:) 28 February 2011<br>(3 February 2011:) 31 March 2011<br>(3 March 2011:) 30 June 2011<br>(1 June 2011:) 31 December 2011<br>(1 December 2011:) 30 September 2012<br>(6 September 2012:) 31 December 2012<br>(6 December 2012:) 28 February 2013<br>(7 February 2013:) 29 March 2013 | |
| Claimed: | Amount in dispute:<br>$\Delta$:USD ...................<br>partially quantified | Counterclaim: None |
| Advance:<br>USD .......... + .......... + USD ..........<br>+ USD .......... + USD ..........<br>= USD .......... | Total advance<br>USD ..........<br>USD .......... +<br>USD .......... +<br>USD .......... =<br>USD .......... | Advance:<br>USD .......... + USD<br>.......... + ..........<br>+ USD ..........<br>= USD .......... |

actual/plannedscheduled/postponed after motion by *Claimant, ** Respondent, ***Parties

☺ Midnight CET, or CE Summer time, as the case may be.

ANNEX (K)

# Cover Letter to Parties for First Draft of Procedural Order No. 1

Dear Party Representatives:

Please find enclosed a first discussion draft of the Arbitral Tribunal's Procedural Order No. 1.[281] Any suggestions and corrections will be welcome. We are ready to discuss this draft and any points you wish to raise with you at our upcoming call-in telephone conference scheduled for ..................

Please note that both our Procedural Timetable and our Procedural Order No. 1 will be issued by the Arbitral Tribunal and will not require your signature.

Looking forward to our conference.

Very sincerely yours,

---

281. See Annex (L), Procedural Order No. 1.

# Procedural Order No. 1

| Under the auspices of<br>TF:+<br>FX:+ | | Date |
|---|---|---|

**Procedural Order No. 1**
issued by the Arbitral Tribunal
composed of

| Tel.+<br>Fax+<br>*Co–Arbitrator nominated by* | **Name**<br>Address<br>ZIP/Place/Country<br>Tel.+<br>Fax+<br>E-MAIL<br>*Presiding Arbitrator jointly*<br>*nominated by the*<br>*Co-Arbitrators* | Tel.+<br>Fax+<br>*Co–Arbitrator nominated by* |
|---|---|---|
| | in the matter of | |
| *herein referred to as Claimant* | | *herein referred to as*<br>*Respondent* |
| | | |
| *represented by:*<br>Tel.+<br>Fax+<br>E-mail | | *represented by:*<br>Tel.+<br>Fax+<br>E-mail |
| | concerning | |

*The Procedural Order No. 1 is only aimed at providing useful guidance, and may be changed at any time, if necessary, by order of the Arbitral Tribunal.*[282]

## A.     General[283]

1. If, on the title page of this order, several persons possibly having different addresses have an asterisk, notification to any of them shall be sufficient, but notification to all persons having an asterisk is requested (two asterisks: two copies).

2. The applicable ICC *Rules of Arbitration* as they are or shall be in force from time to time (currently the ICC Rules in force from 1 January 2012) will apply. The directions which may be given by the Arbitral Tribunal from time to time shall, unless the Parties otherwise agree, be followed.

3. The Arbitral Tribunal may issue *Procedural Orders*, but the Terms of Reference prevail. Procedural Orders need not be signed by all members of the Arbitral Tribunal. They may be signed by the Presiding Arbitrator alone after consultation with the other members of the Arbitral Tribunal. In exceptional circumstances, the signature of any arbitrator, "for the Arbitral Tribunal," or the indication as "issued by the Arbitral Tribunal," is sufficient.[284]

4. The Arbitral Tribunal will seek inspiration from, but not be bound by, the (2010) *IBA Rules of Evidence*, available at http://tinyurl.com/iba-Arbitration-Guidelines.[285]

5. The *Provisional Procedural Timetable* and the deadlines will be set by the Arbitral Tribunal, taking into account, to the extent feasible, holidays as notified to the Arbitral Tribunal (if possible a year in advance). However, once set, the Provisional Procedural Timetable must be strictly observed by the Parties. A counterclaim may be raised no later than with the answer to the main claim.[286]

6. The provisional Procedural Timetable may be modified by the Arbitral Tribunal after consultation with the Parties, including by dispensing with activities previously envisaged, speeding up deadlines, or by inserting further deadlines, but only well in advance. The Parties may not argue that they reserved arguments or points to raise them at some later opportunity offered in the provisional Procedural Timetable, and that accordingly it would be unfair to deprive them of that opportunity. Time limits shall be extended only in exceptional circumstances. Any request for an **extension** must state until which date the extension is requested, why the extension is necessary, and **why the request could not have been made earlier**. The Parties shall refrain from arguments based on an analysis of the Procedural Timetable and the absolute or

---

282. See question 384.
283. See question 626.
284. See question 386.
285. See question 385.
286. See Annex (J), Procedural Timetable. See also question 387.

relative length of time periods derived from it, or on extensions of deadlines previously granted to their opponent.[287]

7. Normally, the local time at the seat of the arbitration applies. A time limit is observed if the written submission or the communication:

- *reaches* the Arbitral Tribunal in hard copy (by hand or by mail) before expiry, local time at the seat of the arbitration, or
- is *sent* to the Arbitral Tribunal by email or fax before expiry, local time at the seat of the arbitration. Any fax or email must be followed by a full hard copy, with all exhibits, sent the next business day at the latest.

if a private courier is used, if the submission or communication addressed to the Arbitral Tribunal, **with all its exhibits**, is *handed over* to the courier service before expiry, local time at the place of dispatch, **provided that the courier's receipt is emailed or faxed to the Arbitral Tribunal the same day**. [288]

8. In case a time limit is not respected by a Party, the Arbitral Tribunal shall, without further notice, be entitled to disregard any submission made by the Party after the expiry of the deadline. Last minute surprise submissions and evidence will be put unread into envelopes, and the envelopes will be sealed.[289]

## B. Prayers for Relief[290]

9. In ICC arbitration, new Prayers for Relief are permitted only within the limits of Article 19 ICC Rules. New Prayers for Relief in Post-Hearing Briefs are discouraged and will normally be disregarded.[291] On costs, see below, paragraphs 85 et seq.

10. Prayers for relief must be worded in such a way that it is clear to the Arbitral Tribunal what it is asked to say in the operative part of its Award. The Parties are encouraged to provide a draft of the operative part that they are requesting. It is the Parties' responsibility to present their Prayers for Relief sufficiently clearly. The formatting is not binding on the Arbitral Tribunal. The Arbitral Tribunal may seek clarification, but will not be required to do so, and may instead reject vague claims outright. A request for "at least" a certain sum will be understood as a request for that sum, not more. Any increase will be possible only within the limits of the applicable rules of arbitration and the *lex arbitri*. See also below, paragraph 22.[292]

11. Please say clearly if a claim is subsidiary, and specify to what, or if a "Stufenklage" (claim by stages) is brought whereby, in a first phase, a Partial Award (for instance,

---

287. See questions 387, 392.
288. See question 392, and see Annex (J), Procedural Timetable.
289. See questions 387, 392, 393, 403.
290. See questions 818 et seq.
291. See Annex (H), ICC Terms of Reference or Constitution Order, paras 134 and 137. See also questions 820 and 821.
292. See also question 824.

ordering certain information to be provided) is requested, to be followed, in a second phase, by a further Award (for instance, for money). Unless clarified, the word **"alternatively" will be understood to mean, subsidiarily**. If it is unclear whether a claim is subsidiary to another, the Arbitral Tribunal will understand that none is, and all claims are to be added and treated separately.

If a claim is presented against several Parties, the Arbitral Tribunal will understand that it may grant the claim only once, either against just one of those Parties or against several of them, but then jointly and severally.

If several Parties present the same claim, the Arbitral Tribunal will understand that it may grant it only once, either to one or to several of the claiming Parties alternatively.

12. If it is requested that a claim should be granted "concomitantly to" (in exchange for) or "subject to" another claim being granted, even only in part, this must be said. Otherwise all claims will be considered separately.

13. Any claim for interest must state on **which principal amount(s), from when to when, and at which rate(s), annual or otherwise, simple or compound, and if so, how often**. Do not roll in (capitalize) interest. The Arbitral Tribunal may request specification or clarification of a claim for "interest" without more, but will not be required to do so, and may instead reject such a vague interest claim outright, or grant interest as it deems fit, without being bound by any applicable law.

14. If "findings," "statements," "declarations," or "orders" are requested, please say exactly what the text of the declaration or order should say, and whether this is subsidiary to *any* money relief being granted on the same matter, which is what the Arbitral Tribunal will understand to be the case if nothing is said. (Please also note that a Party **requesting a declaration** should in due course say **why it needs this relief**).

## C.  Provisional Measures

15. The Arbitral Tribunal may issue Provisional Measures, including orders for security for costs. If a measure *has been* ordered, the Arbitral Tribunal will assume that the Parties complied in due course.[293]

## D.  Related and Parallel Proceedings

16. The Parties are invited to keep the Arbitral Tribunal informed about related and parallel proceedings (e.g. setting aside proceedings, challenges of arbitrators, Provisional Measures, attacks on patents, other arbitrations or litigation between some of the Parties, etc.), even after the proceedings in the present arbitration have been closed. Opening documents in such proceedings and any decisions rendered must always be copied to the Arbitral Tribunal. If it is argued that particular parallel

---

293. See question 446.

proceedings have an impact on the present arbitration, this should be explained in detail.[294]

## E.   Written Submissions

17. Other than skeleton submissions, if any (which shall be limited to six pages, shall not be accompanied by any exhibits, and shall be sent to the Presiding Arbitrator only who will monitor compliance with these limitations), all written submissions, Witness Statements, and exhibits shall be sent to the Presiding Arbitrator in one hard copy, together with enclosures. To make it easy to quote or summarize, written submissions shall also be sent to the Presiding Arbitrator as downloadable and alterable Word documents (not PDF files, and cleaned of earlier versions). At the same time, one single hard copy with enclosures should be sent directly to the two Co-arbitrators, together with a USB Stick or CD-Rom containing the full digital record of documents submitted. However, a rejoinder on the counterclaim and skeleton submissions, if any, should not be sent to the Co-arbitrators and the Counterparty until approved by the Presiding Arbitrator. The Parties shall keep a further full set of all their submissions and all their exhibits, including Witness Statements and Experts Reports, in hard copy ready to be consulted by the Arbitral Tribunal, to be shipped according to its instructions, for instance to a Tribunal-appointed Expert or to a hearing room. All other communications shall be sent to the Presiding Arbitrator and the two Co- arbitrators, in one copy each, by letter, fax, or email.[295] The Arbitral Tribunal will only read and treat as submissions those that are specifically addressed to it, not letters that the Party Representatives may have written to each other, and may just have copied to the Arbitral Tribunal, which is discouraged.

18. Written submissions, Witness Statements, and exhibits shall be sent to the Party Representatives in hard copy, together with enclosures, **at the same time as they are sent to the Arbitral Tribunal and by equally fast means**. Additional hard copies of the briefs, Witness Statements, and exhibits shall be sent directly to the further persons having an asterisk or two (two asterisks: two copies) on the first page. All other communications shall be addressed to the Party-Representatives only, at the same time and by equally fast means (letter, fax, or email).[296]

19. All communications sent by fax or email shall also be sent in hard copy to the Party-Representatives and the Arbitral Tribunal, at the same time and by equally fast means.[297]

---

294. See question 442.
295. See questions 397 et seq. and question 593.
296. See question 397.
297. See question 397.

20. The International Court of Arbitration of the International Chamber of Commerce ("ICC Court") shall receive all written submissions (with enclosures), any Transcript, and all communications, including those on costs, in one hard copy and/or email.[298]

21. Please provide a distribution list on the document itself or on the covering letter (the covering letter should then specify what it is covering, not just say, "please see attached").[299]

22. In the written submissions (divided in subchapters, with all paragraphs numbered consecutively, please do not start with 1 again, and provide a Table of Contents), **the Parties shall present their allegations and denials with reasonable particularity**, offering immediate specific proof (submitting documents and referring specifically to the passage supporting the allegation, and naming witnesses if already known, but not yet providing their Witness Statements if a separate date was foreseen for this) for each allegation and denial. It is insufficient to submit entire binders of exhibits or to plan to particularize one's allegations at the Evidentiary Hearing only, through witness' or Experts' testimony. Take a detailed position on all allegations and arguments of your opponent. If the other Party specifically asks for **further and better particulars**, these **must be provided** spontaneously in due course, unless the Arbitral Tribunal orders otherwise. If you are presenting several subclaims (e.g. for several sub-amounts) please give each an Arabic number and short name (e.g. "Claim 1, Delay penalty") and use number and name consistently throughout the arbitration. Please **do not round any numbers up or down**; leave them as they are. If you convert an amount from one currency to another, give all the details and explain why. The Arbitral Tribunal will consider differences of less than USD 10 for what appears to be the same claim to be *de minimis*. Comment on the law is encouraged.[300] The Parties are encouraged to present **subsidiary points** of view (assuming *arguendo* ...), and to **carry also these to their consequences on *Quantum***. Please explain on which legal **basis** you are claiming **interest** in all its aspects (above, paragraph 13). In a *summary* section, please list all the primary subclaims (principal only) leading to the sum to be awarded (principal only) as in your final *Prayers for Relief*, or refer specifically to such a detailed calculation if already provided.[301]

23. Please provide arguments in law, supported by relevant sources of law (statutes, case law, legal writings, on the *lex arbitri*, conflict of laws, *lex contractus*, *lex societatis*, *lex loci actus*, law of civil procedure, public law, international law and treaties, possibly other laws, and comparative law). In its Award, the Arbitral Tribunal may apply the law as it deems correct under the principle of *iura novit curia*, even without alerting the Parties to particular sources of law, and will not be required to discuss all sources of law invoked by the Parties.[302]

---

298. See question 397.
299. See question 397.
300. See questions 120 et seq., and questions 665 et seq.
301. See questions 397, 398, 451, and 459 et seq.
302. See question 397.

24. Should a Party fail to submit a submission when due, and should a further submission still be due from the same or the other Party, that further submission may still be made.[303]

## F. Language[304]

25. The language of the arbitration shall be *English*. Any request for the use of another language (even if limited to particular instances) must be presented well in advance, not after the fact, and giving reasons. The Arbitral Tribunal shall have full discretion to accept or reject such requests.

26. Any translation shall be at the expense and risk of the Party relying on it. Please provide the source of the translation. Any **translation** must be **laid out and paginated** the same way **as the original** (easy with slightly smaller print). Please give any translation the same exhibit number as the original.[305]

27. All written submissions and other documents created for use in the arbitration (including Witness Statements), shall be either in English or in the original language with English translation (complying with paragraph 26 above).

28. Contemporary documents of fact must be submitted in the original language, always with English translation (both under the same exhibit number). Anything (even handwritten notes in the margin) appearing in another language must be translated or stated to be interlinear translations into a specified language. Sources of law must be submitted in the original language, but in English translation only if the Arbitral Tribunal requests it.[306]

29. In case of translation difficulties, please advise the Arbitral Tribunal promptly, so that translation problems do not hold up the arbitration unnecessarily.

30. At the hearings, any testimony submitted in a language other than English shall be interpreted consecutively (or if the Arbitral Tribunal so directs, simultaneously). The necessary arrangements shall be made by, and at the expense (subject to the Arbitral Tribunal's final decision on allocation of costs) and risk of, the submitting Party. The Arbitral Tribunal shall not select interpreters.[307]

## G. Documents and binders[308]

31. The following applies to all *Documents* submitted as factual evidence or sources of law, also those attached to Witness Statements and Experts' Reports (on these see below, paragraph 44). No loose documents just in folders, please. All documents shall

---

303. See question 397.
304. See questions 139 et seq.
305. See also question 464.
306. See question 464.
307. See question 608.
308. IBA Rules, Art. 3.

be submitted in two-holed A4 (or US-sized) copy, normally in their entirety, in separate binders but at the same time as the main written submissions or Witness Statements or Experts' Reports: "Skeleton" submissions are without exhibits. Please put the date of the document near the top right-hand corner of the first page, using letters to indicate the month. Please **use "Bates" numerator stamp** for easy reference **within an unpaginated document** *before* copying. Any photograph should be accompanied (not on the picture itself) by its date, the person that took the picture, from where and in which direction. Any handwritten notes should be transcribed if not easily legible, and translated or stated to provide an interlinear translation into a specified language. The author, if known, should be identified, or stated to be unknown. If a document was already submitted by the other Party, please refer to that document as already numbered and submitted; do not resubmit it.[309]

32. All pre-existing documents shall be submitted in the original language(s). If a document has original versions in more than one language, submit them all under the same exhibit number. Where necessary, a translation into English (which may be prepared by the submitting Party, **not necessarily by an official translator** – but always state the source) must also be submitted (see above, paragraph 26), again under the same exhibit number.

33. If, by exception, documents are submitted or translated only in part, please include the context and structure in which the excerpt appears to avoid the impression that the excerpt is taken out of context. Please **highlight** in the original text **the portion** (including context) **that is to be considered and is translated**. Please comply with above, paragraph 26. Only the translated portions will be read and considered.

34. Documents should be individually **numbered on the documents themselves** (*before* copying), but binders should also be divided by **protruding numbered thumb-tabs** bearing the exhibit numbers. Each document, one Arabic number. No two documents in the arbitration, and no two binders, shall bear the same number. Date your binders, please. One document per number and tab, please. **Never re-start with "1."** Please **avoid split numbers** such as XIII/27 or having several series of documents such as "annexes," "attachments," "exhibits," "schedules," and "appendices," or numerous series, e.g. one for each witness (but at hearings, using cross-bundles without new numbering is encouraged). Instead, please consider starting document numbering for different types of documents at various points "in the air" (e.g. 701 or 801, see below, paragraph 37), and putting different types of documents into separate binders. Avoid resubmitting a document already on file just because it is mentioned in a Witness Statement. Instead, have the witness refer to the document as it is already numbered. To the extent possible, each binder should be organized in chronological order, preferably with the most recent documents on top. Each binder should have a back, not just spirals. Please, **do not overload arch-folders** (they do not travel well).[310]

---

309. See question 459.
310. See question 463.

35. Claimant, please continue factual documents with C-7. For any parallel proceedings, please start with C-601.

36. Respondent, please start factual documents with R-1001. For any parallel proceedings, please start with R-1601.

**Sources of law** should be presented **separately** in separate binders, and numbered starting "in the air." X law, Claimant, start with CLE-701, and Respondent, with RLE-1701. Y law, Claimant, start with CLE-801, and Respondent, with RLE-1801. Other laws, Claimant, start with CLE-901, and Respondent, with RLE-1901.[311]

37. Legal Expert opinions on the case or decisions from parallel proceedings should be presented the same way as other Expert opinions and Factual Witness Statements.

38. The Arbitral Tribunal welcomes files printed on both sides and shrunk to A5 size, and these preferably in bound form (not overloaded) with a back (not wired) rather than in archfiles.

39. Please provide a dated list of documents, giving them the same names and dates as on the documents themselves, and update the list from time to time.

40. A deadline may be specifically set by the Arbitral Tribunal, after which **no new factual documents** will be admitted from the Parties, except as *nova* for cause shown by leave of the Arbitral Tribunal. If no specific deadline was set, the **cut-off time** will be at the time of **the last main written submission (on the main claim and separately on the counterclaim) before the first Evidentiary Hearing** (no new factual documents may be submitted with a skeleton submission, see above, paragraph 17). Sources of law may be submitted without leave at any time, even with Post-Hearing Briefs.[312]

41. Article 3 of the IBA Rules of Evidence applies for the *production of documents*. Documents shall be produced to the requesting Party only, without copy to the Arbitral Tribunal. Documents shall be produced to the requesting Party in the original language. If a translation (into *any* language) is available, please produce that to the requesting Party also, but no new translation is required. It will then be the requesting Party's choice to submit the document (if necessary with a translation into English) to the Arbitral Tribunal and the opposite Party as appropriate, above paragraph 32.[313] Requests for the Arbitral Tribunal to order production of a document should be in the form of a Redfern Schedule.

42. The Arbitral Tribunal may on its own motion request the production of a document.[314]

---

311. See questions 460 and 463.
312. See question 403.
313. See questions 467 and 468.
314. See question 594.

43. All documents shall be presumed to be authentic and complete (or full and faithful copies).

## H.     Witness Statements and Experts' Reports[315]

44. The **cut-off time** for Witness Statements, Experts' Reports and motions to appoint a Tribunal-appointed Expert is the same as that for documents, above, paragraph 40. The following provisions about witnesses are meant to apply to witnesses and Party-appointed Experts (hereinafter collectively "witnesses") presented by a Party, but not "adverse" or "tribunal" witnesses who do not provide Witness Statements. To these, special rules will apply.

45. *Written Witness Statements* (no joint Witness Statements by several persons, please) shall be submitted as prescribed in the IBA Rules of Evidence (article 4.5) in the original and in English translation where applicable, laid out and paginated the same way as the original. The witness' signature is not necessary, but the submitting Party must state that the witness fully agreed to a text as submitted, see below paragraph 58. **A Curriculum Vitae with a picture should be attached** (not treated as an exhibit). The CV should state the languages understood and spoken. **Witness statements** shall be separately bound and submitted separately for each witness, **not** submitted and **numbered as documents**. Exhibits to written Witness Statements, if newly submitted, should be submitted separately (not bound with the Witness Statement), numbered as in above, paragraph 31.[316]

46. *Party-appointed Experts' Reports* (including Legal Expert Reports) shall be submitted as prescribed in the IBA Rules of Evidence (article 5.2) and above, paragraph 44. Exhibits should comply with above, paragraph 31 et seq.

47. The Arbitral Tribunal will presume that a Party-appointed Experts' Report is endorsed *in toto* by the presenting Party as its own allegations.[317]

48. Should the Parties present, instead of or in addition to, argument on law, Party-appointed **Experts'** Reports **on law** (which is **not encouraged**), these Experts would be treated as any Party-appointed Expert or witness, see particularly below, paragraphs 55 and 59.[318]

49. Motions that a *Tribunal-appointed Expert* be appointed must be accompanied by a separate description of **the profile that the Expert to be appointed should match** and by a **separate list of numbered Expert's questions**. The Arbitral Tribunal shall not appoint any Expert without this, except of its own volition.[319]

---

315. See questions 486 et seq., IBA Rules Arts 4 to 6.
316. See questions 464, 515, and 582.
317. See question 580.
318. See questions 582, 583, and 630.
319. See question 589.

## I.     Evidentiary Hearings[320]

50. Please consider taking the hearing room sideways, with the Arbitral Tribunal seated in the middle and the witness facing it, with any interpreter next to the witness. Claimant shall sit at the Arbitral Tribunal's left and Respondent on its right. Swivel chairs, please, for the Court Reporter and, if possible, for the arbitrators.[321]

51. The *Evidentiary Hearings* (not the Case Management Conferences) shall be *transcribed verbatim* in English by professional **Court Reporters** sitting in the hearing room. The Arbitral Tribunal is ready to assist in the selection of Court Reporters. These shall however be appointed, **provided with advances, and promptly paid directly and equally by both sides** to cover the cost of providing one copy of the Transcript for each member of the Arbitral Tribunal, one for each Party, and one for the ICC. The cost of additional copies shall be borne by the Party requesting those copies. Overnight or "live notes" Transcripts shall be prepared only upon request by a Party, and, for the increment in price, at its expense. The Arbitral Tribunal need not sign verbatim Transcripts. The participants are encouraged to provide "Errata Sheets" separately for each day of Transcript, with copies to the Court Reporter and the ICC. Normally these will be filed with the Transcript of the day in question, and not lead to an improved version of the Transcript. "Corrections" to the Transcript to improve what was said will be disregarded. The transcription costs shall be part of the Party Representation costs, and the final decision on their allocation shall take them into account.[322]

52. Tape recordings may be made only if the persons speaking permit them. Unilateral transcriptions (from a tape or other source) prepared by a Party can be invoked only if made available to the Arbitral Tribunal and all Parties as soon as they were prepared, providing upon request also a copy of their source.

53. The hearings will be conducted generally as described in Article 8 of the IBA Rules of Evidence.

54. Except as directed by the Arbitral Tribunal, there will be **no oral opening or closing statements**. PowerPoint may be used, but only slowly and large enough so that the entire projected text can be read then and there by all present.[323]

55. Witnesses of fact and Party–appointed Experts (hereinafter collectively, Witnesses) shall be generally treated the same way. They shall testify at the Evidentiary Hearing. Witnesses (except adverse Witnesses and Tribunal Witnesses) who have provided **no Witness Statement** will **not** be **heard**. It will be the presenting Party's responsibility to secure any necessary visas in time and to bring its Witnesses to the hearing, subject to the Arbitral Tribunal's final decision on the allocation of costs. With respect to visas, third Party Witnesses and adverse Witnesses, the Parties may request the Arbitral Tribunal's assistance. If a Witness of fact fails to appear, the Witness Statement will

---

320. IBA Rules Art. 8.
321. See Annex (Q) Checklist for Hearing Rooms, and questions 617 et seq.
322. See question 608.
323. See question 629.

normally be disregarded, but in extraordinary circumstances may be considered and given weight by the Arbitral Tribunal, or the Arbitral Tribunal may make special arrangements for the Witness to be heard after all.[324]

56. If Witnesses are heard individually, the following provisions will apply. If the Arbitral Tribunal hears two or more (Expert) Witnesses "side-by-side" (also called "(Expert) Witness conferencing"), the following provisions will apply *mutatis mutandis*.

57. The Witnesses shall be heard as far as possible according to subjects, with Claimant's Witnesses, as a rule, going first.

58. Pursuant to the law at the geographical place of the hearing, Witnesses will be admonished to tell the truth, and will first affirm their Witness Statements.

59. Time management at the hearing, sequence of testimony, and availability of Witnesses (physically or by video-line or telephone) will be discussed at pre-hearing telephone conferences before each stretch of hearings.[325]

60. For time management, it is likely that the Arbitral Tribunal will apply a **chess-clock** *system* as follows: Each Party will have the same pre-determined amount of time for the whole stretch (working out to **no more than one hour per half day** *in the overall average* of the stretch, and assuming that there will be no opening and no closing statements). This time will be available at its discretion for its examination of all the Witnesses and Experts over the whole stretch. Time used by a Party to ask questions of any Witness, and time used by them answering such questions will go against that Party's time. Interpretation time will also go against the questioning Party's time. When the Arbitral Tribunal asks questions, these questions and the answers to them will stop the clock, but not questions interjected for clarification or to speed up, and answers to such questions. If procedural incidents, including interpretation incidents, arise, the clock will be stopped. Opening statements, if any, and oral summations, if any, will be on an equal time basis, but outside the chess-clock system. The Arbitral Tribunal will have **no float-time** reserved to distribute.[326]

61. The Arbitral Tribunal may ask questions at any time.

62. The Witnesses will not provide any direct testimony (sometimes also called evidence-in-chief) beyond confirming their Witness Statements (not adding new text) upon question by the Arbitral Tribunal and after having corrected typing errors and similar details. The Witness may then be **cross-questioned, without** restriction to the scope of the Witness' previous testimony (**Scope Restriction**).[327]

63. Avoid the questions listed in the Appendix to this order. No unreasonably leading questions are permitted on direct or re-direct.

---

324. See question 630.
325. See question 608.
326. See questions 635 et seq.
327. See question 532.

64. A Party may waive at any time its right to cross-question a Witness, which may lead to cost consequences, if a Witness traveled to a hearing only to learn that he or she would not be required to testify. The written Witness Statement will then stand as confirmed, but not necessarily as true, and the Witness will then not testify, subject to below, paragraph 73. If a Witness has confirmed his or her Witness Statement at the hearing, the other Party may even then waive its right to cross-question the Witness, in which case the Witness may not be re-direct-questioned by the offering Party, and the next Witness will then testify. If a Party does not offer a person as a Witness, or if a Witness called fails to testify, adverse inferences may be drawn from this against the Party only if the other Party had also called the person, as an adverse Witness. If a Party withdraws a Witness, the other Party may (even on short notice) call that Witness as its own (adverse) Witness, and, at its option, adopt that Witness' Statement.[328]

65. After cross-questioning, a Witness may be **re-direct**-questioned by the presenting Party **without Scope Restriction.**[329]

66. The Arbitral Tribunal may allow re-cross-questioning, and even further questioning with or without Scope Restriction.

67. At breaks during their oral testimony, witnesses of fact shall neither discuss the case nor their or somebody else's testimony with anyone (Witness Sequestration).

68. Expert witnesses may be present in the hearing room at all times, and shall not be subject to Witness Sequestration.

69. Witnesses of fact who have not yet testified, with the exception of two "client Witnesses" (witnesses who instruct counsel, but are not necessarily presently or formerly the Party itself or employees of the Party) each designated by the Parties in advance and for the entire stretch of hearings (not counting any Party Representative who, by exception, is also to testify), shall not be present in the hearing room before they testify. The Arbitral Tribunal may order otherwise for Witness conferencing.[330]

70. Unless the Parties agree otherwise, witnesses of fact who have testified may remain in the hearing room thereafter, even if there is a possibility that they might be recalled.

71. Should a Witness testify during the Evidentiary Hearing, but, by leave of the Arbitral Tribunal, by way of video link or over the telephone (even at short notice if the Parties agreed on a videolink but this fails), the location from which this will be done will normally be determined by the other Party (normally, the offices of correspondent lawyers), and the testimony will normally be given in the presence of a representative of the other Party (normally, a local correspondent lawyer). The costs of these special arrangements (except lawyer's fees and expenses) shall be advanced by the Party submitting the testimony.[331]

---

328. See question 608.
329. See question 541.
330. See question 659.
331. See questions 561 and 562.

72. No *new* factual documents may be submitted by the Parties after the main written submissions (none with any skeleton submission). Afterwards, and through the hearing, a new document may however be offered as a *novum* if that document could not have been reasonably presented earlier. Developments in parallel proceedings will be treated as *nova*, not as sources of law, and are welcome at all times. If it is intended to offer or use a new document at the hearing, even if it allegedly merely presents or summarizes information already in the record, it should be submitted to the other Party in photocopy as early as possible (but not yet to the Arbitral Tribunal). The other Party may then either accept the new document into the record, or may resist inclusion in the record, in which case the Arbitral Tribunal, after having heard the Parties, will decide whether to accept it as a *novum*.

73. Similarly, for cause shown and after all Witnesses have testified a first time (or, at the Arbitral Tribunal's discretion, earlier), a Witness may be recalled by any Party, or a Witness whose cross-questioning was waived may be called, to testify about matters that came up only after the Witness Statement was prepared or after it was confirmed at the hearing.

74. *Oral summation*, if any, will be on an equal-time basis, and each Party will be heard only once even if it still has time left on the chess-clock. See above, paragraph 60.

## J.    Post-Hearing Briefs[332]

75. *Post-Hearing Briefs* shall be presented simultaneously.

76. Unless the Arbitral Tribunal limits these to specific questions, the Post-Hearing Briefs shall fully wrap up facts, law and Quantum by reference to the final Prayers for Relief – as stated please, not new or newly worded – and to the evidence advanced in their support in the arbitral proceedings including the witness hearings. All paragraphs shall be numbered throughout the entire submission.

77. In particular, in their *factual analysis*, the Parties are invited to proceed to a subclaim-by-subclaim examination. They should: (i) identify the disputes remaining; (ii) discuss the issues as such, including the technical aspects where appropriate; and (iii) for each claim refer, *inter alia*, to the following sources and discuss their relevance: submissions, documentary evidence, Witness Statements, and live testimony.

78. For each claim, where appropriate, a *legal analysis* shall discuss *inter alia:* the applicable contractual provisions and regulations; subsequent agreements among the Parties, if any, what points they covered and how they were reached under the applicable law; the practice of the Parties in their commercial/financial relations; any references to trade usages or commercial practices, supported by references to the evidence, as appropriate.

---

332. This is inspired by directions on Post-Hearing Briefs issued by Wolfgang Peter.

79. The *Quantum* of the final sum claimed as principal for each subclaim or fall–back position shall be stated with precision.

80. Explain all aspects of interest (on which principal amount(s), start and end date, simple or compound, which rate(s), how ascertained) separately.

81. *Quotes* of relevant passages from documents, exhibits, Witness Statements, the Transcript, sources of law (statutes, case law, legal writing), etc., shall be made in full wherever reasonable. If citations are made (by reference only), they shall be made with appropriate precision. No string citations, please. **No citations to entire cases**, please (but submit the entire case). Just quote the entire passage on which you rely, and highlight the relevant portion.

82. *References* to **earlier submissions** shall include the title and **date** of the document. References to documents and exhibits shall state series name, volume, the number, the page, and paragraph.

83. *References* to testimony shall state the date and the name of the person quoted, give the full text, including the context of the passage quoted from the Transcript, and highlight the relevant portion.

84. *No further documents* shall be submitted without leave, with the exception of sources of law (no legal opinions, no decisions from parallel proceedings).

**K.     Costs**

85. The costs shall normally follow the overall outcome, but may be allocated and charged separately for certain issues, particularly if "bifurcated," briefed, or heard separately.

86. The first *submissions on costs* will be **only one-page statements** presenting details as can be presented on one page, not attaching supporting documents. Please leave out all advances made which are just that, advances. Please distinguish between expenses and fees for services rendered. **Please state for each item whether this was billed to and paid by the client, or reimbursed by the client to the law firm, or was billed to the client but not yet paid, or was expected to be billed to the client.** The other Party and the ICC must be copied.

87. On motion by a Party, or *sua sponte*, the Arbitral Tribunal may order further submissions on costs if in its discretion it deems this useful.

**L.     Settlement**

88. The Arbitral Tribunal may begin at any time during the proceedings to facilitate (partial) settlement, but only if it has the prior informed consent of the Parties. Such informed consent will imply a waiver of the challenge of the arbitrator or of the Award

(e.g. on the basis that the settlement talks showed bias or helped a Party more than the other) if the settlement fails.

89. The Arbitral Tribunal will not meet separately with the Parties (shuttle diplomacy caucusing). Its involvement may be evaluative. The process should also be kept simple and short.

90. The Arbitral Tribunal should respect the Parties' freedom of decision and not force settlement.

91. If the Parties settle "out of court," they should advise the Arbitral Tribunal promptly. If the Parties roughly simultaneously withdraw their claims and counter-claims, this shall be treated as a settlement.

92. The Parties should say so expressly if they wish the Arbitral Tribunal to retain jurisdiction until certain payments are made, certain assets are transferred, and the like. Otherwise, the Arbitral Tribunal will assume that it should terminate the arbitration as soon as possible.

93. The Parties should say so expressly if they wish the Arbitral Tribunal to issue an Award by consent, and state its dispositive part expressly (it is not sufficient to submit a copy of the settlement agreement and request a Consent Award reflecting it or referring to it). Even so, the Arbitral Tribunal shall not be required to issue a Consent Award. Otherwise, the Arbitral Tribunal will issue a Closing Order.

94. The Parties should say in which proportion the arbitration costs should be borne. Otherwise, the Arbitral Tribunal will assume that the costs are to be borne equally by both sides, taking into account also any non-refundable registration fee paid to the Arbitral Institution.

95. The Parties should say whether one Party should contribute to the other's Party Representation costs, and how much. Otherwise, the Arbitral Tribunal will assume that each Party will bear its own Party Representation costs.

*

96. This order may be amended at any time by the Arbitral Tribunal *sua sponte* or upon application by either Party after having heard the other.


For the Arbitral Tribunal:


_____

## Appendix to Procedural Order No. 1

### Questions to avoid (Michael Hwang's no-no list[333])

1. Questions about unarticulated intentions of witnesses (e.g. what did you mean when you wrote this letter/these minutes?);

2. Questions about the motives of witnesses relating to actions or omissions (e.g. why did you insert this clause in the agreement? Why did you do/not do [something]?);

3. Questions about a witness' interpretation of letters or contractual documents unless it impacted on his or her subsequent actions (e.g. what does this clause of the contract mean to you? What do you think the writer or this letter meant by paragraph X?);

4. Questions to demonstrate what is or is not in a document (e.g. where in this document does it say [whatever]? Do you agree that this clause does not say anything about [something]? Look at this document – does it contain any reference to [x]?);

5. Questions for dramatic effect which do not add to the knowledge of the Arbitral Tribunal (e.g. I put it to you that you are not telling the truth (unless Counsel has built up a foundation for this suggestion by previous questioning). Could you please read out the third paragraph of your letter?);

6. Questions designed to make the witness concede facts in favor of the opposing Party which are apparent from the record and are not denied (e.g. do you agree that you never replied to my client's letter?);

7. Questions solely aimed at attacking credibility or creating prejudice (i.e. having no direct relevance to the issues, but designed to question the witness' credibility or character by asking him questions on other matters outside the events covered by the existing arbitration);

8. Questions that seek to argue a legal issue with a lay witness (e.g. do you agree that Clause X means ...? Do you agree that my client acted lawfully in terminating your employment?);

9. Questions which take a witness through facts and documents with a view to making the witness agree with the other Party's interpretation of a document or characterization of events (rather than the actual facts themselves) (e.g. do you agree that my client behaved reasonably under the circumstances?);

10. Questions which end ... "answer yes or no" when the question is not a "yes or no" question;

---

333. This is adapted from directions issued by Michael Hwang. The first ten questions were published in The Art of Advocacy in International Arbitration, Second Edition, Chapter 17, *Ten Questions Not to Ask in Cross-Examination in International Arbitration* by Michael Hwang, pp. 431–450, and are here reproduced with permission of JurisNett LLC, Huntington, New York 11743. The further questions are reproduced with Mr. Michael Hwang SC's permission.

11. Questions designed to "cut them off at the pass" (e.g. confirm that the document that you authored is true. Confirm that you read your witness statement with care before signing it. Confirm that you received legal advice before writing this letter.) as these are matters which can be assumed, and the Arbitral Tribunal will be skeptical of any witness who chooses to raise these defenses as excuses for untruths;

12. Questions where adverbs and adjectives are at the core (e.g. do you agree that you acted unreasonably in … ? Would you characterize your behavior as impetuous?);

13. Questions repeating passages in the witness statement and asking the witness to confirm his or her belief in them, or how carefully he or she read the statement before affirming it;

14. Questions as to the witness' belief or intention at the time he or she entered into a contract (e.g. what did you expect to obtain from entering into the agreement with … ?);

15. Questions aimed at getting witness' explicit confirmation of allegations made by your client and which have not been denied (e.g. is it correct that X does not deny Y's position that … ?);

16. Questions which do not end with a question mark and prove to be more comment or argument than a question (i.e. leaving a witness unaware that he or she is required to respond);

17. Questions on the legal position of the other Party which are a matter for counsel, not a witness (e.g. do you agree with X's counsel that … ?);

18. Questions asking a witness about the content of a document not written or read by him or her;

19. Taking the name of the Arbitral Tribunal in vain (i.e. do you expect the Arbitral Tribunal to believe that … ?);

20. Questions that seek to reconfirm what the law presumes in your favor (i.e. do you agree that you are bound by what you have signed?);

21. If matters can be proven by a document, try not to prove it through witness testimony which simply refers to that document without adding any value to what is stated in that document (i.e. look at document X. Do you agree that it says …?).

# Challenge of Arbitrators

*It is not possible to give templates here. The following examples provide just an idea of the style, and the kind of arguments that may be made.*

19 November 2003

**S Arbitration No. ... B vs/ N**

Dear Party Representatives:

This morning, Wednesday 19 November 2003, I found on my desk Mr. X's letter to me, dated 18 November 2003. Mr. X attached his letter of the same date to Mr. Y, and Mr. Y's letter to him dated 14 November 2003, which had as its attachment a letter written on behalf of B to the Z Arbitration Institution on 11 January 2001, in another arbitration between the Parties.

In his letter of 14 November 2003, Mr. Y suggests that B withdraw my appointment by 19 November 2003, which is today, or that I resign by the end of this week, that is 21 November 2003, failing which N would challenge me within the deadline for this, which appears to expire early next week.

Mr. X's letter of 18 November 2003, is to the effect that B asks me to confirm my intention to continue to serve even in the face of a potential formal challenge by N.

Five arbitrations are mentioned.

(a)

It is correct that I was the Presiding Arbitrator in Z Arbitration No. ../C v. N where the Final Award was rendered on 31 May 1996. In the meantime, I heard that the management (and control?) of N had changed.

(b)

It is also correct that I chaired Z Arbitration No. ../A v. K, where the Final Award was rendered on 16 August 2002. That the Award was almost immediately leaked to V seems new to me. I hear for the first time that K is now under common control with N.

(c)

I hear for the first time of another Z Arbitration No. .. between the Parties where the above-mentioned letter of 11 January 2001, was written.

(d)

I also hear for the first time about an S Arbitration No. .. between A and N.

(e)

I know nothing about the present S Arbitration No. .. beyond the names of the Parties and their Representatives. I note that the law firm that represented S in (a) Z Arbitration Nr. … co-represents N in the present S arbitration (e)

I note your comments on the similarities and dissimilarities between these arbitrations. Today I can only say that the issues in the two above-mentioned Z arbitrations (a) and (b) that I chaired were entirely different.

I would like to assure both Parties that I am entirely independent and unbiased and intend to remain so, as the Parties have every right to expect. I also recognize B's right, within those limits, to appoint the arbitrator of its choice. I believe that both these interests are best served if I refuse to withdraw.

Very sincerely yours,

---

5 December 2003

**S Arbitration No. … B vs/ N**

Ladies and Gentlemen at S Arbitration Institution:

Thank you for having granted me, in your letter of 27 November 2003, an opportunity to comment on N's challenge of 24 November 2003, with its 6 enclosures. Much of what I have to say will repeat what I wrote on 19 November 2003 (enclosure 3 to the challenge), but for convenience I will set it out again:

The challenge is based exclusively on my involvement in two previous Z arbitrations that I chaired and the Awards made in those two arbitrations by the two Arbitral Tribunals. Three further arbitrations are mentioned, as is, newly, a case in federal court in New York.

(i) It is correct that I was the Presiding Arbitrator in Z Arbitration No. … /C v. N where the Final Award was rendered on 31 May 1996. In the meantime, I heard that the management (and control?) of N had changed.

(ii) It is also correct that I chaired Z Arbitration No. ... /A v. K, where the Final Award was rendered on 16 August 2002. I now see exhibits 5 and 6. These documents do not refresh my memory. I did not check in my archives, but I have no reason to doubt that they were submitted to me at the time.

(iii) I hear for the first time about the case in the United States District Court (for the Southern District?) of New York.

(iv) On 19 November 2003, I heard for the first time of another Z Arbitration No. ... between the Parties. In this situation, the letter of 11 January 2001, was written. I have not yet seen the Award in that arbitration, exh. C 6 in (vi) S Arbitration No. ....

(v) I also heard for the first time on 19 November 2003, about an S Arbitration No. ... between A and N.

(vi) I still know nothing about the present S Arbitration No. ... beyond the names of the Parties and their Representatives. I note that the law firm that represented O in (i) Z Arbitration No. ... co-represents N in the present S arbitration.

I continue to be unable to comment on the similarities and dissimilarities between all these cases. No doubt the Parties will argue about this in the arbitration. Arguments based on the similarities and dissimilarities between the instant case and other cases are the bread and butter of litigation and arbitration. It also happens all the time that the same arbitrator sits simultaneously or consecutively on various arbitrations involving partly the same issues and partly the same Parties.

I have never met V. All I remember is that in arbitration (i) Z No. ... somebody of that name was depicted by C in an unfavorable light, but my view was then and is today that an arbitration is about applying law to facts, not about who owns what or is good or bad or nice or not.

After due reflection and having studied the IBA Guidelines, I would like to assure the S Institution and the Parties that I am entirely independent and unbiased and intend to remain so, as is only right to expect. I also recognize B's right, within those limits, to appoint the arbitrator of its choice. I believe that both these interests are best served if I remain an arbitrator.

Very truly yours,

---

13 February 2004

**Case No. ...**

Dear Sir or Madam (at State Court):

On 12 February 2004, I received from you a number of documents (all in English, for which I am much obliged) relating to the case mentioned in reference. You invite me to submit my written answer in duplicate within 14 days from the date I was served with the application.

Under Swiss law, a non-Swiss Court cannot serve a resident of Switzerland with process in this way. In fact, I must draw your attention to Article 271 of the Swiss Federal Criminal Code which forbids under penalty of imprisonment or penitentiary the exercise on Swiss territory acts of sovereignty for a foreign state which are reserved to public officers (except by special permission). Any person furthering such acts falls under the same penalty as an accessory.

Under these circumstances I am sure that you will understand that it is probably best if I send you back the entire documentation, herewith enclosed.

Very truly yours,

---

3 March 2004

**Your Case No. ...**

Dear Mr. (at State Court)

I have now been properly served with the documents in the above matter. Many thanks.

Applicant apparently brought its challenge to your Court under Art. ... of ... I do not believe that Art. ... applies.

The same challenge against me was dismissed by the S Arbitration Institution on 22 December 2003. This may be seen from Document 19 in your file.

According to the Arbitration Rules of the S Institution, § 18 Subs. 4 (Document 20 in your file) the S Arbitration Institution decides finally on challenges of arbitrators.

Where this has happened, Art. ... of the Arbitration Act which uses the word, finally, excludes the jurisdiction of your Court.

However, should you have to decide the case on its merits, which I do not concede, may I respectfully refer to what I wrote the S Arbitration Institution on 5 December 2003. Since I do not see that letter in the file I herewith enclose it. I have nothing to add to it.

I assume that it is correct that I copy, without enclosure, the Counsels of Applicant N and of Opponent B, and also the S Arbitration Institution.

Very truly yours,

---

17 February 2005

**Arbitration No. ... B vs/ N**

Ladies and Gentlemen at S Arbitration Institution:

As you know, since January 1 2005, I continue my full-time practice as an international commercial arbitrator, but independently and separately from my previous law firm,... ......., and now from my own separate "boutique" premises. I am not a consultant to my former firm nor do I have any other remaining connection with it. I have no residual financial arrangements with my former firm which would make my income depend in any way on the financial success of my former firm.

In its letter of 11 February 2005, N challenges me again, this time in two respects:

1. That "at some time no later than May 2002" my former partner Mr. .... of the Geneva office acted for the T-Group and filed, on behalf of that Group (or companies within that Group?) civil and criminal complaints against Mr. E and Mr. Q, is new to me.

I also know nothing about an alleged co-operation in the matter at the time or more recently between my former law firm and W and Associates or any other law firm acting for V, B S.A., B Ltd. or A Holdings Ltd.

Mr. E is no doubt well-known in his country and elsewhere, but, no disrespect to him, all I remember about him is that his name is mentioned somewhere in the file of the present arbitration and possibly already somewhere in the A arbitration.

Mr. Q is no doubt also well-known, but, no disrespect to him, his name is totally new to me.

Had I known about some or all of the above matters I would no doubt have considered what to do, but I knew nothing.

The suggestion that I might lack impartiality or independence because I now might be tempted to decide against N to please a former client of my former firm, or to displease the opponents of a former client of my former firm in an unrelated matter, is entirely unfounded, and I reject it.

1.2. Looking at the IBA Guidelines, this case seems to me to be outside the Orange List and even outside the Green List.

The Orange List is a collection of matters that, according to the Guidelines, need be disclosed, but are not *per se* grounds for disqualification. Failure to disclose is not *per se* a ground for disqualification.

The Green List is a collection of matters that need not be disclosed and are not grounds for disqualification.

I do not know whether the T-Group or Messrs. E and Q are "affiliates" of one of the Parties. I do not know whether my former firm indeed acted sometime between November 2000 and March 2002 for or against a Party in an unrelated matter. In any event the firm's actions were taken without my involvement. ... is no longer my firm. The present case thus, for one or several reasons, falls outside Orange List point 3.1.4 and outside Green List point 4.2.1.

2.1. The allegation that I have already taken a position on relevant legal issues was previously presented by N in its earlier challenge of November 2003, which was rejected at the time by the S Institution.

Since the renewed challenge is now geared to a specific question of Private International Law, let me point out that the Private International Law to be applied by an Arbitral Tribunal having its seat in S is not necessarily the same as the Private International Law applicable by an Arbitral Tribunal having its seat in Z. The legal question is not the same. I find the challenge unfounded.

2.2. Looking again at the IBA Guidelines, the present case is again even outside the Green List.

I have never given an opinion on the Private International Law questions in S Arbitration Law that may be relevant in the present case, neither a general opinion nor an opinion focused on the case that is being arbitrated now. The Arbitral Tribunal's decision in the A case was that Arbitral Tribunal's decision in a different case, and based on a different law. Thus, the present case falls outside Green List point 4.1.1.

3. My conclusion is that the new challenge should be rejected in both its aspects.

Very sincerely yours,

---

7 March 2005

**Arbitration No. ... B vs/ N**

Ladies and Gentlemen at S Arbitration Institution:

Reference is made to the letter of N, dated 25 February 2005.

1. My present firm does not represent T-Group in civil cases against anybody or in attempts to open criminal proceedings against Messrs. E and Q.

2. My former firm was ... I know that my former firm's website included, since September 2, 2004, an announcement that I was leaving the firm, effective January 1, 2005. I did not know that a picture showing me at work (without giving my name) was somewhere in the website and remained there until February 28, 2005. On that day, I asked my former partners to remove the picture, and when I checked the next day, it was gone. As I wrote you on 17 February 2005, it is new to me that my former firm represented T-Group in this way at some time before May 2002 (since N seems to believe this to be relevant, let me say that at no time did the Zurich partners receive any income, significant or otherwise, from cases handled by the Geneva office), and that there was or is a link, though shareholding or otherwise, between T-Group's then opponents and N. New to me means that I know nothing about this.

3.1. As you will know, Swiss law firms are not allowed to disclose the names of their present or former clients. I am in no better position than anybody else to obtain information about the case in question.

3.2. I can only note that Exhibit 1 now submitted by N, the letter of 11 June 1999, does not fully bear out the allegations made by N in its challenge. From it, it appears that my former firm acted on 11 June 1999, on behalf of T S.A., a Bahamas corporation, in criminal proceedings against Mr. E and a Mr. I, but not (yet?) Mr. Q, and various companies, several in the British Virgin Islands or in Panama. These, N now apparently claims, were or are linked through shareholding or otherwise with N.

3.3. I can only say that all this is new to me. In other words, I know nothing about any of this. I know nothing about Mr. I or the various companies or their past or present links, if any, with N. Since N seems to believe that any failure to deny specifically and expressly any allegation that it makes amounts to an admission, I herewith deny its allegations expressly.

4. I am puzzled to see that N faults me for saying that had I known certain things to be alleged I would no doubt have considered what to do. I believe that any reasonable and fair-minded person would say this and act accordingly.

5. I am amazed by N's view that my statement that I may "possibly" have come across Mr. E's name in the A arbitration is tantamount an "admission" that I have "received prior pleading and evidence concerning Mr. E in a case involving similar issues." Since N seems to believe that if I do not now deny this expressly, this will be a further admission, I expressly deny it.

6. N apparently insists on faulting me for not disclosing in the present arbitration what I did not know and still cannot verify, or on faulting me for not having known what the legal counsel of R, Ms. ...., claims to have personally discovered just recently, but about which, by its own submission, N must have had, through the personal actual knowledge of its officers, Messrs. E and Q, actual institutional knowledge all along.

7. I recognize that the Parties in this arbitration, as in any arbitration, have the right to expect the arbitrators to live up to proper standards of independence and lack of bias. In the present arbitration, my judgment could not be affected by things that I did not know. It cannot now become affected by, for me unverifiable, allegations about past activities of my former firm and alleged links between N and my former firm's then client's then opponents that are all new to me.

8. I recognize that the actual knowledge test for an arbitrator has its limits where the arbitrator deliberately closes his eyes to possibly relevant facts. This is at the basis of IBA Guideline 7(c) cited by N. Since N now seems to claim *innuendo* that I did not make reasonable enquiries to investigate any potential conflict of interest as required by IBA Guideline 7 (c), I expressly say that in the present case, as in the A case, the S case and all the other cases that I handled with my former firm, I always followed the firm's internal conflict check mechanism.

9.1. In this particular case, it was and is my practice to put the conflicts check documentation into my file of a case. This is where I found it in the present arbitration. I received a phone call on or before 4 June 2003, from Me M of Geneva, enquiring whether I could serve as Party-appointed arbitrator. On 4 June 2003, my assistant sent by internal e-mail a New Case Memorandum to all the partners, including those in Geneva, stating what Me M had told me about the new arbitration (Exhibit 101). None of my partners indicated a potential conflict. I then called Me M to tell him that the firm had no conflict and that I was available.

9.2. In August 2003, Ms. X who was in town on other business dropped briefly by my office to ask me whether I was available as an arbitrator in the matter. I remembered that I had been recently asked the same question, and that there was no conflict. I told her that the firm had no conflict and that I was available.

9.3. On 30 October 2003 (her time), Ms. X sent me an e-mail asking me whether I was still available. My assistant opens my emails and prints out for me those that I should read. In due course (I was traveling at the time) she submitted this print-out to me, with her hand-written remark that we had performed a conflicts check on 4 June 2003 (Exhibit 102).

9.4. On 31 October 2003, my assistant sent an e-mail to Ms. X, in which I confirmed that I was available, and no conflict had arisen since our previous contact (Exhibit 103).

Very sincerely yours,

---

17 March 2005

**Arbitration No. ... B vs/ N**

Ladies and Gentlemen at S Arbitration Institution:

I have seen the letter that N sent you on March 16, 2005.

This is getting repetitive. I can only repeat that the only source of information that I have today, and ever have had, about Ms. E and her relationship with R and N, and the relationship between R and N, is what N alleged in my previous, unsuccessful, challenge, and alleges in my present, pending, challenge as an arbitrator in the present arbitration. Previously, neither I, nor apparently my then partners, had any knowledge, let alone "huge knowledge," about these allegations or facts, if they are true.

I do not accept that I have been "misleading" you or anybody else, "sometimes" or at any time, in this or in any other matter.

Very sincerely yours,

# Instructions to Our Fact Witnesses[334]

Dear ......

**Time and Place of your appearance:** ...................................

**Be well on time and ready to testify.**

**What to wear:** What you would wear for an important business meeting or for an important interview. Wear comfortable shoes.

**Your Witness Statements:**

- 1st Date ................
- 2nd Date ................

Please study these again when you bring them along. You will perhaps be asked to correct typing errors affecting the meaning. Please flag them.

**Your oral testimony:**

Now you are called to testify. Sit down when the Presiding Arbitrator invites you.

Before you are asked questions, you will probably be admonished to tell the truth: "You must tell truth, the whole truth, and nothing but the truth. Knowingly not telling the truth may be punishable by imprisonment up to five years, or a fine, or both." This has nothing to do with you personally; everybody who testifies is told this.

---

334. See questions 514, 515, 516, 519, and 656.

Talk to the presiding Arbitrator, even if a question comes from somebody else. Please talk very loudly, so everybody in the room can hear you.

Please testify in English. Wait for the question. If you do not understand the question, say so. If you need help with a particular question, say so. This is not a test of your English.

Answer the question, no less, no more. Do not ramble. Do not argue the case. That is the lawyers job. There are these possible answers:

" Yes."
" No."
" I do not remember." (This is not a memory test)
" I do not know." (Nobody can know everything)
" Sorry, I do not understand the question. What is the question?"
" Sorry, that was a long question. I no longer remember the beginning. Because of this, I am not sure that I understand the question at the end."

Nothing more.

Do not guess. Do not speculate.

## Tell the truth.

Tell the truth if asked

- whether you talked to the lawyer (What did the lawyer tell you? "To tell the truth.").
- whether you talked to another witness, or anybody else ("Yes, to my husband ...").
- whether you drafted your Witness Statement yourself ("The first draft was mine." Or, "I answered questions orally, and the lawyer produced a first written draft in English and asked me to make sure that it reproduced what I had said, and that it told the truth." "Yes, in the .... language.").
- whether you are being paid to testify. Answer, "Not separately paid, but yes, I am employed by ..., and paid as an employee. This does not prevent me from telling the truth." Or, "Yes, as part of my payment package. My employer also pays my reasonable expenses. This does not prevent me from telling the truth."
- whether you own shares in one of the Parties or companies related to them.
- whether you have options to shares in those companies.

**Your contact person:**

If you still have any questions about testifying or anything else, ask Ms. ...................., phone no. ................. This is your contact person.

This person will also deal with your travel arrangements, hotel, etc.

Other people whom you may meet, and their function, see attachment, "Dramatis Personae," but please do not contact them directly: always go through your contact person.

# Instructions to Tribunal-Appointed Expert[335]

Dear Professor .......

It was a pleasure meeting you the other day at .......... airport. I am writing you this letter in the name of the Arbitral Tribunal that I am presiding which opposes (company A), a German corporation belonging to the (B) Group, to (company X), a corporation belonging to the (Y) Group, and ultimately to the (Z) Government. Both Parties have agreed that we should ask you to act as a Tribunal-appointed Expert in our arbitration, and you have agreed to act in this capacity.

May I remind you that, as a Tribunal-appointed Expert, you must remain in all respects independent from the Parties and impartial. Under Swiss law rendering a knowingly false Expert opinion would be punishable by a fine or penitentiary up to five years, or both.

The questions that you will answer in your report are the numbered questions on the attached list that you and I established together, principally on the basis of questions suggested by both Parties. Please refer to these questions by number.

We discussed the documents on which your Expert opinion should be based, the questions that it should answer, and the method that should be followed to answer these questions.

You have the documents listed on the attached list. Please refer to these documents by their numbers included in the list.

Should you at any point come to the conclusion that you need further documents or further information, or clarification of any kind, please do not contact one or the other

---

335. See question 593.

Party directly verbally, nor both of them simultaneously, not even in writing. In such a case, you should call me straight away, and we will work out a solution.

My Co-arbitrators and I do not exclude that you might have to ask questions or hear explanations, and perhaps inspect plant and equipment on the spot, but in the experience of some of us this can be tricky. It is essential to safeguard the integrity of the entire expertise procedure. Any irregularity could jeopardize the validity of your conclusions and of the decisions that the Arbitral Tribunal might make based on your report, all at considerable loss of time and money.

You should not accept any new documents directly from the Parties, not even from both.

Generally, if you have any questions or problems, please let me know, and we will sort it out.

Your report should set out not only the results of your investigation, but describe very precisely which data you used and which method you followed. Explain why you selected this method rather than another method. State which data you used (only those on the arbitration record! Otherwise please contact me, even if it is about a generally accessible matter such as the specific weight of iron). Specify in which publications the method followed and the data used are described more fully. If you make an assumption, please state clearly what it is and why you are making the assumption. The purpose of all this is to ensure that the Parties (who have their own Experts) can see exactly what you have done, and if they so wish, may challenge the data that you accepted or assumptions that you made, or the methods that you used.

Please never forget that the Parties have different agendas in this arbitration and may disagree on many issues. Your task is to answer our questions as best you can, not to find a middle ground between the Parties.

Please do not communicate directly verbally with the Parties (not even on timing matters) and do not send them your report directly, even though they ultimately provide the funds for the exercise.

We hope to receive your written report by .............. Please send three copies to the Presiding Arbitrator ( ...) and one copy each to the Co-arbitrators. It will be for the Arbitral Tribunal to distribute them further.

Once the Arbitral Tribunal has received your report it will study it. A phase may follow where the Arbitral Tribunal, possibly after having heard the Parties on the subject, may revert to you with additional questions in writing, asking for an additional report in writing.

Ultimately, on ................, at ...... a.m., there will be a hearing with the Parties, presumably in ............... You will be requested to attend. The Parties will have studied your report and will have an opportunity to ask you all and any question they deem relevant. Please be patient with them and keep cool, even if they do not appear to agree with all your statements.

You will bill the Arbitral Tribunal promptly for your actual expenses and your fees (estimated at EUR ..., into a newly-opened account with (bank) in Zurich. As soon as the advances have been credited, I will advise you, and you will start working on your investigation and report.

Should you at any time believe that the advances on deposit are about to become insufficient, you should promptly notify the Arbitral Tribunal since the Arbitral Tribunal is in no position to guarantee the payment of your expenses and fees beyond the deposits received.

To show your agreement with the above, please countersign the enclosed copy of this letter and return it to me.

( ...)"

*List of documents, attached to Letter of Instructions*

- Excerpts from Request, Answer, Reply, and Rejoinder
- Economic Justification of Extra Costs, 27 December 2011
- Numbered Claims Tables
- Synopsis, 20 December 2011
- Minutes of 11/12 July, and 19/20 September 2011 (4 volumes)
- Interim Award of 14 December 2012
- Master Time Schedule as per Annex III of Contract (1)
- 01-0915-900
- Fabrication Erection Time Schedule of 1 October 2007
- Interim Master Time Schedule as submitted by ........ on 6 March 2012
- Theoretical and Actual Master Time Schedule 08980001706871 with supporting Documents
- Schedule and Actual Fabrication Erection Schedule UAN01-0915-900

**Attachment**

**Questions for the Expert**

1. .........
2. .........
3. .........

All these questions should be answered on the assumption that the Interim Award of ...is correct.

The original master time schedule shows the contractual obligations of the Parties. On ...., as explained ..................., the original master time schedule was replaced by an amended master time schedule.

The actual times should have been shown by the Parties in the two "is" time schedules, but they differ! Where discrepancies appear between the "is" time schedules, answers should be given with respect to both extremes, and a reasoned opinion should be given as to which timing appears realistic under the circumstances (which may be one or the other timing, or a specified timing in between).

For activities that bridge the time when the amended master time schedule came into force, please answer with respect to the original master time schedule up to the time when the amended master time schedule came into force, and, for the time thereafter, on the basis of the amended master time schedule.

Before discussing the individual items, you may want to consider grouping them.

The main delaying effect is due to item 084, the gas/gas-heat exchanger, attributable to ............ Is it feasible to quantify the delaying effect of this particular item in its impact on the overall delay penalty claims, prayer for relief III, and item 086g? Is it possible to quantify item 084's delaying effect on item 090? Item 086f seems also to be related to 084.

# Correspondence Preparing for Experts' Hearing

Dear Party Representatives:

The Arbitral Tribunal remained silent for a while because it was hoping that the Parties would be able to sort out the remaining points amongst themselves. To a heartening extent, this now has happened, and the Arbitral Tribunal is grateful. The matter of the setoffs/deductions has now been concluded.

As far as the delay claims are concerned, the Arbitral Tribunal does not believe that it can decide all the points by itself without the help of an Expert. It notes the suggestions of the Parties. Another possibility would be to appoint Prof. Dr. ............... If there are any objections against him, please voice them. If the Arbitral Tribunal hears nothing from either of the Parties by the end of February .........., it will proceed.

Dear Party Representatives:

For the remaining delay claims, allegations and pleadings have been presented. We do not think that the Tribunal requires the Parties' advice on what impact the Interim Award may have on these claims.

However, we do welcome your comment on the Tribunal's idea to appoint an Expert on project management.

For most of the claims an Expert's opinion should not be necessary. As far as the Tribunal would need the support of an Expert, such an Expert should not simply be experienced in project management generally, but rather should have experience in building, especially chemical or even ammonia plants.

Copies to Co-arbitrators, Party Representatives, ICC Secretariat

Dear Professor

Thank you for your report of ...............

We are all looking forward to discussing it with you on .......... in ............. There will no doubt be further questions, but it appears useful to submit some questions to you already, many of which have been suggested by the Parties.

The questions can be grouped in at least three different ways: according to methodology, according to individual identified delays, and according to claims in the arbitration.

I would like to do it in these three groups, one after the other.

I realize that grouping the questions this way may result in some duplication and repetition (which may however be given the fancier name of welcome redundancy).

1. How did you deal with the *change of master time schedule?*

2. There is an explanation of the method followed on page 2 of the summary, but could you give a fuller explanation? Did you identify the *critical path?* What did you do about the delays, which, but for earlier delays, would have been critical, but in the event were not? What did you do about delays that were "in the wake" of other critical delays, where a Party felt that there was no hurry because the critical path was elsewhere anyway, and until the critical activity was completed, any delay in its own activity would not be critical? If you followed a critical path method in this sense, you could perhaps illustrate by examples how it applied, for instance, with the erection of steel structure (page 16 of your report), or the relationship between the delay in the gas/gas-heat exchanger and delay in .....................

3. Or did you use a method where the various delays are weighed against one another? What were the criteria to give a particular weight to a delay? Were there instances where one delay was cancelled out by another? If that is the method that you followed, please again give examples, for instance see page 25 of your report, with respect to engineering delays in foundation and earth work.

4. Was the waste heat boiler problem taken into account? How? If not, why not?

5. It is suggested that piping erection was completed only at the end of March ......, which would mean, if it started in early May, ......., that it took nine months rather than six months as according to the Master time schedule, correct? If so, to whom did you assign those extra three months, and why?

Looking forward to meet you again on .........................

Dear Party Representatives:

Many thanks for your help at our Experts' hearing.

Please find enclosed the supplementary report to the Expert's Report by Professor
...........

The Parties are now invited to present their comments in writing by ............. These comments should cover the assessment of the evidence on delay, that is the first report, the hearing of ..................., and the supplementary report. Could you also comment on the methodology question? Is Swiss substantive law relevant in this connection? If so, what does it say?

Copies to Co-arbitrators, Party Representatives, ICC Secretariat

# Checklist for Hearing Rooms

1. Does the hearing room have natural light?
2. Is there space to seat up to ... persons in a U configuration, with one or two rows behind counsel (with tables), and sufficient bookshelves? Is there a witness table across the gap, with a seat also for an interpreter next to the witness?
3. Are there swivel chairs for the arbitrator and the Court Reporters?
4. Are there full facilities for taking of Transcript, amplification, PowerPoint, terminals for live note Transcript, and screening or projection of called-up documents, and other usual facilities such as copiers and printers? Will the provision of live note be followed by hard copy overnight Transcript?
5. Will the room be available in the evening and not have to be vacated for some wedding reception?
6. Will there be free wi-fi access?
7. Are there adequate retiring rooms, preferably with windows, for Arbitral Tribunal, Parties and witnesses?
8. Are there arrangements for lunch and tea refreshments?
9. Who is the contact person at the hearing venue?
10. Hotel proposed for Tribunal members ................
11. Liaison person at the hotel: ..................
11. See sketch of layout of hearing room.

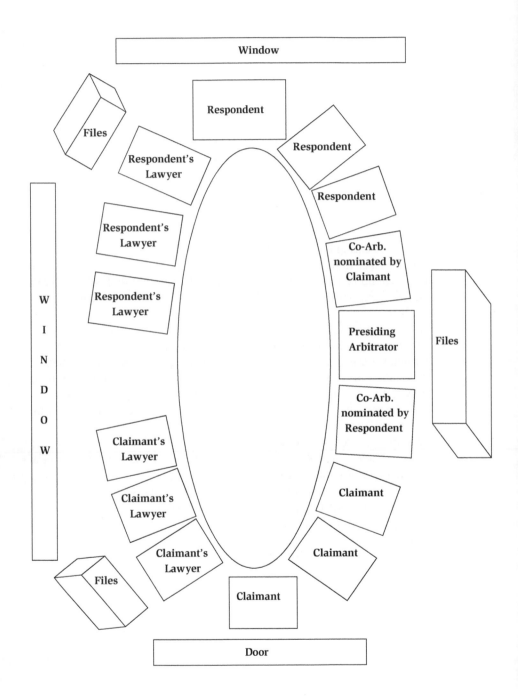

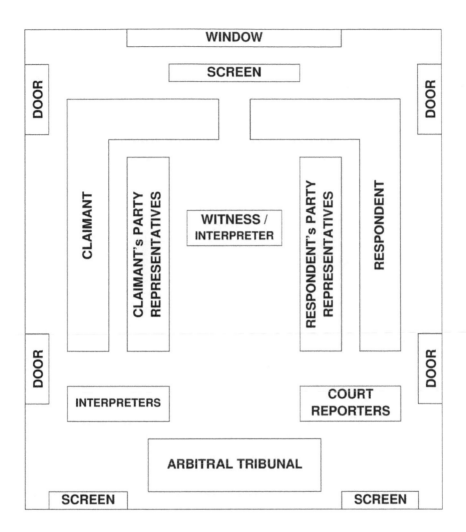

# A Few Tables of Contents of Awards[336]

**Example 1**

### Table of Contents of Final Award

A. Introduction
B. Proceedings to the Terms of Reference, Deadlines
C. Proceedings after the Terms of Reference
D. C's Objection to Jurisdiction
E. R's Response to C's Jurisdictional Objection
F. Discussion – Law Applicable to the Arbitration Agreement: Swiss International Arbitration Law
G. Interpretation of Arbitration Clause: Swiss or Y Private Law?
(a) Is there a text?
(b) Applicable law to interpretation of text
(c) C's objections based on the wording of the clause
(d) Conclusion
H. Offer and Acceptance on Arbitration in Swiss or Y Private Law: Special Agreed Form?
I. Text Form Requirement of Article 178 of the Swiss Private International Law Statute
(a) Special text form for offer?
(b) Special text form for acceptance?
K. Offer and Acceptance Meeting form Requirements of Y or Swiss Private law, as provided by Article 178 Subsection 2 Swiss Private International Law Statute?

---

336. See question 759 and the ICC Checklist which can be used also in Non-ICC Cases.

## Example 2

### Table of Contents of Final Award

(a) Off-balance-sheet items
(b) Attempt to transfer to ... required?
(c) If an item is prescribed, is it still the same?
(d) Diligence
(e) Law of bills and notes, or private law?
(f) Endorsement to ... required?
(g) Three-year statute of limitations?
(h) Effect of bankruptcy
M. Article 1.5 Argument and Articles 2.5 and 3.5 of the ASG
N. Y law
O. Are the Receivables Items Covered by the State Guarantee Even If Not Transferred to ... and Later Returned?
P. Is a Prescribed Item Still the Same Item?
Q. Is the State Guarantee Unconditional or Did C Have a Duty of Care?
R. Law of Bills and Notes or General Private Law, or Both? Statute of Limitations?
S. Interruption of Statute of Limitations in a Bankruptcy
T. Effect of Revocation of Bankruptcy Decree and Subsequent Reopening of Bankruptcy
U. Summary: Due Care
V. Principal and Interest
(a) Principal
(b) Interest
W. Consequences for C's Prayers for Relief
X. Consequences for R's Prayers for Relief
Y. Costs
(a) Assessment of arbitration costs
(b) Assessment of party representation costs
(c) Costs follow the event
(d) Allocation of arbitration costs
(e) Allocation of party representation costs Operative Part of Final Award

# Example 3

## Table of Contents of Final Award

A. Introduction
B. Constitution of the Arbitral Tribunal
C. Lex Arbitri, Jurisdiction, Applicable Law, and Language
(a) Lex loci arbitri
(b) Jurisdiction
(c) Applicable law
(d) Language